Deaf Killers

Peter Jackson

First published in Great Britain 2006

Published by
Deaf print Winsford
PO Box 93
Winsford
Cheshire CW7 3FU
England

British Library Cataloguing Data

ISBN 0-9532206-7-2

Printed in England by JEM Digital Print Services,
Sittingbourne, Kent ME10 2NH

To

Nancy

Other Crime Books by Peter Jackson

Deaf Crime Casebook
Deaf to Evidence
Deaf Murder Casebook
Deaf Target
Death Around the Green

History Books

Britain's Deaf Heritage
A Pictorial History of Deaf Britain
A History of the Deaf Community in Northwich and
Winsford 1880 – 2002
(with Maureen Jackson)
Deaf Lives (Ed. with Raymond Lee)
Manchester Memoirs (Ed.)
Preston Pride (with Maureen Jackson)
The Gawdy Manuscripts

Contents

Acknowledgements

There are many people to whom I owe a debt of gratitude for their help during my research activities in various parts of the world. For this book, my research has taken me to the United States (four times), to Turkey and Egypt. In addition, I have acquired a devoted readership of my books, some of whom have been willing to put themselves out and assist in some of my research, especially in places that I could not get to.

In Turkey, I am indebted to my good friend Basak Kutlu, a teacher of English in a primary school in Istanbul, whom I met about ten years ago on a holiday in Bodrum. The story of Sultan Süleyman the Magnificent could not have been completed without her translation of several articles from Turkish into English.

In Egypt, I am greatly indebted to the Airtours Holiday group and representatives in Sharm el Sheikh who went out of their way to make special arrangements for me and my wife to visit Cairo and carry out research with the assistance of a guide, Mona Go'maa, and our personal driver. We were also fortunate to meet up with a Deaf man, Mohammed Ahmed, who filled in for us some useful background in the murder of Waheeda Ghanem.

In the United States, there are so many to thank, especially in various courthouses in California (Holmes), Annapolis (McCullough), and Nebraska (Curtright). Special thanks must be given, I think, to Aszelea Delly of the St. Louis (Missouri) Civil Courthouse Criminal Records Office for photocopying for me the trial records of two cases, *State of Missouri v. Randolph* and *State of Missouri v. Spivey*. I also wish to thank Tom Bastean of the Missouri School for the Deaf and I must not forget the valuable help given to me by D. A. Sachs of Oakland, California with West Coast of America Deaf murder cases.

In England, too, Deaf and hearing friends went out of their way to find me information to help to fill in the missing details of a story, especially my devoted reader Simon Hesselberg.

Two of my American research trips were undertaken with my interpreter, Samantha Anderson, whose support made an enormous difference to the quality of information that I received. Samantha also made numerous telephone calls to contacts in the United States which because of the time difference often meant the calls being made in the middle of the night.

On the other two trips to the United States, I was accompanied by my wife Maureen without whose support it would have been difficult to complete this book. Not only did she assist in the research, often spending hours in libraries both in England and the States, and also on the Internet, but she also typed a large part of this book!

I am also indebted to my assistants Pauline Tolfree for some of the secretarial work and Laura Warriner for some telephone research.

Finally, to all my readers, my great thanks. Without your enthusiasm for Deaf crime, there would be no motivation for me to write these stories.

Peter W. Jackson
Winsford, Cheshire
May 2006

Chapter 1

1554: Turkey

Murder in the Ottoman Court

The Age of Sultan Süleyman the Magnificent from 1520 to 1566 heralded the growth of the Ottoman state of Turkey into one of the greatest empires ever, embracing all or part of the territories of present-day Turkey, parts of southern Russia, the Middle East countries southwards into Saudi Arabia, eastwards into Iraq, westwards into Hungary and Yugoslavia as well as the north African countries of Libya, Tunisia and Egypt.

In his conquests and subsequent rule over millions of subjects, he was helped by his many sons and by the people he employed in his royal court, known as the Ottoman Court. What is not commonly known is that sign language was in widespread use within the court, because many of the servants were deaf "mutes", who were not able to speak. The use of sign language was not confined to the deaf servants; hearing servants and other people associated with the Ottoman Court picked up the language, which was said to be capable of expressing ideas of great complexity.

The deaf servants were mainly used as doorkeepers to the Sultan's harem, where he kept his many wives. In common with many sultans of his time, Sultan Süleyman had a large number of wives, but his

1

favourite and his greatest love was Hürrem Sultan who cultivated the loyalty of her deaf doorkeepers.

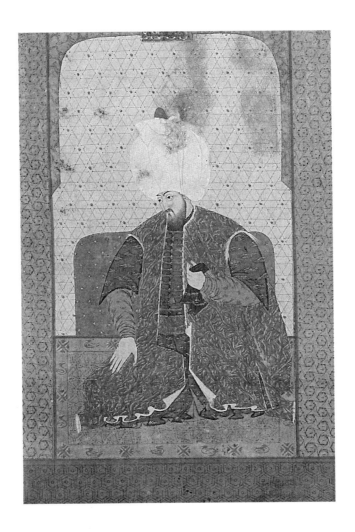

Sultan Süleyman the Magnificent

"Under cloak of darkness, love will find you. Fearing the dark, you will never find love."

—Unknown

Chapter 1

London, April 1817

She is dead.

Katherine, Lady Egerton, stared at the still form lying on the bed. Beloved sister, friend of the heart...Anne was gone. One minute she was struggling for breath, the next she lay silent and still. The only person in the world Kit loved more than life had left her.

They are all gone now. The sudden solitude tore at her heart.

Kit smiled sadly, gazing through eyes filled with tears at the frail body lying before her. *The brown mouse.* Anne's name for herself. Delicate even as a child, she had not long survived her marriage to the cruel Earl of Rutledge. Kit knelt at her sister's bedside, assailed by grief and guilt, and reached for Anne's hand. Could she have done more to save her sister from the dread disease? Could she have done more to protect Anne from the heartless man who was her husband?

Pale in death, Anne was still beautiful. Kit had often sketched that heart-shaped face. *Not a mouse, but a much-loved sister with a kind, unselfish heart.*

Kit had seen the end coming in the last few months, months through which she'd faithfully cared for Anne. The coughs that wracked her sister's slight frame had grown worse as Anne seemed to fade before Kit's eyes. Kit knew she was losing her even as she willed that weak body to heal. The physician said he could do nothing; each time he left shaking his head and telling Kit to make "the poor girl" comfortable as best she could. Kit had tried to save Anne, doing the only thing she knew by giving her syrup of horehound and honey. But such a small measure was not enough. Then, too, her sister had seemed to welcome death.

Suddenly, the room grew cold. Kit felt his presence, a looming evil behind her. She took a deep breath and summoned her strength.

"Leave her and come to me." Rutledge's tone was harsh and demanding. Kit had no need to see him to know his face would be twisted in an odious scowl, his lips drawn taut. "It is time."

"I must see to my sister."

"You need do nothing. I have arranged for the burial. Come away now."

Kit knew what he wanted, for she had seen the lust in his dark eyes. What at first had been sideways glances became leers and unwanted touches. Though she'd lived in his home since the death of her husband the baron, Kit had avoided the earl, rarely leaving her sister's bedside. She had been thinking of a way to escape, but her exhaustion in caring for Anne these last days left those plans incomplete. With meager funds, her options were few.

When she failed to rise at the earl's direction, his hand roughly gripped her shoulder. She stiffened at the pain of his fingers digging into her skin.

"I have waited long for you, Katherine, enduring that mockery of a marriage to your sister while all the while it was you I wanted, you I was promised. Now I shall have what is mine."

"No!" She rose swiftly, stepping back as she turned to face him. Revulsion rose in her throat. What did he mean by those words? She never had been promised to him!

His smirk transfigured what many thought of as a handsome face. Hadn't Anne at first been fooled by his aristocratic features and wavy brown hair? One had only to look closely to see his nature reflected in those thin lips and narrow eyes now focused on Kit. A deep furrow between his brows bore witness to his long having insisted upon having his way. When Kit sketched him, it had been as an attacking hawk.

"What will you do?" he asked smugly. "Where will you go, m'dear? You are alone and without funds. I am the one who has provided food and shelter for both you and your weak sister, though I wanted only you. You are *mine*, Katherine, and I will have you."

Terror seized her. Cornered, her eyes darted about like an animal snared in a trap. His tall figure blocked the door to the corridor; the only way out led through his adjacent bedchamber. She fled toward it.

She hastened into the room as he stalked after her, knowing she had but seconds, and her eyes searched for a weapon, something to hold him at bay. At the side of the fireplace were tools, short bars of iron that could fend off a man. But could she reach them in time?

He lunged for her just as she ran toward the fireplace. His body collided with hers, and she fell upon the wooden floor with a thud. Pain shot through her hip. His body crashed down upon hers, forcing the air from her lungs. She gasped a breath just as his mouth crushed her lips, ruthlessly claiming dominance.

Tearing away, she pushed against his shoulders with all her might, but his greater strength held her pinned to the floor. His hand gripped one breast and squeezed. She winced at the pain, but that was quickly forgotten the moment a greater terror seized her: His aroused flesh pressed into her belly.

Violently she struggled, but to no avail. His wet lips slid down her throat to her heaving chest as his fingers gripped the top of her gown and yanked at the silk. Kit heard the fabric tear as he ripped her gown and the top of her chemise, and she felt the cool air on her naked breasts. Frantic, she mustered strength she did not know she had. Twisting in his grasp, she reached for the iron poker now a mere foot away.

His mouth latched onto her breast where he voraciously sucked a nipple. Lost in his lust, he did not see her grasp the length of iron, raise it above him and bring it crashing down on his head. Stunned by the blow, he raised up, his eyes glazed. Kit let the bar fall again, this time with greater force. Blood spattered her chest and face as his body went limp. He slumped atop her.

Kit's heart pounded in her chest like a bird's wing beating against a cage. Frantically she shoved his face from her breast and rolled his body to the floor.

Unsteady at first, her breath coming in pants, Kit rose and looked down at the crumpled form lying before her, every nerve on edge as she gazed into that evil face, now deathly pale. Blood oozed from a gash in the earl's left temple. There was no sign of life, no movement.

I have killed him!

Fear choked off her breath as she wiped blood from her face with a sleeve, and with one last look toward her sister's bedchamber she raced from the room. Footsteps sounded down the hall. Alarmed at the prospect of encountering one of the earl's servants who would summon a constable, Kit knew she must find a place to hide, and there was nowhere to hide in the house. Quietly stealing into her bedchamber, she grabbed her cloak and reticule, stuffing inside it the one piece of her jewelry that could be sold to sustain her, and fled the dwelling.

Out on the street, she paused to draw her cloak tightly around her, desperate to cover her torn and bloody gown. Where could she go? Who would shelter her in the state she was in, given the deed she had done?

Only one name came to her.

Willow House.

Chapter 2

His collar turned up and his hands stuffed into his coat pockets, Martin braced himself against the unusually bitter April wind and stepped off the gangplank onto the London dock. He was happy to at last set foot on English soil. It had been a cold crossing from France.

Glancing at the young man who'd followed him off the ship, Martin spoke his thoughts aloud. "It's been ten long years since I left for France, John. So much has happened in that time. Who would have thought Napoleon's war on a 'nation of shopkeepers,' as he called us, would end the way it did?"

"Aye, sir. Though I only saw the last of it, and that from Calais, I know 'twas a long and hard-fought victory. But we sent the Corsican running in the end, didn't we?"

"That we did. We certainly did."

The English tongue felt foreign to Martin's lips, like exercising a stiff leg after long holding it still. He would lapse into French at times, he was certain, but it was best to try and return himself to the language of his countrymen. He had no desire to cross the Channel again anytime soon.

The cold wind off the water blew a lock of dark hair across his forehead, and Martin brushed it from his eyes as he studied the merchant ships lined up in the Thames. The cluster of tall masts stood like a forest of swaying trees bare of leaves, stark against the cold blue sky, but the familiar sight warmed his soul. His senses embraced the familiar smells of the river, the wood of the ships and the dock, salted sails waiting to be mended, sour ale from the taverns and the stench of sewage. One never forgot the smells of home even if they were not always pleasant. The sounds of the busy river, men shouting instructions while they loaded and unloaded cargo, captains calling to their crews and gulls shrieking as they vied for scraps of garbage were the sounds of his youth. The Powell family of merchant seamen had grown wealthy in the trade both war and peace had brought them. Of the four Powell sons, he was the only one who had left the sea. The only rebel. Oddly enough, after choosing to leave it, he missed that life and was looking forward to a return.

Why, at thirty-two, did he feel so old? Perhaps, he considered, it was because in the last decade he had lived another life, a life that was now coming to an end. As the Frenchman Martin Donet, he'd been England's eyes and ears in Paris during the war with Napoleon. A spy for the Crown. But that was done. With the battle at Waterloo and the Bourbon king restored to the throne, by Prinny's order Martin was coming home. Not that there wouldn't still be English spies in France, he mused; the allies had little trust for each other. But Martin would no longer be one of them.

He watched John studying the ships in the river, excitement causing the young man's brown eyes to glitter. The boy looked younger than his twenty years, but trained as he was in both weapons and stealth that youthful appearance was deceptive. Like Martin and the others who'd served the British Crown in France, John Spencer was more than he seemed.

"'Tis a right pretty sight, sir," the slim Englishman said.

"Are you glad then you've joined me, John?"

"Oh, aye, sir. I am. Though it will be good to see my family and my sisters before ye have need of me."

"Well, then," said Martin, handing over a small purse. "Here's some coin. Enjoy yourself, for soon you will have no time to frolic. Be at Ormond's townhouse tomorrow at the hour agreed. Do you have its location in mind?"

"Aye, sir. I recall it well. Though I were only there a few days, I'd not easily forget such a grand place."

The young man strode away, weaving through the dockworkers, his step light and his head of brown curls bobbing up and down. John was obviously glad to be included in what he thought would be a grand adventure. Martin remembered a time he might have felt the same. Now he just wanted his work for the Crown to be over.

As he started to turn away, Martin caught two seamen arguing as they left a dockside tavern. While he could only hear snippets of the conversation, a few harsh utterances were clear.

"I says His Majesty got what he deserved, livin' high while some poor curs don't even have bread!"

"Ye sound like one o' those bloomin' marchers, Davie, the ones they call the Blanketeers. Nothin' will change by yer throwing rocks and ye know it."

"Might not," the other man allowed, scratching the stubble on his chin. "Then again, it might."

The two had ambled too far away for Martin to hear the rest, but their exchange set his mind wandering. What exactly had happened to the Prince Regent? And who were the Blanketeers?

He supposed he would gain the answers soon enough. Ormond would know.

* * *

A short time later, Martin walked up the steps of his friend's Mayfair townhouse. It was an elegant abode indeed, as John recollected.

Martin had not seen Ormond or Ormond's wife since the year before, in France. Once a rake, attracting women in both Paris and London, the marquess had finally settled down with the mischievous bluestocking who captured his heart. Martin smiled as he thought of the adventure-loving Lady Mary. Had she changed from the hellion she'd once been now that she was Lady Ormond? Recalling what his friend told him, Martin rather doubted it. The pair was alike in that way. Heir to a dukedom, the marquess was also the Nighthawk, a legendary thief of Napoleon's most guarded secrets. Not many knew the truth.

A butler opened the door, bowed and took Martin's hat. He was expected.

"His lordship will receive you in the study, Sir Martin. Please follow me."

The butler led him to an open door, beyond which Ormond rose from behind a large carved desk. "Martin. Come join me. I was just pouring myself a brandy."

Martin examined his friend. The British peer looked happy. "A drink would be most appreciated. The crossing on my father's ship was a bit rough."

"You sailed into London on one of your father's ships?"

"Yes, the *Claire*—one of the new schooners, named after my mother. The captain stopped in Calais to pick up some cargo."

Pouring them each a glass of the rich brown liquor they'd often shared in Paris, Ormond cast him an assessing look. "You seem well, old man—though a bit tired around the eyes, I daresay."

Martin ran his hand through his hair, a nervous habit picked up in France, a lingering vestige of the stress from his occupation. "I do not always sleep well, as you know."

Ormond's dark eyes were sympathetic. "Mary and I were glad to hear of you returning to England. The change will do you good. Is it to be permanent?"

"It is," Martin said, accepting the proffered glass. "When the Prince Regent bestowed on me the Order of the Bath, I agreed to one last assignment. So, here I am."

"Ah, yes, the assignment. But what then?"

"I am certain Prinny would have another task, should I want one. But my plan is to return to the family business. I'm retiring as a spy. It's been a long time since I took a ship to sea, and I find myself curiously anxious to get back to a moving deck—at least for a while. My father was so delighted his rebel is coming home that he welcomed my order for a new schooner when I placed it some months ago. Then, after a few sailings, perhaps I shall take up the business side of Powell and Sons."

"I've never seen you near a ship, though I knew your family owned them. Paris has only the river."

"I'll not be missing Paris."

Ormond raised a brow. "The war?" When Martin did not reply, he added, "Elise...?"

After all these years, hearing her name still brought a bitter pain, as did the memory of their last night together; Martin's nightmares were testament to that. "You were wise to remain a bachelor then, Ormond. Ours was a dangerous business. A spy's wife is never safe. She'd be alive today if I'd not married her."

Before his friend could respond, the door to the study flew open. Mary, Marchioness of Ormond, burst upon them like a storm cloaked in sapphire silk, her skirts crackling like lightning. Martin had forgotten how beautiful she was, with golden hair and piercing green eyes. Her presence filled the room. She carried a bundle held tightly to her chest.

"Sir Martin! You're here! Hugh told me you would be arriving sometime in the next few days. How wonderful it is to see you. I understand you're here for a new assignment."

"Just Martin, please. I'm not used to the added title and prefer not to use it in the company of friends. To answer your question, my lady, yes, I've returned for the last of Prinny's tasks. What's that in your arms—the young heir I've heard about?"

Lady Ormond smiled proudly and held out the sleeping baby for Martin's inspection. He reached for the bundle, cradling it in his arms.

"Another like his father, I see. What a glorious head of dark hair. Are his eyes dark brown?"

"They are," said Lady Ormond, beaming with pleasure. She gave her husband a knowing glance. "They were blue for a brief while and then turned the color of brandy. Henry will be the very image of his father." The proud papa had come over to peer at the sleeping baby as if to verify her conclusion.

"He is a handsome boy, Ormond," Martin said, handing the baby back to his mother. "The first of many, I assume."

Lady Ormond blushed as she took him. "Well…at Christmas little Henry should have a new brother or sister."

Ormond put his arm around his wife and drew her close, kissing her temple. "I am very pleased at Mary's recent news."

Lady Ormond returned her husband a warm look, and Martin was suddenly envious of the two, of they love they shared, and without thinking he let out a long sigh. He had lost not just Elise on that cold December night but the babe she carried.

"Darling, I was just coming to tell you it's time I leave," said Lady Ormond. "Henry's nurse is waiting for me." She gave her husband a quick kiss and turned to go, then glanced at Martin and added, "I'll see you tomorrow. You are joining us for dinner, yes?"

"Dinner would be fine. Most gracious of you to ask."

"Perhaps you will consider staying with us, too? Hugh and I would welcome your company. It would give us a chance to hear the news."

Martin opened his mouth to protest, but Ormond answered for him. "I will see if I can talk him into it, love."

"Wonderful!" came Lady Ormond's reply. She then departed in a rush of silk, and Ormond refreshed their brandies and gestured to the two chairs in front of the fireplace.

"Stay with us, Martin, or my lady will be gravely disappointed. We have servants aplenty to tend your needs."

"All right," Martin agreed, taking a seat. It was an easy enough demand. "Some time with you and your lady before I face the task ahead would be welcome. My belongings are still on the ship. I'll have them delivered here."

"Good. And tomorrow we will all discuss the new assignment?"

"Of course. By the by, that reminds me. I heard two old salts arguing on the dock about something involving Prinny. Did something happen to him?"

"Yes. It was a scare, but he's fine now. I'll spare you the details until tomorrow when we can all discuss it together. I imagine you need a break."

"All right. You can expect John and me about six o'clock, as I'll have some other errands to run during the day. Tonight I just want to forget my work. As you say, I need some time away from Prinny's problems."

"What you need is a good woman, Martin. Mary has made all the difference in my life. Suddenly living is very enjoyable. Of course, she tries my patience at every turn"—he stared out the window as if remembering a particular event—"but I can't imagine life without her. She and little Henry are very dear to me. You need a wife, if you don't mind my saying so. It's been too long."

Martin grimaced. "It had not occurred to me to marry again. But a woman's warm body just now would be pleasant." He peered over his brandy at Ormond, and his lips quirked up in a grin. "Know any good bawdy houses?"

"Not I. Even before Mary entered my life I did not frequent them. I had mistresses in those days, and the last one brought me much trouble." Ormond seemed to think for a moment. "I did hear Eustace remark one evening at the Club about a place called Willow House. Something about them catering only to gentlemen and their guests. As Eustace told it, the women are supposed to be quite fine. Some have even become mistresses of his friends. I can ask him to recommend you."

"The thought occurs that times have changed in London. A recommendation is needed for a *brothel*?"

"Apparently one does for Willow House."

Raking his fingers through his hair, Martin chuckled. "Well, I agree it has been awfully long. Too long, in fact. Yes, I think I will take that recommendation."

Chapter 3

Abigail Darkin took a last look out the tall window at the green lawn, pleased with the recent additions to her property. The new pond surrounded by rosebushes gave a feeling of serenity to the sheltered environment of Willow House. Named for the weeping willow trees that wrapped around two sides of the elegant white manor like the arms of a welcoming lover, this had become more than her home. It was a refuge.

She remembered fondly the distant uncle who bequeathed her the house upon his death. It had been a great boon—and a surprise. She hadn't known the uncle very well, and she'd just left her position as nanny to two young ladies now grown. Of course, she'd had only a little money and no idea how she would keep up such a wondrous residence; still, she had been happy to have it. Who could have foreseen that her soft heart and reputation for kindness would draw girls of the night to her, young beauties who wanted a safe place away from the bawdy houses of Covent Garden or worse? Willow House soon became known as the most elegant brothel in London, members of the *ton* and their wealthy friends its only clientele. Abby had standards after all.

"Miss Abby! There be a young woman to see ye. The lass seems very upset."

Abby raised her head from the ledgers on her desk to find a young maid at the door, cheeks flushed and a distraught look upon her round face. It was only late afternoon, so the house was quiet. Clients did not arrive until late evening, and those few who stayed the night were gone after breakfast.

Tucking a dark brown curl into the coil of hair at her nape, she set aside her business. "Relax, Emma. The house is not burning. Did she give her name?" Sometimes the young maid failed to remember her manners and was quick to overreact, though Abby had been schooling her to become a proper servant.

The maid shook her head, causing errant blonde curls to fall around her face. "No, ma'am. I did not think to ask her." Sucking air through her teeth and wrinkling her forehead she added, "I suppose I should've, shouldn't I? But she looked so pathetic, even frightened, and she seemed ta know ye."

Used to seeing desperate girls on her doorstep who'd heard of her kindness, Abby was unsurprised. She tried to help all find legitimate work. Of course, the most beautiful, well-spoken and gracious were allowed to join those who lived and worked at Willow House, if such was their desire and there was an opening.

Casting a last glance at her unfinished ledgers, she sighed. "All right, Emma. Show her in."

The girl arrived quite disheveled, with strands of dark flame-colored hair falling about her shoulders and cloak, but Abby recognized her immediately. It had been years since she'd seen the young women whom she'd served as nanny, the girls she had raised as her own, but she would know Kit, Lady Katherine Endicott—no, now she was Lady Egerton—anywhere.

"My God, Katherine, what has happened to you?"

Katherine fell into her arms, sobbing. "Oh, Abby! Anne has died, and her husband, Lord Rutledge, he…he tried to rape me! It happened so suddenly I didn't have time to plan where I'd go and then I thought of you." Pleading blue eyes stared up at her. "May I stay the night, Abby? I've nowhere else to go given the…the circumstances."

Abby stroked her hair and held the overwrought girl close, sad to find that she had lost one of the dear Endicott children and now the other was in dire need of help. "You were right to come to me, child. Of course you may stay the night, and longer if it will help. Did the man know you were coming here?" She was prepared should any unwanted guest seek entrance to her establishment, but she preferred to be warned.

Katherine's face turned ashen, and her head jerked toward the door.

"What is wrong, child? Do you fear he followed you? My doorman will protect you. He's a big fellow and can be quite fierce if need be."

The young woman took a deep breath and let it out as if trying to calm herself, then turned and looked into Abby's eyes. "No, Abby. I fear the man is dead. Rutledge lies bleeding and still. I…I think I've killed him."

"Oh my," Abby said, helping her frightened ward into a chair. "Come sit. There is nothing for it now. If you killed the man in defense of your honor, surely you will not be held responsible. Do not think of that." She had her doubts about how the House of Lords would respond to the slaying of one of its own, but she would not share them. "I have a special room never used by our clients that you may have."

Yes, she would help this child who sat sobbing before her, whose scrapes she had once tended, whose nightmares she had soothed. Anne and Kit had been the children of her heart. She began to pace in front of the fireplace, followed by the eyes of the young woman as Katherine surveyed her surroundings for the first time. Abby wondered if the girl was noting the richness of the room, the polished cherry wood furniture and shelves full of classic books. Behind Abby, a fire crackled in the stone fireplace.

Abby's gaze fell on the decanter of French brandy gracing a small table next to the brocade-covered chair where Kit sat in front of the desk. "Perhaps a drink might be appropriate just now, my child. Something to warm you?" She walked to the table and poured a generous helping.

"Is it true what I have heard, Abby?" Kit asked with faltering speech as her eyes drifted around the room. "Is Willow House a…a brothel?"

"Well, yes," Abby conceded. The label, while accurate, still offended her. She handed the glass to Kit and admitted, "I didn't start out to make it one. It just happened as the girls came to me. Though I helped some leave that life, others wanted to stay and pursue their former occupation. They are all quite lovely, and they will all be kind to you, Kit. Many have had hard beginnings and would well understand your tale of a man trying to force himself upon you. That is one reason they feel at home at Willow House. We entertain only *gentlemen*."

Kit sat looking at her hands, cradling the glass of brandy in her lap, tears falling from her eyes. "I love you, you know that, Abby. If you have found peace in this place, I'll not judge you or the girls."

"You always did have a kind heart, Katherine. I see that has not changed."

Kit looked up with reddened eyes. "Once I had such wonderful dreams, Abby. You remember. Dreams of a life with a husband to love me—and children. I've no dreams now."

"Do not despair, child." She patted the young woman's back in sincere comfort as Kit sipped her drink. "Things will seem better in the morning. Emma will show you to your room, and while you are having a nice hot bath I will find something for you to wear. The girls here are all most elegantly attired and willing to share. Some hot food and a good night's rest will put you to rights."

"Oh, Abby, I don't think I shall ever be right again. What can I do? Where am I to go?"

Abby thought for a moment. "I have a friend who places young women in the homes of the gentry...to act as servants, mostly, but in special cases, such as yours, as governesses and the like. She may be able to help you. As an earl's daughter and a baron's widow you should have a better future, but perhaps for now this will give you something to do. A place to find solace while we sort this out. I'll give you her information when I bring you the gown."

* * *

Martin raised the brass knocker, but before he let it drop the black door opened and a well-attired butler with gray hair inclined his head and accepted Martin's hat.

"Good evening, sir. Please follow me. Miss Abby will see you in the parlour."

Martin followed the servant through a black and white marble-floored entry hall, passing a wide staircase leading to the next floor, at the base of which stood a large man with blond hair looking straight ahead ignoring them. Down another corridor they went, to the right, and Martin noted the impressive furnishings of the rooms he passed. They would compete well with those he'd seen in Mayfair. Finally the butler stopped and bade him enter a small, well-appointed room. The first thing Martin noticed was the crystal chandelier hanging above two brocade sofas flanking a marble fireplace. A gilded mirror set over the mantel made the room appear much larger than it was.

The butler departed, closing the double doors. A well-attired woman in her late forties, dark brown hair pulled back into a knot, faced Martin with appraising hazel eyes.

"You are Sir Martin Powell?"

"Yes, ma'am. And you would be...Miss Abby?"

A genuine smile spread across the woman's face, and Martin relaxed. She might have been a treasured aunt, this woman with the twinkling eyes, someone you might tell all your secrets. A comforting presence. Not at all what he'd expected.

"I am Miss Abby, and this is Willow House. Lord Eustace commends you to me as one who has the trust of the Prince himself. That is a high honor. Welcome. How may I serve you, Sir Martin?"

"Well...I was hoping to meet one of your girls this evening. You come highly recommended by Eustace in return. I have been away from London for many years, and have no...attachments."

"You speak with a slight accent, Sir Martin."

"Ah, yes. My mother is French and I've been living in Paris."

"Of course," the woman said as she poured him a brandy. He accepted the drink and took a healthy swallow, appreciating the gesture and the fact she asked no further questions. The war had been over for more than a year, but he was reticent to speak of his time in France. Even to a favorite aunt with twinkling eyes.

"You may stay the night if you like," Miss Abby continued, "and even stay for breakfast. Or, you can leave earlier. As you desire. We are very flexible and very discreet. No questions will be asked."

"Right, then." Martin was suddenly anxious to move forward. He set down his half-empty glass.

"Do you have any preferences, sir?"

"Ah...no." He felt himself smiling. "Just 'beautiful,' but then I've heard that is never an issue at Willow House."

The madam returned his smile. "If that is your only requirement, I believe we can meet your needs rather well."

Martin was done with polite conversation. "If you will just tell me where to go?"

"Upstairs, the next to the last door on the right. If you need assistance, the rather large Scot in the entry can assist you."

Martin thanked her and left the room, thinking he heard a soft chuckle behind him. Had it been so long since he'd been with a woman that he appeared anxious? The thought was disconcerting. After many years of serving the Crown, he was no randy youth.

He headed quickly in the direction he'd come. In the entry he passed the large blond man standing guard. The Scot, Martin guessed. Up the carpeted stairs he went, but at the top he struggled to remember what exactly Miss Abby said. The end of the corridor was dark. Which door on the right? The last door? Yes, that was it.

Martin slowly opened the door and moved into the shadows. Inside, a young woman stood before the room's only window, the light of the fire behind her dancing in waves of long auburn hair that fell nearly to her waist. Moonlight from the window cast pale rays of light across her profile, revealing delicate features, a slim neck and ivory skin. He was surprised to find such a treasure in a brothel, even a high-class brothel. The girl appeared otherworldly, ethereal, like something out of a dream.

He was drawn to her as if summoned.

* * *

Kit stood at the window, lost in thought and staring out into the night. What had happened to her life, to her dream of a husband and family? How had it come to this? She and Anne had been raised as daughters of an earl!

Anger rose within her, an anger that caused her teeth to clench. It was the fault of her father, who, lost in grief upon her mother's death, gave himself to gambling and drink. Caring little for life, he had not survived to provide for his daughters, abandoning them to husbands he would never have chosen. Kit had determined she would never lose herself in a love like that, nor would she cling so desperately to a memory that she would welcome her own demise. She had been strong for both herself and Anne. But she wasn't feeling very strong tonight. Just weary and alone.

Oh, God. What's to become of me? If only someone would hold me and tell me it will be all right.

As if in answer, a deep voice came out of the darkness. "Come to me," it said.

Kit spun, her blood running cold. A tall figure stood in the shadows. Deep in her thoughts, she'd failed to hear the door open or close.

"Who are you?" she asked, her voice quavering.

The figure took a step forward. Firelight cast a warm glow onto the sculpted features of the tall man, and sooty black hair framed a handsome face with high cheekbones, a strong nose, and curving, sensuous lips. To Kit's artist's mind, the man was very nearly beautiful. Like a painting by Thomas Lawrence. Like the knight she'd dreamt would one day come for her.

His mouth twitched up on one side, almost a smile. "Miss Abby sent me."

What was Abby thinking, sending such a man to her door? But before Kit could think of what to say, he took another step forward.

"Come to me," he repeated.

Perhaps it was the two glasses of brandy she'd had, or perhaps it was the man himself who drew her. He was a stranger, but his voice, so warm and soothing, was hypnotic. Her doubts slipped away and she went to stand before him. His hands caressed her arms as he slowly drew her to his warm chest. Eyes like blue flames held her gaze, so intense she could feel them reaching into her soul.

"What's your name, beauty?"

Still in a daze, she responded. "Kit."

"Well...*mon chaton*, my kitten, we will take this slow. It has been a long time for me. You need do nothing. Just let me love you."

He inclined his head, and his lips touched hers ever so softly. His arms wrapped around her. The embrace promised every comfort Kit desired. For a brief moment she allowed herself to melt like wax before a flame.

The man pulled away and looked at her, his eyes falling to her curves barely disguised in the thin silk wrapper she wore. "So beautiful...are you real?" His indigo eyes glowed in the soft light of the fire as he ran his fingers through her hair sending shivers down her spine. His throaty whisper came to her as if across a great gulf. All she could do was stare.

His warm lips soon nuzzled her neck, brushing over the rapid pulse at the base of her throat. Kit closed her eyes, and a long sigh escaped as she lifted her hands to his shoulders then entwined her fingers in the waves of his ebony hair. She had never been with a man like this. The old baron never excited her, and Rutledge terrified her. The responsible thing would be to send him away. Obviously he thought her to be someone else. But perhaps for once she could follow her own desires; she could let this man continue to kiss her. Like a drug, he was taking away all of her pain.

The touch of his warm lips on her throat sent another shiver up her spine. His hands roamed her wrapper, gently cupping her breasts, and it was as if he touched her bare skin, leaving tingling heat in the tracks of his fingers. He offered warmth and comforting words, everything she wanted. Perhaps that was why she did not turn away. Why not let him love her as he intended?

His lips returned to her mouth. She responded, opening to him. His tongue slipped inside to stroke hers, slowly, erotically. She had never been kissed like this. Once again he was gentle, handling her as if she were precious, and Kit responded with a passion she did not understand. She had dreamt of being touched like this: by a gentle man, by a knight with eyes of blue flame. Was it wrong to let it happen?

As if reading her mind, he picked her up and carried her across the room. Another vague thought to protest quickly faded. She would not deny herself what she desperately wanted. Not tonight. Perhaps just once she could pretend she lived a fairy tale.

Dark blue velvet curtains were drawn back at the four posters of the large bed where he laid her. The soft down cover rose up to cradle her body, embracing her like a welcoming cloud. She sat with half open eyes as the man undid her robe, sliding it from her shoulders, and the garment fell away to reveal her naked form. Quickly he shed his clothing, returning and covering her with his body as if he knew instinctively that she craved his warmth.

His rigid manhood, ready for her, pressed into her thigh. She was surprised she felt no alarm. No, she wanted this man, needed him like her very next breath. The overwhelming passion rising within her was new.

He kissed her again, this time deeply, and then shifted to one side, bracing himself on an elbow as his warm hand traveled from her neck to her breasts. His leg slipped between hers, and the warm skin of his leg pressed against her inner thigh. She reached for his nape, pulled his mouth back to hers and turned in toward his body. When his palm caressed her nipple, she pressed her breast into his hand, wanting more.

He bent his head to her breast, gently licking, and then he took the sensitive tip into his mouth. Heart beating faster, Kit entwined her fingers in his hair and held him close. A moan escaped her when he brought his lips back to hers, wooing her with kisses and roaming hands. His manner proclaimed she was his. She reveled in that possession, for she wanted to be his if only for this one night. He could take away the terrible memories, the loss, the pain.

As if he heard her thoughts he whispered, "Kitten, you are mine tonight. I intend to love you well."

His warm hand moved across her belly and down to the nest of dark red curls at the apex of her thighs. Gently he touched her there, parting the folds of her most sensitive flesh with his fingers, and she shivered but welcomed the caress of that responsive bud. She was already wet for him, the honey liquid having flowed unbidden in response to his first touches. It might have been a long time for him, but he must have once loved well.

"You are sweet innocence in your responses, Kitten, as if I'm your first man. I cannot wait much longer to be inside you."

Kit knew little of lovemaking. The old baron she married had been kindly enough, though he was more like a grandfather, which made their wedding night a perfunctory affair. Then, a mere two weeks after they wed, the old lord died of heart failure. Never before had she experienced the feelings, the sensations or the response that this man drew so easily from her.

He rose above her, letting his erection settle into the cleft guarding her most intimate center. Her flesh was slick, sensitive and hungry for him, and when he rubbed himself over the opening it caused her breathing to speed. She lifted her hips in invitation.

He entered her slowly, as if savoring the feel. Though he was large, she was so wet that he slid forward unimpeded. Deep within her he stilled, and she responded to the fullness by gripping him with her inner muscles, imprisoning his warm hard flesh. Then, with a single thrust, he drove deeper still.

"Ah, God, Kitten," he rasped as he started to move—slowly at first, rhythmically, then faster. The slight pain that had come with his first hard thrust quickly disappeared. She wasn't a virgin, but she had only been taken twice by the old baron, and he had been small she now realized.

Who was this man who claimed her? What magic had he woven to take one who in her heart had never been taken before? She moved now in a dance so instinctive that she needed no instruction as she wrapped her legs around his. Her body responded to him as if he'd always been her lover, and Kit raised her hips to take him deeper, wanting all of him. He kissed her passionately—even, it seemed, desperately.

Her breathing came in pants as she raised her hips again, digging her fingers into his warm muscled shoulders. A tension had begun to build, one she'd never before experienced, pulling her to the crest of an unfamiliar mountaintop she yearned to reach. Wrapped in the throes of passion, they moved as one. Closing her eyes tightly, Kit willed the pleasure to continue as it swiftly built. Then, with a burst of stars, spasms welled up deep within her. They rolled over her as her muscles gripped his hardened flesh. Kit was infused by a pleasure she had never known.

A soft cry escaped her lips just as the stranger's body stiffened and released a flood of warmth within her. Small echoes of pleasure radiated from where he was lodged deep inside. Sinking into a trancelike state of bliss, she clung to him, and he held her in return, whispering French words she recognized as words of love.

* * *

Martin had never before experienced any woman like the one he held now. Elise had died so young. Their lovemaking had been sweet and joyful, enthusiastic…but nothing like this. He told himself it was just because it had been a long while since he'd known a woman's body. But he knew it was more. It was this woman. It was everything about her.

It was as if his body recognized hers. They had moved in tandem like two who had long been lovers, though in other ways she seemed so innocent. Because of that innocence, he had been most tender with her.

Moving to one side, he pulled her close, stroking her long hair that to his fingers felt like silk. He kissed her forehead as she rested her head on his shoulder, her full breasts pressed against him, warm pillows of pleasure. Through barely opened eyes, he glimpsed her pale skin and long limbs glowing in the dim moonlight. A goddess in repose. Drawn to that beauty, he began to stroke her, reveling in the warmth of her body and the softness of her rounded breasts with their soft, dusky nipples. And with each touch of her silken skin, his body responded.

He whispered in her ear, "*Tu m'ensorceler.*"

She had, indeed, bewitched him. She was an enigma: while seemingly innocent, still so passionate, so responsive. There was nothing practiced about her. Was she new to this life? As they lay together, he wondered. A fallen dove perhaps. Whatever she was, whoever she was, somewhere during this night she had become precious to him. She had become *his* kitten.

Finally, he could fight sleep no longer. Holding her close, his last thought before slumber was to make her his mistress.

Yes, he would see Miss Abby about it in the morning.

Chapter 4

Kit woke before dawn. There was a misty quality to the room, a soft glow, a gray light, an unreal twilight. Then, instantly, she was fully awake.

Where was she?

Abby's.

The heavy arm draped over her and the hand caressing her breast almost caused her to panic until she remembered the night before and its events. Remembered *him.* Feeling that warm wall of his chest behind her, she turned her head on the pillow and looked into his sleeping face framed by thick raven hair. The memory of their lovemaking flowed into her mind bringing heat to her cheeks. Happiness.

Shame followed. *Oh God. What have I done? I've made love to a stranger in a brothel.* Gripped by the reality of her situation, Kit was suddenly desperate to leave. She must escape before he awoke. She could not face him. She could not face Abby!

Carefully she lifted his arm from her chest. Lost to Morpheus, the stranger did not move, and Kit slipped from the bed and crept silently to the armoire where she had hung the new gown and underthings Abby gave her. She dressed hurriedly, thankful for the front-lacing corset Abby provided. Then, anxious to be away, she took her cloak and reticule and tiptoed from the room—and from Willow House.

* * *

It was the warm sun hitting his face that woke Martin from the deepest sleep he had experienced in a very long while, the first time in a fortnight he'd not had nightmares. He could still smell her scent of spring roses on the pillow, but he quickly realized the enchantress he'd held in his arms was no longer lying beside him.

Quelle beauté!

He sat up, letting his legs fall over the side of the bed and dragged his fingers through his hair. His body responded as he thought of having the beautiful redhead again, but where was she? Perhaps downstairs having breakfast.

Hurriedly he dressed and descended, anxious to see her. He had already begun to think of the enticing woman as his. He had not forgotten his plan of the night before. If anything, that need had grown stronger.

At the base of the stairs, a young woman with dark hair and wearing a yellow gown lingered briefly in the entry hall, giving him a long perusal before smiling and gliding away. Martin barely noticed. The big bruiser was missing, so no one stopped him as he hurried down the corridor where he'd first met the proprietress, searching until he found a room that appeared to be a study. Through the open door he saw Miss Abby sitting behind a desk poring over papers.

"Where is she?" he blurted, forgetting his manners and not bothering to greet her.

Raising her head, Miss Abby looked surprised. "Who, Sir Martin?"

"The woman I was with last night. She said her name was Kit."

A look of horror crossed the proprietress's face. "Did you say *Kit?*"

"Why, yes. The girl with the auburn hair. I liked her very well and want to discuss terms of having her become my mistress. Taking her off the rolls, so to speak. I wanted to speak to her again before I did so."

Miss Abby rose and covered her mouth with her hand, eyes frozen in shock. Without a word, she ran past him and out the door. Puzzled, Martin followed. He had to hurry to keep up. Miss Abby moved fleetly down the corridor, up the stairs and then into the last bedchamber on the right. Martin was intrigued to discover what she was about. Kit could not have returned so fast, could she? What necessitated this rush?

Kit had not returned. In the empty room, the proprietress did a full circle then dropped into a chair at the side of the fireplace, letting her face fall into her hands. "Oh, no. No, no."

Martin remained puzzled but his instincts were on alert. Something was terribly wrong. "Miss Abby?"

She raised her head to stare pointedly at him, eyes still full of horror. "This was not the room I sent you to! It was the *next to the last* door on the right." Her head fell back into her hands and she sobbed.

Martin shook his head. "I do not understand why you are so upset. It matters little to me which girl you intended. I like the one I had. Where is she, Miss Abby? Where is Kit?"

The proprietress sat up, straightened her back and let out a ragged sigh. "Not Kit, Sir Martin. She's…"

Martin felt frustration well up inside, for the proprietress was clearly reticent to continue. "You can trust me, Miss Abby. I've kept the Crown's secrets for many years. I can certainly keep yours."

Miss Abby's gaze was full of hopeful trust. "She's Katherine, *Lady* Egerton."

* * *

What had befallen her beloved Kit? Abby was indeed horrified. As if the girl had not suffered enough, and now this? But she would not seek answers from Sir Martin. He was only a man after all. No, he would never understand why a young, gently-bred widow whose dreams were destroyed and who had just survived an attempted rape would give herself to a stranger she did not know. Abby did not understand it herself. She could only surmise there was something very special about this man who had been entrusted with the Crown's secrets, something that had spoken to deep longings in the young woman's aching heart.

Abby had liked Sir Martin herself when she'd greeted him the evening before. She considered herself a good judge of character, and she believed him a man of honor. Lord Eustace had spoken highly of him. Still, how much could she safely tell him? How much could she reveal without betraying Kit's trust? She supposed limited information would do no harm. Perhaps it might even help.

She spent some minutes telling him Kit's story and what brought her to Willow House. She did not want him to think ill of the young woman or believe Kit to be one of the courtesans who worked there should he ever encounter her again.

"The girls' mother died of consumption, you see. Their father, a dear man, slowly succumbed to a broken heart. Of course, the world just saw another reckless member of the *ton* lost to drink and gambling. When he finally passed away, he left his two daughters near penniless. In the middle of Kit's first Season, their guardian hastily arranged marriages for both her and her older sister, Anne to Lord Rutledge and Kit to old Lord Egerton."

"To be torn from such a life of privilege…" Martin reflected, incredulous.

"It was wrenching," Abby agreed, "and it broke my heart, though I was powerless to do anything to help. Both marriages, it seemed, were doomed from the beginning. The baron died soon after Kit wed him, she told me, and the meager allowance provided her was swallowed up by the losses of the property held by the baron's sons. In truth his sons had no desire to help her. So, Kit fled to Anne. When her sister took ill—the same sickness that befell their mother—Kit took up her care. But as Anne's health worsened, Rutledge made clear his lecherous intent."

Abby was gratified that Sir Martin listened so patiently, and by his look of both sympathy and anger as she told him of the assault by Rutledge and Kit's actions in self-defense. His expression grew grave as the story finished, and when she was done, he thanked her and departed, vowing to search all of London if he must to find her. Abby bid him success in his search but wondered if Kit wished to be found by him. For herself, she had other ways of finding her friend.

* * *

"How was your evening at Willow House?" Ormond asked as he welcomed Martin into his library. Neither Lady Ormond nor John had yet arrived. Martin assumed it wouldn't be long. He had spent most of the afternoon beginning his search.

He hesitated to answer, thinking of what to say as he surveyed the room, allowing the furnishings to distract him. They bespoke not just wealth but a desire for comfort. Burgundy velvet curtains drawn back from the windows that faced the street allowed into the room what lingering daylight remained. Leather chairs flanked a marble fireplace. Above the mantel was a painting of a foxhunting scene. All was very masculine. All was very Ormond. Martin wondered what sort of home he would create for himself if he ever settled down again. It was a question he'd thought long abandoned.

"An interesting question," he finally said, but he offered no more. Where to begin?

He took the customary brandy Ormond handed him and settled into a comfortable leather chair. A moment later he said, "I found a woman."

"Well." Mouth curving into a wry smile, Ormond took the chair beside him. "Since we are talking about Willow House, I hardly find that surprising."

"You misunderstand, my friend," Martin corrected. "Not just any woman."

Ormond did not reply at first. Then: "You found this woman at Willow House?"

"It's not what you think. This is a lady I desire above all others, and she has since disappeared. Worse, the trail grows cold."

Ormond shook his head. "I must say you have me a bit confused. Start at the beginning. Who is she?"

"Katherine, and she is a lady."

"What the devil was a lady doing there?" Ormond asked.

"I know it sounds strange, and I would ask you to say nothing to anyone about her being there. The circumstances are most unusual. It seems her former nanny owns the establishment. The girl came there seeking refuge, and, well, there was a mix-up. Do you know the name Egerton?"

"There was an old Lord Egerton my father knew quite well. I thought he died. Is she his daughter?"

"Ah, no. But if it's the same Lord Egerton, she was his wife. Now she is his widow. They weren't married long before he died. Rather a sad tale, really. Lady Egerton's only sibling, a sister, died as well as both parents. Kit—that is what she told me to call her—has few funds and nowhere to go, and according to the former nanny she is fleeing a desperate situation. In defending her honor, she killed her brother-in-law, the Earl of Rutledge."

Ormond's eyes were wide. "That sounds grim. Rutledge... I know the man. Not well, but I see him now and then. He has—or had—a nasty reputation for violence. It is even rumored he takes on the devil's tasks when they serve his purposes."

"Poor Kit." Martin shook his head, truly dismayed.

"And in one evening you know you want her? She must be quite a prize."

"She is, but perhaps for the sake of the lady's honor I'll not go into details. I vow I will find her if I have to turn over all of London, and you know I can do that."

"Yes, I daresay you can." Ormond shrugged. "When you find her, bring her here. My wife would welcome her. Mary is not a woman who judges. When we were betrothed, she mistakenly believed my former mistress was carrying my child and insisted I marry her instead!"

"That sounds quite the tangle."

"I assure you it was. For weeks I carried with me a special license thinking I'd never get to use it. Fortunately it all came right in the end, but you can see why my wife would have no qualms about giving shelter to your Lady Egerton, whatever it was that happened."

A knock came at the door, followed by Ormond's "Enter," and the butler stepped into the room. He waited to be acknowledged and at his master's nod spoke.

"A young man has arrived, my lord. He says his name is Mr. John Spencer and that you are expecting him."

"Ah, yes, we are, Jenkins. Let Cook know we'll be another hour before dinner. Has her ladyship returned from visiting her mother?"

"Not yet, my lord. I will show the young man in and then see about Cook. Will there be anything else?"

"No, Jenkins. Thank you."

The butler left and shortly returned with John, who was dressed as quite the dandy for dinner, no doubt wanting to impress the man he knew was the infamous Nighthawk. A flash of emerald green waistcoat peeked out from a royal blue jacket over cream-colored pantaloons, and the young man's brown curls had been neatly combed.

Ormond chuckled as John stepped in. "Good evening, John. It is good to see you again. I trust you are well?"

John bowed his head. "Good day to ye, my lord. Aye, quite well."

"Come in, then," said Ormond. "We were just about to get started."

"I heard ye married the Lady Mary, my lord, and now she is Lady Ormond. Will she be here?" the young man asked anxiously. "'Tis a year since I've seen her."

Clearly John was taken with Ormond's wife. It did not surprise Martin. He remembered his own first reaction to the blonde beauty.

Ormond smiled. "Yes, John. It is just as you say. The former Lady Mary is now my marchioness. I expect her in time for dinner, if not before." He pulled out a chair for the young man and sank back into the seat next to Martin. "Prinny's new task will require all our efforts. My desire, just so you know, is to keep my adventure-loving wife out of it if I can."

"What's it all about, then?" inquired Martin, setting down his brandy.

"The situation has been brewing for quite a while, and it involves some discontent among the common people. Even riots."

"Riots in England?" Martin said, astonished. John, sitting beside him, gaped.

"Fortunately for you, Martin," Ormond continued, "your sojourn in France allowed you to miss them. Indeed, I missed the beginnings while I was there. They have roots going back many years. While we were in Paris chasing Napoleon's secrets, the followers of a General Ned Ludd caused quite a stir in the north counties."

"Ah...the Luddites. I've heard of them." Martin had a vague memory of someone passing through Paris telling him of the strong reaction of the textile workers to the machinery replacing their livelihoods.

"My wife argues vehemently for their cause, as you might imagine," Ormond said. "The lace and hosiery workers lost jobs when the machines were brought in. They couldn't feed their families. Since then, the weavers have joined in."

"Interesting. We did not see this in France. Perhaps the war made this a lesser concern?" Martin suggested aloud.

"I suspect so," said Ormond. "But in England it has become a problem of great magnitude. The economic depression, made worse by the wars with France, even led to an attack on the Prince Regent this last January."

"An attack on Prinny?" Martin felt his brows rise. "So that's what the old salts were talking about."

"Gawd," said John.

"Quite," said Ormond, eyeing him. "His carriage was mobbed as it left Parliament, and the rabble threw rocks and shouted insults to the monarchy. The windows were shattered and glass flew everywhere. It must have been terrifying."

"You said he is fine now. Was he hurt?" asked Martin.

"Amazingly, no. But the incident has sent ripples through the government."

John stared, agog, and Martin shook his head at the attack on the monarch. It was bleak news indeed. Still, Ormond didn't stop there.

"Parliament fears the revolutionary fervor in France has spread to our shores, and has, as you might find unsurprising, overreacted. They're passing one law after another designed to keep the populace in their place. The Home Secretary, Viscount Sidmouth, the fool, and his sidekick, Viscount Castlereagh, have managed to get Parliament to suspend habeas corpus, making it possible for those suspected of treason to be imprisoned without trial. George Cruikshank, the caricature artist, has already published a drawing depicting Castlereagh hanging Lady Liberty."

Martin shook his head.

"It gets worse," Ormond said. "Sidmouth has also ordered the arrest of all printers and writers of materials considered inciting, so the press is up in arms. All this has only stirred the pot, I'm afraid."

The marquess rose, pulled a map from a drawer and spread it on top of his desk, and Martin and John gathered around him. Pointing his silver letter opener to a spot in northwestern England, Ormond directed their attention to a certain town. "There was an incident. Just here." The three men peered closely as Ormond continued, "Manchester, wouldn't you know. In March there was a demonstration. Hundreds of cotton workers carrying blankets in the cold protested the government's actions. Their aim, I'm told, was to march on London to gain the Prince Regent's attention. It is said they were hoping for some say in government. It's been dubbed 'the March of the Blanketeers.'"

Martin nodded his head. "Ah, the Blanketeers. I can see Cruikshank's caricatures now."

"The government did not find it amusing, I can assure you," Ormond chided. "The leaders of the march were arrested, but the fears of a revolution spreading to England have not faded in the weeks that followed. Sidmouth is sending out spies all over Britain to investigate what he believes are 'centers of discontent.' My own information suggests they may be making the situation worse. I even begin to wonder just who was behind the attack on the Prince Regent."

"Are you suggesting these spies are acting as *agents provocateurs*?" Martin asked, horrified.

"Your French is exactly right. These spies might be creating disturbances rather than quelling them, increasing the opportunity—even the justification—for further repressive measures."

"What does the Prince Regent expect me to do about it?" Martin wondered aloud. "I am a spy, myself."

A smile spread slowly across Ormond's face. "Ah, but that's just where you come in, don't you see?"

Perplexed, Martin held his breath.

"Prinny wants action taken but doesn't trust Sidmouth's lackeys. In that, I believe he is right. You, my friend, are to spy on the spies."

Martin let out his breath. "*Bon Dieu*," he whispered.

To which John added, "Blimey!"

Chapter 5

Her heart beating in her throat, Kit knocked on the door of the elegant townhouse in Grosvenor Square. Surely she could do this. After all, she and Anne had several governesses over the years, so she knew the role well.

She had no choice, either. She needed a place to hide and was not afraid of hard work. Abby had been wonderful to take her in, but Kit could not stay at Willow House, particularly not after what had happened there. Images of the dark-haired man with the indigo eyes and gentle touch stole into her mind sending shivers up her spine. She could still feel his hands on her skin. She could still feel the shame of what she'd done. Like a tarnished silver pitcher, Kit worried she wore her terrible secret on her face.

Mustering her strength, she took a deep breath and forced from her mind all thoughts of the man and the night, and tried to focus on the present and the task at hand. How hard could it be to help twin sisters with their coming out? To be a finishing governess? It was in the middle of her first Season that Kit's life had changed forever, but she'd experienced enough of the *haut ton* to guide another. And compared to her other options, helping two girls who'd spent years on the Continent become ladies of London society was a readily acceptable task. The woman whose name Abby had given Kit, Mrs. Pendergast, had been most enthusiastic about the opportunity.

A maid in a black and white uniform opened the door. "Lady Katherine Endicott?"

Kit nodded. Knowing of her circumstances, Mrs. Pendergast had suggested she use her name before marriage.

"Please forgive me for keeping you waiting, m'lady," the maid said, dipping into a small curtsey and opening the door. "The butler is out this afternoon and the footman has been sent on an errand, so it will be me showing you to the mistress." She swung the door wide to allow Kit enter and bade her follow. "My name is Gertrude, but the twins call me Gertie. 'Tis sweet, really."

Kit smiled at the friendly, talkative girl whose ramblings about the twins became exuberant. Looking more closely, however, Kit reconsidered. The servant wasn't exactly a "girl." She might be in her mid twenties, older even than Kit herself. The maid's brown hair was drawn back into a tight knot topped by a white mobcap, which Kit thought a bit severe, but the plump young woman's blue eyes twinkled and there were lines at their edges that said she smiled often. No wonder the twins called her Gertie. She had a face that suggested her answers to all their questions would be yes.

They passed through a set of double doors opening into a large room filled with light. Red and tan Toile de Jouy fabric depicting a hunting scene covered two large sofas facing each other before a stone fireplace. On a low walnut table between the sofas sat a silver tray bearing tea and scones.

"Welcome, Lady Katherine." A middle-aged woman rose to greet Kit, and Gertie excused herself. "Please join me," the woman said, gesturing to one of the sofas. "We are being quite casual this afternoon, and Gertie has already seen we have tea so we can be private for a moment." As Kit accepted the seat on the sofa, the woman continued. "If all I have heard about you proves true, I expect you will suit the position just fine. Do make yourself comfortable, my lady."

"You may call me Miss Endicott. It's important that I not be known as Lady Katherine."

Her would-be employer smiled, obviously relieved at not having to deal with appropriate address. "You will find the twins easy, Miss Endicott, though giddy at times, and mischievous. You'll meet them soon enough. They are very excited about their first Season." Glancing up at the door as if expecting her daughters to miraculously appear she added, "They're around here somewhere."

"Oh?" Kit accepted the cup of tea handed to her.

"Yes, dear." Taking a deep breath as if she'd just recalled something, the woman said, "Oh, I've been remiss. Allow me to introduce myself. I am Madelene de Courtenay…but then you probably already know that."

Kit thought the woman was what some would call handsome. She fussed with light brown hair streaked with gray that resisted the knot to which it was confined. Sincere brown eyes found Kit as the woman added, "We've been living on the Continent, you see, for several years now, mostly in Austria. My husband's affairs of state kept us there longer than we expected. That business with the Congress of Vienna, you know."

"Yes, I am familiar with that effort. It decided how Europe would be aligned for the future, did it not?"

"That is what my husband tells me, dear. I was not involved, of course, except for social events. Well, anyway, I have quite forgotten how it's done in London—the Season, I mean." The woman continued to fidget. "That is one reason we decided to bring the twins home. To London, I mean. You do understand, don't you?"

Kit nodded, unwilling to interrupt and desperately fighting a grin. Her prospective employer was already flustered enough, perhaps at the possibility of employing nobility, and given her situation Kit found that nervousness endearing.

"It's time we considered husbands for the girls, and we want them to marry Englishmen. Mr. de Courtenay is a gentleman of good birth and considerable wealth owing to his many successful business ventures, and so invitations to the balls will come. He carries no title, but our daughters Priscilla and Penelope will be well dowered. It is our hope they will marry well—perhaps to members of the nobility in need of money, to be perfectly frank. They must be men of good character, however. We insist upon that. It is my fervent hope you can help prepare Pris and Pen for their Season, Lady Kather—I mean, Miss Endicott. Can you?"

She eyed Kit with such hopeful blue-gray eyes, Kit realized the woman didn't want to interview anyone else. Whatever Mrs. Pendergast told her, it must have been a firm endorsement. Kit was glad of it.

"Why, yes, I believe I can. There will be a need for certain tutors and a dancing master to instruct them. There are customs to be understood and observed, and a suitable wardrobe will need to be provided for each. But I shall be most willing to help." Kit would even look forward to the task if the girls were anything like their mother. Madelene de Courtenay seemed kind and obliging.

"Whatever you need will be provided, my dear. You will find us most generous. But one last thing. While of course we will attend all the balls ourselves, I will want you to be with the girls for their first few to assure they follow your directions."

It was an unusual request, and Kit was instantly uncomfortable. She wasn't worried about being recognized. Before her short half Season, she and Anne had been raised outside of London, and afterward she'd had few visitors. But she was ill equipped for such a ball. Her clothing in particular.

Setting down her tea, she gripped her hands in her lap and said, "Mrs. de Courtenay, I have no funds at present for gowns to wear to any ball. I had to leave my things behind." Even if she hadn't left them, her ball gowns were out of fashion.

"Don't you worry at all, my dear. I understand you've had an unfortunate setback."

Kit felt the color rise in her cheeks, embarrassed to have her rather dismal circumstances acknowledged by a gracious woman clearly intending to offer what could only be labeled as charity. "But, I don't—"

"Think nothing of it," Madelene de Courtenay interrupted. "We will provide all you need to comply with our wishes to attend the twins, and you will have the say in all things having to do with their first Season. When you accompany them to the modiste to select appropriate gowns, I insist you select a few for yourself as well." The woman must have seen that Kit was about to object, for she held up one finger and repeated, "I *insist*, my dear."

And that, thought Kit, was that. She hadn't been offered the position, exactly, nor had she accepted. But it appeared she had obtained it all the same.

* * *

Ormond smiled at his wife as the footman served out the fish course. "Darling, if you were, as you are, a young woman of good birth but looking to hide out with no funds, where would you run to in London?"

Martin shot his friend a look of caution, but this seemed to deter Ormond not one whit from his intended inquiry. The men were having dinner after their meeting, and Lady Ormond had joined them. Martin found his thoughts torn between the missing beauty with the auburn hair and Prinny's ridiculous new assignment to spy on English spies.

"Well, if it were me," Lady Ormond opined, holding one finger up to her chin, "I would want something to engage my brain. Something I wouldn't mind doing while providing for my existence." She thought for another moment. "I suppose I would seek a position as governess—a position that did not involve small children, because they might require too much attention."

"Brilliant, darling! I hadn't thought of that. Of course, that is just what she might do." Ormond was clearly proud of his wife's cleverness.

"Why, may I ask," Lady Ormond inquired, green eyes boring into her husband, "do you want to know? I assume it is not hypothetical."

"No, actually," Ormond agreed. "Martin has…er, lost just such a woman, whom, he has learned, has fallen on hard times and might be seeking a place of refuge. She is but a year or two older than you."

Lady Ormond turned. "Lost a woman have you, Martin? Hmm. Already?"

Martin knew when he was being toyed with. He shot John a glance, but the young man was engrossed in his food. "Enough, you two," he whispered.

"Do not be so touchy, Martin," Lady Ormond said, studying him and likely seeing more than he wanted. "Anyone would think this woman has gotten beneath your skin." She paused and added on a more serious note, "If you like, I can make discreet inquiries as to whether any women of the *ton* have recently retained a lady of quality as a governess."

Martin eyed her. "I don't want to frighten her or make her think she is being hunted. Could you inquire so as not to raise anyone's suspicions? I also would not wish to alert Lady Egerton to my interest."

"Of course not," said Lady Ormond, green eyes twinkling. "You know how I love this sort of thing. Think of it as me helping our friend the spy. Yes, I'd quite like to do it."

Ormond gave Martin a look, clearly annoyed that his wife was off on another adventure. "Then, yes," Martin said, amused that the tables had turned. "Please make your inquiries—if Ormond has no objection." As if there were anything his friend could do to stop her. "I am making some as well."

* * *

Kit recognized the shop as the same one she and Anne had frequented, a modiste on Bruton Street with a good reputation for dressing debutantes and women of the *ton*. The bay window with small glass panes displayed several gowns in the current style, with high waists and low necklines, done up in pale silks, brocades and satins with ribbons, flounces and lace.

They entered the shop to a jingle of a bell hanging over the door and the practiced greeting of an older woman with dark hair wearing a blue morning gown. The first things Kit noted about the woman were her high cheekbones and the professional confidence etched in her face; she would make an interesting subject to draw. Mrs. de Courtenay had been delighted to learn Kit was an artist, asking her to teach the girls a bit of her craft. Now they all three had new sketchbooks and pencils, and Kit had begun to draw the twins and the faces of the de Courtenay servants as well.

"Good day, ladies, I am Mrs. Singleton. How may I help you?"

"Good day to you, Mrs. Singleton. I am Miss Endicott, the girls' governess for the Season. We seek your assistance for their wardrobes. Appropriate gowns for day and evening, including those they will need for the balls they will attend. And perhaps a pelisse or two."

"Ah yes, Miss Endicott. Now I recall. Mrs. de Courtenay sent me a note. You are to have whatever you need and she will receive the bill. She was most insistent that you, too, should have gowns as well as her daughters."

Kit felt the heat rise in her cheeks. This was so hard, taking the charity of the kind de Courtenays. But it wasn't as if she could return to Rutledge's home to pack a valise. The servants would long ago have discovered his body. Not for the first time, she wondered why she had heard nothing of his death; but facing the issue at hand, she had to admit she must accept the gift of the gowns if she were to accompany the girls to their balls and other entertainments as their mother insisted.

"Oh yes, Miss Endicott! You simply must," pleaded Pen with her soft blue-gray eyes and a few freckles sprinkled over her nose that Kit thought charming even if the *ton* would not. "You simply must choose fabric for your own gowns. We will help. It will be such fun!"

Looking at Pen's sweet face, Kit gave up all resistance. "All right, but only because your mother insisted." Smiling at Mrs. Singleton she said, "Perhaps one or two gowns for me."

"Mrs. de Courtenay was very clear, Miss Endicott. A few gowns for evenings and a few walking gowns as well, I should think."

"Very well, then," said Kit, resigned. She could see there was nothing for it but to go along with Mrs. de Courtenay's generous plans.

She put her arm around Priscilla's shoulders and made the introductions: "This is Miss de Courtenay." Pris smiled briefly; she had no love for elaborate display. "And this"—Kit wrapped her other arm around the second girl—"is Miss Penelope." Pen beamed at Mrs. Singleton, eager to please.

The modiste exuded confidence as she stood ready to begin, tucking a strand of dark brown hair behind her ear and steepling her fingers in front of her. "Very well. You girls are both lovely. I am quite certain our creations will render you the most beautiful young women at the balls. Let us get started, shall we?"

The girls exchanged excited glances and followed the woman to a trestle table holding bolts of fine muslin and silk in white and ivory. Kit eyed them as they eagerly handled the luxurious fabrics, looking toward their future and the Season. In the weeks she'd been with them, she had grown quite attached to Pris and Pen. Though twins, they looked nothing alike and had very different personalities. In the sketches of the two she had just begun, their differences were most apparent. Pris, the older by only a few minutes, was intelligent and levelheaded, her demeanor quite adult. Even now she was commenting affably on the practicality of the various fabrics, but her light red hair hinted at the temper Kit had seen on a few occasions.

Pen, on the other hand, had a softer appearance, with light brown hair and a rounder face, and she had a more malleable temperament. Both girls had blue eyes, though Pen's were paler, more of a blue-gray like her mother's. In their demeanor, the twins were as different as Kit and Anne had been—and they were equally as close. Kit kept hidden deep within her the twinge of pain she felt at knowing she'd never see Anne again.

She smiled to herself as she recalled how Pris had announced one afternoon the search for the proper husband was a mission of utmost importance and it was essential he be someone she could respect. Pen, on the other hand, was quite biddable, happy just to be included in any parties and dances. Any man who wanted her would do just fine if he were the choice of her parents.

It was a busy afternoon. Mrs. Singleton devoted herself to working with Kit to assure the girls selected appropriate gowns for the remaining events of the Season. The girls were arguing over the choice of ribbons and trimmings when the modiste finally turned her attention to their governess, giving Kit a long, studying appraisal.

"You seem quite familiar to me, Miss Endicott, even your name. Have you been here before?"

Kit shied from reminding the woman that she had been there before as a lady, as an earl's daughter, but she would not lie. "Yes, I was here ordering a gown some years ago. It was lovely. Your work is excellent."

Distracted by the praise as Kit hoped, the older woman thanked her and turned her attention to the fabric she had chosen. "This will go nicely with your fair complexion, Miss Endicott. And the silver moiré will set off your hair. That auburn color is most unique, so dark, so rich. And there is a slight blue cast to this fabric that will bring out your eyes, don't you think?"

Kit was thrown by the woman's compliment but not certain why. Perhaps because her hair had brought her to the attention of the Earl of Rutledge when she and her sister were first introduced to him at Petworth House in Sussex. Her father had visited the grand estate at the invitation of the Earl of Egremont, and Kit had never forgotten the great collection of art the old earl amassed. And she had never forgotten the Earl of Rutledge, whose watchful eyes never left her and her sister.

"Thank you, Mrs. Singleton." Kit's hand brushed the shimmering fabric. It had been a long time since she'd had such a gown. "You are most kind. Yes, the silver will do nicely."

Mrs. Singleton continued to hunt through the fabrics on the table when Pris came up behind her. "Miss Endicott, you must have a blue gown, too. Your eyes—"

"A good suggestion, my dear," said Mrs. Singleton, interrupting as she pulled out a bolt of blue satin. "Yes, with your eyes, Miss Endicott, a gown in blue would do nicely. This lapis satin, perhaps."

"I will be happy to take all your recommendations," said Kit, looking into the older woman's determined eyes. At least she'd be relieved of the burden of choosing the precise nature of the charity bestowed upon her.

Mrs. Singleton suggested several other fabrics to Kit while Pris and Pen offered their opinions as well. Then the older woman returned her attention to the twins, joining their discussion on sashes to complement the ivory silk they had selected for their first ball. Not surprising to Kit, Pris chose bold accent colors, including plum and dark green, while Pen stayed with the pastels most debutantes wore. Kit had come to love these girls. They often brought to mind another part of her long-ago dream: a daughter of her own.

Kit turned to face the bay window and strolled a few steps to peer out between the displayed gowns onto the street. In truth she stared at nothing; her only goal was to be alone with her thoughts. As the twins' chatter faded into the background, Kit remembered the day she and Anne visited Mrs. Singleton's shop for their own coming-out gowns. Her eyes misted over with the memory. She was the one who had chosen a royal blue for her sash, while Anne chose a paler shade. Her eyes squeezed shut as she fought for control, glad the de Courtenay girls and the modiste could not see the tear slipping down her cheek. She quickly brushed it away. How she missed Anne. How she regretted not being able to say a proper goodbye, not even able to wear the proper mourning clothes. Of course, Anne would understand. She always had.

Wiping away another tear, Kit forced herself back to the present and looked out the window, this time in earnest. On the street, a man doffed his hat to a passing woman and paused to greet her. He was tall, with very dark hair.

For a moment her heart stopped. Could it be the man from Willow House? From the side he appeared so, but no, this man was shorter. He turned his face as he spoke with the woman, and Kit was suddenly certain this was not the man she remembered, the man who was always in her thoughts. This man's face looked younger, not as wise in the ways of the world. Nor were this man's features as perfectly formed.

Kit wondered what had happened to that man from Willow House, where he was, what he was doing. *Who* he was. She did not even know his name. Somehow that made him seem less real, as if he had only been an Adonis from her dreams. But no, he had been very real. She still recalled the feel of his skin beneath her fingers, the feel of him moving inside her bringing her the most amazing pleasure she had ever experienced.

Her cheeks warmed, as if others could hear her thoughts. But what would she say to him if she encountered him on the street? *"Why, sir, you don't know me but we shared a bed one night"?* No, it was unthinkable, improper and shameful. But she could not deny that she wished to see him again, albeit from afar. And she was glad her courses had come and she need not face the prospect of telling a stranger she carried his child.

As she continued to watch the pair on the street, they said their goodbyes and departed.

"Miss Endicott!" She heard her name being called and turned to see Pen's blue-gray eyes pleading, her manner anxious. "You simply must tell us which fabric will be best for the pelisse."

"Of course." Jerked back to the present, Kit crossed the shop to join the twins. Pen directed her attention to a selection of fabrics, and Mrs. Singleton handed her a picture of a design for a long coat.

"For you?" Kit asked Pen.

"Yes," said the girl, nodding. "Pris has already chosen the dark blue one she will have."

Kit pointed to a light brown cloth tending toward peach. "This one, I think," she said as the girls' voices collided. Pris still argued for a deep blue for her sister, but Pen quickly nodded approval, signaling her agreement to Mrs. Singleton. The light brown it would be.

They had exhausted the modiste, Kit realized. "I think we are about done, are we not, Mrs. Singleton?" she asked. Seeing the woman's relief, she aimed her next question at the twins. "How about returning home for tea?"

"A good idea," said Pris. "I am getting very thirsty…and hungry."

"Oh yes, let's!" said Pen, ever eager to please.

And they were off.

Chapter 6

Martin watched Lady Ormond set down her breakfast roll and pick up her cup of chocolate before looking directly at him. Her expression was bleak. "I've been asking ladies of my acquaintance, Martin, and not one has retained a new governess or a woman matching Lady Egerton's description. I must have been wrong about where she would go."

Martin set down his coffee and swept his napkin over his mouth. He was having breakfast at the home of the Ormonds, where he was now ensconced as their houseguest, at least for the time being. Several weeks had gone by, and he was becoming re-accustomed to London. For several days he and John had been attending meetings at Westminster, absorbing information about the disturbances that had taken place around the country. What he had learned was most disconcerting.

"Seems we've both little to show for our efforts. My own inquiries have turned up nothing thus far, my lady—but I thank you for trying."

"The thought occurs she may have left London altogether," said Ormond, setting down his newspaper. "Interestingly, there has been nothing in the *Morning Chronicle* or *The Morning Post* that speaks of the incident with Rutledge."

"And not a single *on dit* floating about my circles," added Lady Ormond.

"If the papers have been silent I am grateful," said Martin. "Perhaps his family is keeping quiet Lady Egerton's supposed crime—and what prompted it."

"Do you think she fled London, Martin?" asked Ormond's wife before she took a bite of her roll.

"Not unless she traveled with friends," Martin replied. "And, from what Abigail Darkin told me, her friends are in short supply just now."

"So," said Lady Ormond, "she is likely still in Town. But you say she has not returned to Willow House."

"No. I have checked there." But he had an odd feeling she was near, still somewhere in London. He wasn't sure how he knew, but he did. And with what he'd recently learned...

"Well, there's nothing for it, then. The hunt continues. With your skills, you will certainly find her," Ormond encouraged. "Just allow the matter some time."

"It seems I've no choice—but I worry about her," admitted Martin. He worried about her all the time. Against his will, the auburn-haired beauty haunted his thoughts. "Particularly with the new development."

Ormond and his wife abruptly ceased eating and turned expectant gazes upon him.

"The man she thought she killed," Martin said. "The Earl of Rutledge..."

"Yes?" Lady Ormond prompted, her expressive green eyes focused anxiously on him.

"He's alive."

"Oh, my." She sounded disappointed, and her lips formed a pout. "No wonder the papers have said nothing. I was rather hoping she killed the beast. He well deserved it."

"Really, darling." Ormond scowled, though it seemed to Martin he only feigned disapproval. "The fellow may be despicable, but I did not wish him dead. You sound like one of my drinking cronies, ever seeking duels and blood."

"Ormond, she was *attacked*. I want to slay the man myself, and I don't even know the dreadful cur."

"At least she will not be facing a murder charge," said her husband. "Though she may have had a valid defense, a trial before the Lords would be most unpleasant."

"Yes, well, there is that," Martin agreed. "All the same, being the kind of man he is, based on what you told me, he will likely be seeking revenge at the very least. Worse, he may still think to take her by force. Thwarted once, he will pursue her again, only this time with more vigor." Martin imagined his kitten fleeing before the crazed earl bent on possessing her, and the thought drove him mad. "I must find her to warn her, must protect her from him."

Ormond and his wife exchanged a glance.

"What?" Martin's eyes darted from one to the other. "I mean only to see the woman remain unharmed."

"Just so," said Ormond, a wry smile spreading across his face. "As would any man who cared for a woman."

Lady Ormond shook her head. "You're teasing the man, darling. I say, let him alone. Martin's playing the gallant, and I, for one, applaud his coming to the aid of a damsel in distress. After all, he *is* an honorable knight of the realm."

At the reminder of that relatively new honor, Martin smiled inwardly. Only once had he returned to England in all the years he'd been in France: the day George, the Prince Regent, awarded him the Order of the Bath. He remembered the droll smile that crossed the monarch's face while conveying the mark of distinction. Prinny was a sly dog, phrasing his justification for the grand gesture in suitably vague language. No one observing would have guessed Martin's real work for the Crown involved espionage, but the award had been presented all the same.

He was a knight indeed, and a baronet.

* * *

A week later Martin found himself none the wiser regarding his kitten's whereabouts, and his desire to find her had not dimmed one bit as his eyes drifted up to a huge chandelier, one of six hanging from the ceiling above him in the ballroom of the Dowager Countess of Claremont. While this ballroom provided a most elegant setting for what Ormond promised would be a high point of the Season, it seemed an unlikely locale for a woman trying to escape notice. No, he would be surprised to find her here. But then, that had not been his reason for coming.

In the crush of lavishly attired men and women Martin could see little of the floor, but the few glimpses he'd caught displayed an impressive blond hardwood that had been chalked in patterned designs for both beauty and the dancers' sure footing. All done according to exacting standards, he surmised. Gilded mirrors covered one wall, reflecting a thousand candles. Tall columns stood at one end of the room like giant soldiers guarding a palace. A small palace, perhaps, but a palace nonetheless.

He'd already located the four exits, including the one to the terrace with stairs leading down to the gardens. Several hiding places off the main ballroom had caught his trained eye, and though no one else would notice, he'd identified each of the armed footmen scattered about the room. Old habits of his days as a spy would be with him forever.

"You are certain they will be here?" he whispered to Ormond, who was standing next to his wife. The marquess had taken care with his appearance this evening; even his dark brown hair, usually a bit tousled, had been tamed. Martin assumed this was owing to Lady Ormond's influence, just as was Ormond's claret brocade waistcoat. Ormond's wife was herself a vision in silk the color of her sparkling green eyes.

"I was assured Sidmouth's cohorts would be attending. Neither Foreign Secretary Castlereagh nor Chancellor Eldon should be terribly difficult to find. They might not attend all the events of the Season, but they would not fail to be seen at this one. The dowager countess can be a formidable ally or enemy, and neither would dare offend her."

Martin waited as Ormond scanned the room, but before either could sight their quarry, their hostess approached like a ship under full sail. Clothed in a cream brocade gown with matching feathers shooting up from her silver hair and jewels sparkling from her neck, the buxom countess reigned as a veritable queen.

"Good evening, my lord, my lady." The dowager countess smiled graciously at the Ormonds, and Martin thought her voice quite deep for a woman. The voice of authority. But those soft gray eyes suggested a kind heart beneath the finery and formal greeting. "So good of you to attend."

"Countess," Ormond said, bowing. "My wife and I were most pleased to accept your invitation."

The woman paused for Ormond to finish then quickly turned her attention to Martin. Raising a bejeweled quizzing glass, she slowly perused him, as if inspecting a new horse for her stable, while directing her words to the marquess. "*Who* is this dashingly handsome man you've seen fit to bring with you tonight, Ormond? And *where*"—she paused with dramatic emphasis, allowing her quizzing glass to drop on its chain—"have you been keeping him?"

Martin chuckled. "Sir Martin Powell at your service, Countess. And, to answer your question, I have been living on the Continent. However, I am most grateful to be included in your lovely soirée this evening."

"We can always use another knight to attend our many damsels, Sir Martin. I'm delighted you've come." The countess raised a silver eyebrow. "Do I detect a hint of the French in your voice?"

"Very perceptive, my lady." He gave her a mischievous grin. "Yes, you might."

He said no more, and when it was clear he would not, the countess offered her hand. Without a word Martin took it and bowed low. When he glanced up, it was to see her eyes shining with apparent delight. He really did love older women of great character, and he suspected that the countess was one of these, formidable in all things with a well hidden soft heart. The smile he gave her was sincere.

Straightening, he gave her a wink, to which she returned a "Humph." At least, that's what it sounded like. But the older woman seemed to enjoy his impudence, just as he'd thought she might.

"I must be off, children. See that you dance with the young maidens, Sir Martin. I expect they will all be gawking at you. Perhaps having been in France you can manage that new dance the Prince Regent introduced at Court last year, that outrageous waltz. I've avoided it as long as possible, but with all the fuss I've had to include it in tonight's repertoire." Then the countess dipped her head at the threesome and turned to leave. Glancing over her shoulder at Martin, she glided away just as he thought he heard another "Humph."

"It appears you've made a conquest, Martin," Lady Ormond said with a small laugh, "one that will serve you well in London society. If my eyes did not deceive me, our intimidating hostess was quite taken. It's rare to see her so enamored with a man. Few impress her."

"She reminds me of my mother, another grand lady," Martin noted as he watched the countess sail smoothly away. His mother was one person Martin had particularly missed while in France. Claire Donet Powell was a warm soul who tolerated many absences from the men in her life, from her seafaring husband

Simon, who adored her, to Martin's older brother Nick, both captains of their own ships, to his two younger twin brothers who often crewed for their father. And then there was Martin. Martin the spy. The outlier. He hadn't seen his family since returning to London, but he would remedy that soon now that he was back in his father's good graces.

"Say, where is Griffen Lambeth this evening, Ormond?" Martin asked his friend. "I would have expected to see our colleague by your side, or at least somewhere in this crush looking for you."

"Mr. Lambeth is staying close to home these days," said Lady Ormond. "Lizzy, his wife and my dearest friend, is very close to delivering their first child. He won't leave her, which I think is most admirable."

"Another devoted husband. I feel surrounded," Martin said, and he began to wonder if it was fate's campaign to convert him. He was looking more like the lone bachelor as each day passed.

Ormond smiled broadly. "Careful, old thing, it may be catching." But Martin could see his friend was only too eager to bring him into the fold.

"Oh, look, darling," exclaimed Lady Ormond. "It's Peter and Emily. Martin, you may not have met them. They are the Earl and Countess of Huntingdon. Ormond and I had only just met when we attended their house party over a year ago, though it seems like yesterday." She gazed fondly at her husband, who returned her regard as if he, too, was remembering. "We haven't seen them since Henry's christening. Ormond, they are headed toward us. Come, Martin." She tugged on his sleeve. "You will want to meet them. They are Henry's godparents and dear friends."

Lady Huntingdon reached them first. She gave Lady Ormond a hug, running her eyes protectively over the younger woman like a hen examining her chick. "I see motherhood agrees with you,

Mary. You are all aglow." Turning to face Ormond, Lady Huntingdon inquired, "And how is our godchild, young Henry?"

"Growing, my lady," Ormond replied proudly.

The earl leaned forward and shook his hand. "Glad to hear it. You must bring the lad to see us. A weekend in the country would do you all well."

"We will, sir. And soon," replied the marquess.

Mary presented Martin to the older couple, and he was soon drawn into the warm circle of friends. Lord Huntingdon was distinguished-looking with brown hair graying at the temples; his wife had the ageless appeal of a wise woman, her light brown hair curled at the sides of her face, her gray eyes reflecting contentment. They were a handsome pair, and Martin's instincts told him they both could be trusted with secrets. Perhaps they had kept a few for Ormond.

"*Sir* Martin," Lord Huntingdon noted, "you must be one of our decorated war heroes. I had heard the Prince Regent was giving our most valiant on the battlefield some well-deserved knighthoods after Waterloo. I suspect congratulations are in order. Well done!"

Martin always felt awkward when praised for battles won by other men, especially when the only reward for some of them had been a quick death. But he could not speak of his real work far from the battlefield, so his only response was a speaking look in Ormond's direction and a quiet, "Thank you, but others did far more than I."

"Ah, yes," said Huntingdon. "We know of Ormond's work. Our mysterious—and for many years missing—marquess did much for the Crown. But his lady has helped him to retire from all that, hasn't she?"

"Just so, Huntingdon," Ormond said. "Like you, I am now a country gentleman living in London during the Season with only my family and my business interests to tend."

"I wonder," said Huntingdon.

"Ormond," Mary interrupted excitedly, and to Martin's thinking it was strategic. "You must tell Huntingdon about your success with the breeding of Thoroughbreds." To Huntingdon she added, "There is a splendid three-year-old chestnut colt from my husband's breeding stock running in the Epsom Derby at the end of the month, this very May. Azor may not be as fine as my Midnight, but all the same he's quite a worthy piece of horseflesh."

Ormond looked heavenward. "No horse will ever compare in my wife's mind with that huge black Friesian stallion of hers. And I suspect she is needling me because, now that we're expecting our next child, I won't let her 'ride with the wind' as is her wont."

Emily Huntingdon gasped. "You two are expecting another child? So soon?" Turning to Ormond's wife she inquired, "How are you feeling, my dear?"

"I feel wonderful, Emily, really I do. Do not be anxious, or my husband will tether me to our home."

"A playmate for our godchild," announced Peter Huntingdon with obvious delight. "Good job, you two!"

Lady Ormond darted a glance at her husband, chagrined, then patted her flat stomach and smiled. "Well, now that the cat's out of the bag, I expect I should qualify my dear husband's announcement by saying our next little one won't arrive till Christmas. I've months to ride Midnight yet."

Ormond rolled his eyes, and Lord Huntingdon laughed.

Martin enjoyed the banter between Ormond and his wife all the more for having been there at the beginning of their love affair. But the warmth reflected in their many glances and furtive touches brought again to mind the woman he'd been thinking about since Willow House. Where in England was she? She had entirely eluded him, and it was unusual for him to run into so many blind alleys in a concerted search. His frustration knew no limit.

"Darling," said Ormond, "may I leave you with our good friends for a short while? I've just spotted someone I need to introduce to Martin. It concerns his business affairs."

Speaking for Mary, Lady Huntingdon said, "Of course we'll be delighted to spend some time with Henry's mother." The older woman looped her arm through Lady Ormond's as if to claim her. "You two go off on your mission and leave her to us."

Martin and Ormond made their exit, and when Martin shortly thereafter asked why the sudden departure, his friend was quick to explain. "I saw Castlereagh and Eldon repair to the card room just a bit ago. It would be best to encounter them there, where we can share a brandy away from the crowd."

They made their way through the crush to the card room, which seemed more the province of men than of women though a few old dowagers lingered there. Small tables were artfully scattered about an expanse half the size of the ballroom, and the lighting was more subdued, reminding Martin of a men's club. Well-attired servants scurried about efficiently refilling drinks for the guests engaged in games of chance.

"Just there, Martin." Ormond gestured with a nod of his head to two men standing in the corner. "Viscount Castlereagh and Baron Eldon sharing a drink and conversation. Let us join them."

Accepting a brandy from a passing waiter, Ormond sallied forth with Martin in tow. Soon they drew up in front of the two men, and addressing the more senior man whose bushy white hair gave him a distinguished look, Ormond courteously interjected, "Eldon, may we join you? I've someone I'd like you to meet."

"Why, of course, Ormond. Haven't seen you around the club much of late. You know Castlereagh, of course."

Martin studied the viscount as Ormond acknowledged him. Castlereagh was somewhere in his fourth decade but still quite young-looking with dark eyes and wiry red hair tinged with gray.

So, this was the leader of the House of Commons who had introduced the bill to suspend habeas corpus at the urging of the Home Secretary. Perhaps Castlereagh had also been the one to send out spies at Sidmouth's biding. Martin had a hard time believing such actions of the older man. Lord Eldon had been a distinguished barrister and member of the House of Lords long before he accepted the role of Chancellor. However, Martin knew well the lengths to which some men would go if asked to preserve the government.

"Allow me to present my friend of many years, Sir Martin Powell."

"Powell..." Eldon drew his brows together. "The name is familiar. Are you any relation to Simon Powell? *Captain* Simon Powell?"

"My father, my lord."

"Ah, yes." The older man's eyes gained a sudden light. "His Majesty's government employed your father with great success during the war with France. As I recall, he made some excellent raids as a privateer in His Majesty's service. Were you a part of that, good sir?"

"My father and older brother, I suspect, my lord. I have been away for many years. But in the last few, I believe Powell and Sons has confined itself to the work of merchants on the high seas."

"To earn that knighthood," interjected Castlereagh, "you must have served on the Continent."

"Yes, my lord, I was employed opposing Napoleon for the Crown." That was the most Martin could say. They would assume, of course, that he had been a soldier or a naval officer, not a spy for Prinny living as a Frenchman in Paris. Few in the government had any idea of Martin's role, and fewer still would know his face.

As Castlereagh opened his mouth again, Martin was spared further inquiry by Ormond's timely comment. "I hear you are working with Sidmouth to stem the tide of protests that have arisen this spring."

Seizing on a subject that obviously stirred his passion, the red-haired statesman plunged in. "Quite right. That bit of bad news is causing us all much worry. We don't want the fires of the French Revolution to spread to England, now do we?"

"Is that really something the government fears?" asked Martin, hardly believing it. "The political climates are quite different." Personally, he believed England had suffered her revolution under Cromwell, centuries before, and was in no danger of another.

"Unfortunately, the fear is sufficiently real to clamp down on the freedoms the populace would otherwise enjoy," said Eldon, regret showing in his dark eyes. "I, for one, hate to see the gains of the past lost, but it appears it must needs be for now."

"The press is contributing to the unrest with their articles glorifying the protestors and printing caricatures criticizing the leaders of government," Castlereagh growled in his own defense. "They are only reminding the rabble of the current economic situation. I assume you heard about that appalling incident in Manchester they are calling the 'March of the Blanketeers'?"

"Yes, I've heard the story," said Martin, "though I was not in England when the events transpired."

"Well, according to our...er, contacts...it seems hundreds of the unhappy weavers were marching in the rain to London to harass the Prince Regent. Fortunately, many were arrested outside Stockport, and the rest turned back as they were about to enter Derbyshire. Sidmouth was certain they were gathering an army. Couldn't have that now, could we?"

"An army?" echoed Ormond. "Hungry men carrying blankets through the cold rain?"

Martin knew his friend well enough to see his suppressed rage, but the two older men seemed oblivious to Ormond's biting sarcasm.

"Well, it was the numbers don't you know. So many. Sidmouth believes the seat of the rebellion is in the Midlands." Castlereagh continued to pontificate, unaware of the reception of his words, while Eldon looked as if he were becoming increasingly uncomfortable.

"I do believe my wife will be looking for me," the older man said abruptly, gazing toward the ballroom. "I'd best wish you gentlemen a good evening."

As the Chancellor strode off, Castlereagh made his apologies and followed.

"Well," said Ormond, "that was short but illuminating."

"One cannot help but wonder just who their 'contacts' are," Martin remarked. "And whether they hired them or used one of their fellow peers more willing to engage in such activities."

"That question looms large in my mind as well," said Ormond. "That was a bit awkward for Castlereagh, didn't you think?"

"Quite. And I had the feeling Eldon was not at all at ease with the subject. Perhaps he is disquieted with all that Sidmouth is doing, especially if he is worried about being drawn into it."

"Indeed. Well, at least you've now met some of those central to the government's schemes. Your task will be to find the rest and learn all they are doing." Ormond's eyes suddenly darted toward the wide doorway into the ballroom and he said, "I had better see what my wife is up to. It is never wise to leave Mary alone for too long."

It was most unusual for Ormond to be distracted, but Martin understood. A wife had changed many things in his friend's life. And, Ormond was correct. The former Lady Mary could easily become involved in something controversial, though it seemed the hoyden had settled down a bit with her marriage. "I'll join you."

They stepped into the ballroom just as the orchestra stuck up a waltz—and Martin froze. Standing not twenty feet before him was the object of his long search, shimmering in a silver gown that reflected the lights above, her only other adornments her auburn tresses and a string of pearls. Even here, amidst the *ton*'s finery, she stood out, once again an ethereal creature.

"Kitten," he muttered under his breath. She stood with two debutantes and an older man and woman, her back to the dancing couples. She appeared unaware of the attention she was drawing from the men around her, but Martin saw the looks they were giving her and felt a wave of jealousy sweep over him.

"What is it, Martin? Why did you stop? What are you staring at?"

"She is here. Just there."

Out of the corner of his eye Martin saw Ormond's head turn toward Kit. At the same time, Kit turned her face to the side and it became a mask of horror. Whatever she saw had shaken her badly.

A man. She was looking at a man.

"Who is that?" Martin said, gesturing for Ormond.

"That," Ormond informed him, "is the man you have been asking about. The Earl of Rutledge."

Chapter 7

Martin's eyes were fixed on Kit as she hurriedly spoke to her companions then headed out of the ballroom—to, Martin assumed, the exit. Her quick strides and fluid movement caused her silver gown to shimmer as she hastened through the crowded room, and Rutledge's head rose above those of his companions. Spotting Kit, he narrowed his eyes.

Martin took no time to excuse himself, he simply bolted after her. Over his shoulder he saw Rutledge moving in the same direction, but Martin was faster and closer. He intercepted Kit just as she reached the corridor. Seizing her wrist, he spoke in an urgent voice that told her there was no time to explain.

"Lady Egerton, come with me."

She turned in panic and opened her mouth as if to object, then her blue eyes flared with recognition.

"Yes," Martin said, "it is I. Come. I will get you away from him."

Grateful for his habit of noting places to hide, cubbyholes hidden from obvious view, Martin pulled Kit along toward an alcove he'd earlier committed to memory. They entered the small space only moments before Rutledge stomped past, his heels a pounding thunder on the wooden floor.

The alcove was clothed in darkness, the only light from one small candle, that seeping in below a heavy velvet curtain. Martin held Kit close. Her breath came in pants, her breasts pressed into his chest. Relieved to have her finally back in his arms, it was all Martin could do to not to give his passion free rein. Her familiar scent of roses swirled about his head. God, he'd missed this woman. But when he felt her shiver, the need to protect was the only emotion he allowed himself and he tightened his arms around her in comfort.

"Not dead," she murmured, her forehead nearly touching his lips.

"No, Kit. You did not kill him. And though I certainly want to see the man dead for what he did to you, I thought it best for your reputation he not be confronted here."

"You know?" She tilted her head upward, her lips within an inch of his. It was all he could do not to claim them.

"Yes. Miss Abby."

"Oh. Oh, dear." Her body tensed. "I must leave."

She began to pull away, but he held her firmly against his chest.

"But he will be after me." Even in the dim light he could see the desperation in her eyes.

"No, my kitten."

She pushed hard against his chest. "I'm not your kitten! I'm not anyone's...anything."

He allowed her to step back. Her voice reflected unshed tears and a vulnerability that pulled at his heartstrings. A feeling of tenderness swept over him. Damnation, she *was* his kitten, and he was not giving her up.

"Shh," he said, pulling her gently back into his arms. She came without protest, rested her head on his shoulder. The alcove had taken on an eerie light.

"I must leave here," she whispered as Martin held her, content to have her close but wanting so much more. She seemed calmer now.

"No, Kit. Not yet. For weeks I've been combing the streets of London for you, and now that I've found you, you'll not be escaping me only to risk being caught by an enraged Rutledge. We must wait a few minutes at least."

"But I cannot stay here." Her voice was soft, almost a whimper, and it made him want to hold her, to protect her. To have, once again, these soft curves and warm skin pressed against his flesh. God, he was hungry for her.

"You will come with me," he said.

"No! I cannot."

"Yes, you can and you will." He bent his head to look directly into her eyes, hoping she would see his desire to protect her, his resolve. She would not be getting away.

"But I don't know you. Not even your name."

Martin would have been amused under other circumstances. She knew him quite well. They had made beautiful, passionate love together, and held each other through the night. But he would remind her of that later.

"If you must have a name, it is Martin Powell."

She raised her head, studying him in the pale light of the alcove. It reminded Martin of the night at Willow House when the only light they shared came from the moon and the dying fire. It was enough.

"Martin Powell," she said aloud, as if trying the name out to see how it fit.

"We will wait just a bit longer and then I'll get you to safety."

"Where?"

"Trust me."

The look on her face said she far from trusted him, but he knew she would come nonetheless. She had few options if she wanted to escape the earl. Martin could not protect her if she returned to her friends or left on her own. He had survived the years in France by his wits and the cloak of stealth he could wrap around himself in an instant. Surely he could do the same for her.

But into his mind came the unbidden memory of a night when he failed to safeguard another woman, a woman who had even greater claim to his protection.

With a deep sigh and a resolution that belied his fear for Kit's safety, he silently stepped toward the curtain. "Come."

He would get her out of Claremont House unseen.

* * *

It was after midnight, and rain had begun to fall when the carriage stopped in front of a house in the area of London known as Adelphi Terrace. Just south of Somerset House on the Thames, the neighborhood was familiar to Kit as one of her tutors had lived near there. Though more of the *ton* lived in Mayfair and Albany, Adelphi was home to many prominent people, and she knew the homes to be costly. Whatever this man Martin's status in London society, he had to be a man of means. But then, had not Abby promised Willow House catered only to the wellborn and their friends?

The silver fabric of her gown was thin, but her rescuer had given her his coat to protect her from the cold. There had been no time to gather her cloak, no time even to bid the de Courtenays goodbye before she fled. It seemed to Kit she was always saying goodbye to someone she held dear. Now all she had was a man she considered a stranger.

The warm superfine wool wrapped around Kit retained the heat of her supposed rescuer's body, and it was much appreciated. Drawing the warm coat around her, she inhaled the scent of him. Martin Powell, he'd called himself. The coat was almost like having his body next to her again, for it brought back the memory of that night she lay in his arms.

"This is my family's residence," Mr. Powell explained as they reached the door. "I have not returned in more than a year, even for a visit, so we'll be finding out together who is at home tonight." He must have seen the concern on her face because he added, "Not to worry, you will be welcome."

He took a key from his pocket and slipped it into the lock. As the door opened, he whispered to her, "Just as well it is late. The servants will be asleep."

Tiptoeing across the threshold, he took her hand and guided her into the entrance hall. Kit could see it was beautiful, even in the faint light. A brass chandelier above reflected a crackling fire from a room off to the right.

Someone is awake.

A thick rug cushioned her slippers as she took a few steps. Ahead, a wide stairway curved up to the next floor. Mr. Powell tugged her toward it. Kit wasn't certain she wanted to go upstairs, where she knew the bedrooms would be located, but she had come this far so she followed. Could she trust this man whom she did not know? He was a man whose very presence, she reminded herself, made her heart flutter like the wings of a bird against a cage.

As they climbed the first steps, heavy footfalls sounded behind them. A deep voice very much like her rescuer's asked gruffly, "Martin, is that you?"

Mr. Powell backed down the staircase, pulling her along. His quick reaction protectively thrust her behind him, but his posture was relaxed. He recognized the voice.

"Ah…Nick. Thank God it's you. I thought perhaps Mother and Father would be gone, as they usually are, but I'd rather not deal with servants or our younger brothers tonight."

Kit peeked around Mr. Powell's shoulder to see the man named Nick staring intently at her. He resembled Mr. Powell with his disheveled ebony hair, though he was perhaps a bit older, a bit taller. His face, even in the dim light, was bronzed and weathered as if he spent a great deal of time in the sun. She could not discern his eye color. It was obvious to Kit he had not been expecting company.

She had never seen a pirate, but this man surely looked the part; the only thing missing was the golden earring. He wore a linen shirt, open at the neck, and black breeches tucked into tall boots. There was something of the gypsy about him, too, a suggestion of another place and another time.

"You'll not be facing the family soon, brother," Mr. Powell's kin said as he leaned against the doorpost to what had to be a study, the source of the firelight. Crossing his arms over his chest, he casually slipped one booted foot over the other. "Mater has sailed with Pater, and our two younger siblings have tagged along as crew. The great run to the east for tea, you know. They will be gone for months. The only ones here tonight are Cook, a new maid, and our old butler Morris. All of them retired for the night. It's a skeleton crew with the parents at sea."

"Just as well. I'll deal with the servants in the morning," said Mr. Powell.

Glancing at Kit the brother said, "I'll be gone when you greet the day. I'm taking the *Raven* out."

"Oh? Where?"

"To the Caribbean, then up to Baltimore." Nick's eyes darted from Kit back to his brother, lips twitching up at the ends. "You will have the place to yourself." The light was dim, but Kit didn't miss his white teeth and wolfish grin as he added, "I see you brought home another stray—a beautiful one."

"Stray?" Kit repeated, her eyes narrowing.

"Oh, he's always bringing home strays," the man explained. Then, to Mr. Powell: "Remember the time you rescued the cabin boy? The one who had fleas?"

Kit was annoyed at being compared to a boy with fleas, and she returned the pirate a glare. He just laughed and said, "Mater never let you forget that escapade."

Mr. Powell gritted out, "The boy would have been beaten if he'd returned to his ship. I could not allow that to happen."

His brother flashed white teeth in another smile, this one aimed at Kit. "I say, brother, are you going to introduce me to your friend?"

"I'd rather not, but I suppose I must. And, please keep this encounter to yourself. These are unusual circumstances." Mr. Powell reached back to pull Kit next to him, but he kept his arm protectively around her waist, the intimacy of the posture making her uncomfortable. "My lady, may I present my older brother, Captain Jean Nicholas Powell. Nick, the Dowager Baroness of Egerton."

Nick stepped away from the doorway and came toward her. Though there was nothing proper about being alone with two men in near darkness, Kit held out her hand in proper fashion. The sides of the coat she wore fell away to reveal a slice of her expensive silver gown.

Nick bowed over her hand. Glancing up to see the scowl on his brother's face, Nick gave his brother a teasing smirk and refrained from touching his lips to her fingers, which Kit was certain had been his intention. He rose and said, "My pleasure, Lady Egerton, and please forgive my comment about the stray. It was aimed at my brother, not you."

"I forgive you, Captain Powell," she said, as graciously as she could under the circumstances.

When it appeared his brother might continue the conversation, Mr. Powell said, "Ask no questions, Nick. Just tell me if the far guest room is unoccupied."

Captain Powell nodded. "'Tis. And of course your room is always kept waiting for you, though you do not live here any longer. The Mater will have it no other way, though the Pater keeps insisting you're gone for good."

"Thank God for Mother."

"A frequent saying of our sire," the captain offered Kit as an aside.

"If I don't see you before you sail, have a safe voyage." Mr. Powell announced. "Oh, and I'm home to stay."

Captain Powell reached out a hand, which Mr. Powell clasped with both of his own. "Happy to hear it, brother. Truly. The Mater will be pleased to know you've managed to survive the Corsican. She worries, you see."

Kit had no idea what Mr. Powell's brother referred to, but she suspected it was the war with France. She did know the Corsican was Napoleon. So, Martin Powell had been on the Continent? Had he fought with Wellington at Waterloo? He did not seem a soldier, more quick and lithe than strong and sturdy. There was nothing military in his bearing. But a long sojourn in France would explain his accent, which she'd noticed that first night they spent together. Then there were the French words he'd whispered as he made love to her. Yes, he was quite comfortable with the French language. Her body quivered at the memory.

As they left the entry hall and Mr. Powell pulled her up the stairs, she glanced over her shoulder to see his brother once again leaning against the doorpost, still watching, smiling like he had a great secret. She hoped he would not share it. She could only imagine what he would say. But hope stirred when she recalled he was leaving in the morning for the Caribbean. And the parents had sailed east.

Mr. Powell never let go of her hand, entwining his fingers with hers as his long strides ate up the corridor. Though she rather liked the feel, and while she remembered well that same hand caressing her body, she was becoming concerned about their destination and was tired of being treated like an errant child.

"You needn't pull me so. I can walk."

Ignoring her plea, he tugged her behind him. "Perhaps, but I am anxious to be alone with you."

A feeling of nervous anticipation gripped her stomach. What was he planning? Then her thinking strayed again to the man they had left at the bottom of the staircase. Would he hear this exchange? "Your brother is a man of the sea?"

"Aye, my whole family. Merchant seamen."

Ah. If Mr. Powell's father and brothers were seamen, it explained why they lived so close to the Thames. From the Adelphi Terrace, one could easily travel by small boat to the ships docked further down the river. "And you?"

"Not for a long time. But yes, I once captained one of my father's ships…for a brief while."

Finally they arrived at the end of the corridor. Mr. Powell pushed down on the door handle and waved Kit ahead. With some trepidation, she went. Stepping over the threshold into a large bedchamber, she could see soft tones of subdued elegance even in the pale light from the windows. A large canopy bed with pale gold and blue bed curtains stood prominently before her. Her anxiety increased.

Mr. Powell walked to the small table next to the bed and lit a candle. "I'll find you something to wear." He looked back at her. "My mother is of a size with you. You can borrow some of her things."

"But that would not be proper."

"Do not be silly. You heard Nick. She is gone for months, and if she were here, I assure you, she would insist upon it."

"What are you planning to do with me?"

"That"—he faced her with a wry smile—"is yet to be decided."

He walked to the fireplace and, crouching, struck a match to a well-laid fire. Then he rose, took off his cravat and tossed it aside before loosening the neck of his shirt. The light of the growing fire was reflected on the skin of his throat and the dark chest hair now displayed. Kit remembered the feel of that hair on her breasts, and her nipples tingled. What would it feel like to have her mouth once again on his naked flesh? She felt a sudden craving for the pleasure they had shared.

"Where are *you* sleeping?" she asked, breathless.

"Here, of course." He slowly walked toward her, his eyes dark with desire.

She stepped back, though something deep within her urged her forward. And, there was that smile again. Kit was unnerved. Did he think just because she'd given herself to him once he could have her again? She had simply taken refuge in his arms and he had made her feel safe for the night, safe from Rutledge. No. Without the brandy, and thinking more clearly than she had the last time they were together, she had no intention of sleeping with a man to whom she was not wed. She perhaps wanted to feel safe again with him, but she was not willing to pay the price.

"You told your brother the guest room…?"

"Yes, well, that was for Nick—and for your honor." He stopped a foot in front of her.

"You cannot stay *here*." Even as Kit said the words, she realized how absurd they sounded. It was his home after all, so she added, "With me."

"Why not, Kitten?" He stepped closer. "We have already shared a bed. We have made love." A faint smile crossed his lips. "And I am hungry for you."

Kit felt her cheeks warm. A shiver ran down her spine, and she backed up. "That should not have happened." She twisted her hands together at her waist and stared down at the floor, reminded of their passion and also of her shame. How could she have made love with him that night knowing how wrong it was? Worse, how could she want him again?

He closed the distance between them, his blue eyes staring into hers. She was suddenly very aware of him as a man. Tall, handsome and lithe, he smelled of brandy and that masculine scent that was his own, perhaps exotic sandalwood. It was the same scent she'd smelled on his coat, and it brought back more memories of their night together. Standing so near, she could feel the heat radiating from his chest.

Taking his coat from her shoulders and tossing it on the bed, he lifted her chin with his curved finger. "Perhaps it shouldn't have happened, Kitten, but it did. And there is something between us you cannot ignore."

His voice was low, a seductive lure drawing her in, reminding her of how she had come to him so willingly once before.

"No," she said, shaking her head as if saying the word could make it true, could erase their night of passion. She was not that woman. But she could not deny the things she had done with this man. The things she wanted to do again.

"Is making love something you do not wish to do?" he asked. "As I recall, you seemed to enjoy it as much as I." Then, more tenderly: "Besides, I have missed you, Kitten."

"No, I cannot. I am not your...your..." She could not bring herself to say the word. Their one night together had been a wonderful, amazing and, yes, passionate experience, but it could never happen again. She had escaped one dreadful night into a dream. Into his arms. As much as she wanted his arms around her again, wanted to lie with him, she could not allow it. This was not who she was. Not who she was raised to be.

Placing his hands on her waist, he pulled her against him. The heat from his broad chest overwhelmed her as she tilted her head up to look into those stormy indigo eyes now dark with desire.

"You opened a door, Kitten, I'm unwilling to close."

Chapter 8

Suspended in the glow of those irises that were the blue of a sky over a calm sea, Martin's only thought was to once again taste her lips. In the weeks since they were last together he'd grown ravenous for Kit. He could not wait another minute.

Wrapping his arms around her and drawing her tightly to his chest, he bent his head to breathe in her scent of roses, and he touched her lips tenderly, as he had the night they first met. Reining in the fierce passion threatening to overtake him, he wooed her with kisses, and she melted into him just like before. He reveled in her softness, anticipating the rejoining of their bodies.

Abruptly she broke the kiss, brought her hands to his chest and pushed. Hard. He could have held her but decided he didn't want to fight her tonight. He let her go.

"No. I cannot do…this," she insisted.

He stepped back to ponder the vision before him. Flaming auburn hair now tumbled about her shoulders, the pins having fallen out long before. Her pale oval face held pleading blue eyes. It was apparent to Martin she was not denying him so much as denying what lay between them, the powerful draw their bodies had to each another. She might be a proper lady, but her physical response told him all he needed to know. The words coming from her mouth didn't match the desire in her eyes.

Alas, he could see her mind was made up. They would not be resuming their relationship tonight. He sighed. After all, he reminded himself, she was not the courtesan he had first thought her. She was a dowager baroness. Patience was called for if he were to win her heart. And he very much wanted to win her.

Years of spying on the French had taught him restraint. Still, he could not help being incredulous. "You are serious?"

She lifted her chin, determination displayed in every feature of her beautiful face. "I am, Mr. Powell. Quite serious."

He crossed his arms and stood back, amazed at her strength of will when he knew she wanted him as much as he wanted her. "I see." Then, leaning close so that their lips were nearly touching: "And what would you have me do with you this night, my beauty?"

"I appreciate your helping me to avoid Lord Rutledge, Mr. Powell, I really do. But being here alone with you is not…proper. If you insist on my staying, at least allow me to take the guest room for the night."

She probably had no idea how alluring she was, standing there in that silver gown, insisting upon her own room and all that was proper. With that fire in her eyes she reminded him of a red tabby cat his aunt owned that was ever quick to draw its claws. But he also remembered quite accurately what she looked like beneath that gown, what he had seen when she was attired only in moonlight and her claws were digging into his back. The image made it particularly difficult to quell his desire.

"'Mr. Powell is it?" He hesitated, allowing her to consider him. He didn't want her to think he easily accepted this ludicrous choice.

She said nothing, just stared. Finally he drawled, "Very well, Kitten, the guest room is yours—for tonight." He walked toward the still open door without looking back, assuming she would follow. "It is just next door."

He did not take her to the far guest room, the one he'd asked Nick about. He wanted her close should she need him—or better yet, should she change her mind. Covering the short distance to the next room in the corridor, he paused, aware she was following closely. "You will be comfortable here, Kitten," he promised.

He opened the door, allowing her to enter ahead of him. Following, he lit a candle then the fireplace, watching her out of the corner of his eye as she made a short examination of the bedchamber. It might be more comfortable for her, but it certainly would not be more comfortable for him if she slept here alone. He doubted he would sleep at all.

"Allow me a few minutes to find you some nightclothes and a gown for the morrow. After breakfast we will talk about what comes next."

"Next?" Her voice quavered. "What do you mean?"

Was that fear he detected? Surely she did not fear him. He would protect her with his life.

"Now that I'm assured you are safe, I cannot allow you to stroll about London with a half-mad Rutledge hunting you. I have friends you can stay with, Kit, at least until other arrangements can be made. I rather think you will like Lady Ormond."

"Lady Ormond?" Now that she had her own room, he could see she was calmer—and curious.

"The Marchioness of Ormond. Like you, she is an earl's daughter. She is but a few years younger. I believe she's rather looking forward to meeting you."

"She is?"

What was it about this woman that made him want to be her protector? She had displayed great spirit in refusing the invitation to share his bed, and he liked that, but it was also her vulnerability that drew him. Martin wanted to keep her safe. Even now, he could see the fatigue beginning to overtake Kit as she leaned against the bedpost.

"Why, yes. I told you I've been looking for you. Lady Ormond has been assisting me in a way. You were not easy to find…not until tonight, when all of a sudden there you were."

Kit yawned. "Tomorrow, then."

He did not want to leave, and he thought of trying to calm her fears with assurances he would be just next door, but he could also see she needed sleep more than words. And if he touched her again, he might not leave at all.

"I'll return in a moment, Kitten, to bring you those clothes."

* * *

Kit paced the room, staring down at the unusual Chinese rug while she waited for Mr. Powell to return with the promised nightclothes. Her mind was full of him, this man with the seductive sapphire eyes and warm lips who had rescued her yet again.

She glanced up to see flowered curtains drawn over two large windows, a gilded ivory dressing table gracing the space between them. He'd given her a lovely room. But what did it matter? It wasn't her room. It was merely a guest room in the house of a man she did not know. *Kitten!* He kept calling her that, as if to remind her of the first time the word slipped from his lips, the night she had so willingly gone to him. What *had* she been thinking? Truth to tell, she had not been thinking at all. She had gone to him so shamelessly. They'd made love, clung to each other while they slept. She could never forget.

A knock disrupted her thoughts. She crossed the room and slowly opened the door, and Mr. Powell smiled and handed her a pile of clothes. "These should do for now."

She accepted them with a grateful, "Thank you."

"Do you need any assistance? I can play the lady's maid," Mr. Powell said with a wry smile. She was sure he'd had much practice in handling women's clothing, but she would not be accepting his offer of help.

"No, I can manage myself." She still had the front-lacing corset and was glad she had worn it this night. He had once soothed her fears in the most intimate of ways, and she was only too aware of how easy it might be to give in to him again. She would not—*could* not—do that. His was the smile of the cat that had captured the mouse. She didn't mean to be ungrateful, but she was no mouse. Thanking him, she abruptly said, "Good night," and closed the door on both him and the passion he offered.

Among the clothes he had brought were a soft nightdress and a blue day gown with butter-soft leather shoes to replace her silver slippers. There was also a soft woolen cloak in a warm honey color. Holding it up in front of the standing mirror, she thought the gown would fit. It was close to the color of her eyes, and she wondered if he had selected it for that reason. Though she was pleased with his choice, she was tired of living on charity. Taking clothing from this man, even if borrowed, felt wrong. The fact that she had so little control of her life grated. Had it only been several weeks ago that Mrs. de Courtenay had insisted on buying Kit gowns?

Weariness overcame her, and too tired to object she decided it was futile to torture herself with things she could not change. She took off her silver gown and underthings, donned the nightgown her rescuer had provided and thought about how things would progress from here. The day had been a long one, getting the twins ready for yet another of their balls. Seeing the faces of her two charges brought a smile to her face. She had fallen in love with them, but now they were launched most splendidly. Their parents, who always accompanied Pris and Pen to the balls, would be all they would need. She didn't feel badly at having to leave behind the governess position, but she would miss the family. The de Courtenays had been good to her.

She was relieved she had not killed Rutledge. That had been one piece of good news. As evil as she considered the man, to face an accusation of murder would be ruinous. And the earl's family likely could produce witnesses to swear she'd attacked him. A new worry flooded her mind. He'd survived the blow and sought her at the ball. Was he now looking for revenge?

Sitting on the edge of the bed, she wondered what tomorrow would bring. Another move certainly. But where, and for how long?

Fatigued, she blew out the candle and slipped beneath the covers, but as she did, she brought her fingers to her lips remembering Mr. Powell's kiss. She had come close to repeating her prior mistake, nearly seduced once again into his welcoming heat. Only at the last moment had she pulled away. Would she be able to pull away if there was a next time?

* * *

Martin had thought he would not sleep, but he was wrong. After one glass of brandy he laid his head on the pillow and soon fell into a fitful state of dreaming. A few hours later, after much tossing and turning, he woke from a nightmare, dripping with sweat though the fire had died long ago and the room had grown cold.

For a moment he had no idea where he was. It was a familiar strangeness; he had awakened in so many different places over the years. He raised his head from the pillow. The rain had stopped and moonlight poured in through the large window. One glance around told him he was in his family's home in London, in his own bedchamber. *My God.* It had been so real this time. Like it happened yesterday.

The nightmare of Elise's death never varied, his mind recalling perfectly the details of that night in Paris. How he had failed. His business was always dangerous; he should have seen the potential for calamity. But in the spirit of celebration he'd ignored his instincts. He had failed to protect his young wife and she was gone in a moment, lost to time, living now only in his memories and his nightmares. A nagging question that always lay beneath the surface, one he did not look at too closely, was whether he'd been the real target that night, not Elise. Perhaps the soldiers had only been feigning drunkenness. Such a possibility only added to his guilt. But he was unquestionably the reason she and their unborn child were dead. Their loss was a constant reminder he never should have married.

Sitting up in bed, he took a deep breath and ran his fingers through his hair. Then he remembered. This night the dream *had* been different, for when he looked down at the girl lying in the street, the eyes in the vacant stare had not been Elise's dark brown. They had been blue.

The eyes of Lady Egerton.

Chapter 9

Kit was unsurprised to learn the friends of Mr. Powell—no, he insisted she call him Martin and it felt hypocritical to refuse—lived in Mayfair. A marquess would have a home in Town, and Mayfair was the choice for much of the *ton* during the Season.

They argued when Martin told her over breakfast that he was taking her to stay with Lord Ormond and his wife. She was tired of her life being controlled by others, yet what choice did she have? Blown along like a leaf before a strong wind, she saw her options as few at the moment, and grateful for his kindness she had finally, reluctantly agreed. Still, it was with some trepidation that she climbed the few steps to the arched door of the elaborate stone townhouse.

Located on Charles Street, the residence was only a short distance to Hyde Park where the nobility took their afternoon carriage rides. The name Ormond was not one she knew, but she did recall that the old baron, her husband, and her father had both known the Duke of Albany, Ormond's father, according to Martin.

The door opened in response to Martin's quick knock. "Afternoon, Jenkins," Martin said, handing the butler his hat.

"Welcome back, sir."

The dignified butler almost smiled, and it seemed to Kit he liked this houseguest. Martin Powell was charming, she had to concede.

"Is Ormond at home?"

"No, sir. Would you like me to announce you to her ladyship?"

"That would be fine, Jenkins, and please let her know Lady Egerton is with me."

Lady Ormond must have been listening, because as she stepped over the threshold Kit heard a rustling of skirts like the wings of a flock of birds. "Martin! We were so worried about you, disappearing like that," said a vision in rose-colored silk. "The countess asked most directly where you'd hied off to, but Ormond covered your tracks." Then, facing Kit, the woman with golden hair remarked with a smile, "Thank heavens you found Lady Egerton, Martin." She took Kit's hand. "You must call me Mary. I have been hoping to meet you. Now that you are here we shall have a grand time."

Kit knew she must have blushed, wondering what Martin had told the Ormonds about her. Had he mentioned Willow House? The very possibility caused her to feel exposed, as if everyone knew the horrible truth of her night in a bordello with this man standing at her side. Still, she instantly liked the woman who would be her hostess.

"You are too kind…Mary. Please, call me Kit."

"I shall, Kit. Come into the parlour." Then Mary turned to Martin and instructed him with an impudent smile, "Kit and I will have some tea, but you, Martin, are wanted at a meeting with Ormond."

Reaching the parlour, her hostess invited Kit to sit on a sofa of pale green silk and then picked up an envelope sitting on a side table. "Here, Martin. Ormond left this for you. I suspect it will tell you where to meet him."

Kit watched Martin's face grow serious as he collected the envelope, furtively casting a concerned glance at her.

"You need not worry about Lady Egerton, Martin. I will see her settled. We will have no trouble occupying ourselves without you two men. So, be on your way."

"All right, my lady, but keep her close. Best not to venture out in public until we know what Rutledge is about." Martin proceeded to tear open the envelope and read the note.

"Will you return for dinner, do you think?" Mary asked.

Still reading Martin replied, "I will return whenever Ormond does. It seems he has scheduled some meetings for John and me this afternoon."

"Well, then, we shall see you tonight, for my husband promised me he will be here in time for the evening meal."

Martin asked the butler to take the valise he'd had packed for Kit to the room she'd been given upstairs. He paused at the door, staring at her, and for a moment their eyes met and held. She was somehow reluctant to see her rescuer go, but with a wave he turned and left.

Mary asked the butler to see that they had tea and returned to Kit, taking a seat on the sofa across from her. "I just know we shall be great friends, Kit."

"This is so awkward, Lady Ormond—"

"Mary," the marchioness reminded her.

"Mary. What I mean is…my life seems to be in such turmoil just now." She was afraid to ask but had to know: "What has Martin told you about me?"

"I can't say we know everything, but allow me to say I would have tried to kill Rutledge myself if he attacked me as he did you. At least, I like to think I would have had your courage."

"Did he say anything else?"

A maid entered with a tray of tea and scones, suspending conversation. Mary thanked her, and a moment later the maid left, closing the doors and leaving them again in private. Mary turned to the tray and poured Kit a cup of tea and one for herself. Kit took a bite of the warm sweet bread and tasted honey on her tongue. Mary made herself comfortable, lifted her cup of tea and calmly returned to Kit's question.

"Oh, I know about Willow House, if that's what you are asking." She must have seen the shock on Kit's face, for the marchioness immediately added, "Please do not worry, Kit. I do understand. Some love matches have unusual beginnings."

"It isn't what you might be thinking. Ours is not a love match. Martin and I hardly know each other."

"Well, Kit," said Mary, "if Ormond and I are any model, it can occur quite suddenly. Before you realize it your heart has given itself away. The job is done. Then it takes you weeks, even months, to realize what happened. Neither Ormond nor I wanted a marriage when we first met, but staying away from each other proved impossible. Now look at us."

"Not in my case," Kit replied.

Mary's mouth twitched up at the corner. "If you say so. But enough of that. Tell me where you have been all this time Martin has been searching for you."

"Well, I took a position as a finishing govern—"

"I knew it! I told my husband as much. That is just what I would have done. Tell me about it."

Mary seemed most curious to know all that Kit had lived through since leaving Willow House, so Kit settled back with her tea and told her of the de Courtenays and of the twins, Pris and Pen.

"What a delightful family!" Mary said at the end.

"They are, really."

Mary rose to pour them more tea. "No wonder we did not find you. I was asking around my friends, but of course the de Courtenays are new to Town... Since they have been on the Continent, we would not know them. Or at least I would not, unless I'd met them in Paris. Ormond might have heard of Mr. de Courtenay. I simply must be introduced."

"They were very kind to me. Mrs. de Courtenay even bought me several lovely gowns so I might accompany the twins to their entertainments."

"We must fetch your wardrobe for you," Mary determined.

Kit did not see how she could ask the kind Mrs. de Courtenay for the garments after abandoning the family as she had, even if her work with Pen and Pris had been for the most part accomplished, but then a thought occurred. "I know the gowns were costly, but perhaps they would consider trading them for my wages."

"An excellent thought," conceded Mary. "I will go there this very afternoon and inquire."

"Could not a footman be sent?" Kit was mortified at the thought of a marchioness running an errand for her.

"Nonsense! And deprive me of an adventure? I have so few these days." Looking out the window rather wistfully she explained, "My dearest friend Lizzy is so great with child she never gets out anymore, and I have had no one to go adventuring with. Our young son Henry is but a few months old and very sweet, but he requires little of my attention just now. He sleeps rather a lot, as babies do. But now that you are here," Mary crowed, a gleam in her eye as she returned her gaze to Kit, "perhaps my prospects will change. In any event, Martin is right. It would not be wise for you to be seen on the streets of London. Rutledge may be having the de Courtenays' home watched if he saw you with them last night at the ball."

"Oh, my." Kit covered her mouth with her hand. "I hadn't thought of that, but yes, it would be just like him."

"If he is as ruthless as we all believe, it is quite likely."

"He *is*. He never treated my sister Anne—his wife—with any kindness." Kit couldn't stop the tears. They welled up in her eyes and flowed down her cheeks. She cried for a sister who deserved love and never found it in the husband fate had given her, and she cried for herself, for the dreams she had left behind in her first Season, dreams of an honorable man who would be her true love. "I'm so sorry. I don't seem to be able to stop."

Mary crossed to where Kit was sitting and wrapped her arm around Kit's shoulders. "You have been through a lot. More than any woman I know. Do not apologize for having a good cry."

Kit took a deep breath, forcing herself to regain control. Taking the handkerchief Mary offered, she dabbed at her eyes.

The marchioness smiled and made an obvious effort to cheer her. "Remind me to tell you of what I went through before Ormond and I finally married. Suffice it to say, I shed many tears before it was done."

The mention of Mary's husband recalled the question that had been rumbling around in Kit's mind. "What will Ormond say if you go to the de Courtenays'?"

"Ormond? Oh, he would prefer I send a servant to be sure, but he will not be surprised if I go myself. He is aware of my…tendencies. Besides, I would not be deprived of meeting these two charming girls of whom you are so fond. I imagine they will want to be assured you are doing well."

"And if—as you suggest—Rutledge is having their home watched?"

"Oh, do not worry about that, Kit. I have often worn disguises on my adventures. I will dress in a more common fashion, in something a shop worker might wear, and take a hired coach with a roundabout journey back here. If anyone is watching that house, they will think me a tradeswoman. To tell it true, you have no idea how I have longed for such an outing."

Kit could not argue with the sparkle in Mary's eyes. The marchioness seemed to be in her element.

A thought occurred: "Mary, if you can go in disguise, why not me as well? I would dearly love to say a proper goodbye to Mrs. de Courtenay and the twins."

Mary seemed to consider. "Well, I do have a disguise I once used in Paris, a stable boy's clothes…. Yes, it might work. I even have a cap that will hide that beautiful auburn hair."

Feeling like she had taken back some control of her life, Kit brightened. It would be right to see the de Courtenays again, at the very least to thank them. "Oh, Mary, that would be wonderful. Let's do it."

The marchioness smiled. "I had a feeling you would be a worthy partner."

* * *

Martin arrived at the government building to find Ormond and John ensconced in a small windowless room, sitting at a table, bent over a stack of documents. The marquess glanced up as he entered.

"Ah, Martin," he said, waving a sheet of paper in his hand. "You are just in time to examine the evidence."

Nodding to John, Martin drew up a chair. "What evidence?"

Ormond handed him the paper, a page of handwritten notes. "John and I have uncovered a spy Sidmouth recruited out of Fleet Prison, where the man was biding his time with other debtors."

"How did you learn this?"

"The Prince Regent has made available to us the work of the Secret Committees in the Commons and the Lords, formed following the attack on his coach. They were supposed to deal with the so-called conspiracy threatening overthrow of the government, but it seems Liverpool may have gone too far."

"And the spy?"

"Recall when I first told you about your assignment that I said one of the ways Sidmouth intends to keep track of what is going on in the Midlands, if not to influence events there, is to enlist his own spies. In this case his name is William Richards, though he goes by the name William Oliver. According to our source, when he is in London he meets with his contacts at a public house, The Guardsman. It is in the mews where Wellington's barracks were once located. I think you and John might want to pay him a visit."

"Why would Sidmouth choose such a man?" asked John.

"A man from debtors' prison might seem an odd choice for a government agent," Martin said, "but consider that he would blend in well with the disgruntled. There are many unhappy men in Fleet Prison who blame the government for their circumstances."

"Martin is right," Ormond acknowledged. "As one who served time in debtors' prison, he could more easily gain the confidence of the unhappy workers in the north. And he is not unintelligent. His occupation was that of building surveyor according to these records."

"That is likely why Sidmouth sought him out," Martin conjectured. "He would be able to read and write to report to the officials who are his contacts. And he probably speaks well enough to persuade those simple men in the north of the correctness of his ideas."

Ormond picked up a file before him. "According to these records, Oliver traveled in April to the northern towns with a letter of introduction directed to the local officials. Its author was none other than Addington, the Undersecretary—and, not coincidentally, Sidmouth's brother."

"What did the letter say?" Martin asked. Sidmouth and his brother were deeper into this than he had at first imagined. The web of intrigue was growing ever larger.

Ormond shot John a glance. "Do you have it?"

The young man hurriedly sorted through a stack of papers. "Aye, here it is, m'lord."

Reading silently the note he was handed, Ormond summarized. "The letter urges local officials to cooperate with Oliver and describes him as an 'intelligent man deserving of your confidence.'"

"I see. Well then," Martin decided. "John, I've only to stop by my family's townhouse to change into my working clothes and then"—he leaned toward John—"you and I shall be raising a pint at The Guardsman."

John grinned at the prospect.

"I think," Martin continued, "it may be time for Martin Donet, the man whose parents were French revolutionaries, to make an appearance. Under the circumstances, I believe my parents will forgive me the lie."

"A good choice, Martin," said Ormond, chuckling. "Such a story should stir the heart of any man committed to bringing revolution to England, and that old disguise from your days in France will certainly work better than the garb you wear as Prinny's shiny new knight. Sorry I am to be missing the performance!"

"Aye, sir," John agreed. "And I'll be happy to see it as yer assistant. My French is good enough for that."

* * *

That afternoon, Martin and John climbed the short flight of stairs to The Guardsman. It was in a very old, plain, three-story Georgian brick building that once had been home, as Ormond claimed, to the First Regiment of Foot Guards, and was famous as the Duke of Wellington's officers' mess before becoming a London public house.

They stepped over the threshold into a small room with a bar to one side, and rays of bright sun from several large paned windows fell across a dozen scattered wooden tables. The air smelled of ale. Only a few tables were taken, and none looked to be occupied by a man who might be Oliver meeting with his friends. Through an opening at the rear Martin could see another room, so John paid the barman for two pints of ale, handed one to Martin, and they headed to the back. William Oliver—or the man Martin thought might be Oliver—was indeed holding court there, several men sitting around him, each nursing a tankard of ale.

Oliver appeared tall even while seated, with light red hair and a round, whiskered face scarred by smallpox. He was dressed better than the others, in a brown coat, black waistcoat, dark blue pantaloons and Wellington boots.

As Martin and John seated themselves at a table on the far side of the room, Oliver and his comrades turned to scrutinize them. A moment later their conversation resumed, but in hushed tones.

Martin had very good ears. Oliver's speech revealed a man who had knowledge of worldly matters and a command of the English language far above his apparent station. The incongruity of the man's dress, manners and speech would serve well the Home Secretary's nefarious purposes.

"I tell ye, petitions are a waste of time!" Oliver's voice rose above the whispers. "It's only force that those bastards understand."

"And ye told this to the men in the provinces, Oliver?" asked a swarthy man in dirty breeches and jacket.

"Aye, I did. And they listened, too."

"Just how did ye make friends with them workers?" another asked, taking a swig of his ale and wiping his mouth on a rough woolen sleeve. "Why would they trust a Londoner?"

Oliver's eyes narrowed. "My friend Joseph Mitchell was my guide. I told him 'twas the desire of the London Committee, which I represent, to form a connection with the country friends. He obliged me when I asked to be taken along on his next trip to the provinces. Only last month, Mitchell introduced me to the reformers in the Midlands."

"Where is Mitchell today?" asked a man who had not yet spoken. "I would like to meet him. He has long been a leader speaking for reform."

"Aye, well, that was a bit of a tragedy, that. He was just arrested and now lies in prison, I'm afraid," Oliver replied.

The man's sadness was surely feigned. Most convenient, Martin thought, that Oliver's contact in the north was suddenly eliminated, leaving Oliver as the only link between the "London Committee," which Martin doubted was real, and the "country friends." The man was sly. Or perhaps Sidmouth had arranged it.

"What about this here London Committee?" the swarthy man asked. "Mayhap it is time we met this committee of yours."

"Nay, the time isn't right," Oliver cautioned. "It's too dangerous to call them together, as some are well known. But ye can be sure they are many and will rise to demand change when the time is right. Aye, they will fight for it, along with thousands of others. Liverpool's government is weak after the war with France. The time is right!"

Martin was now certain there was no London Committee, nor any London friends. But the time had come to make himself known.

Allowing his French accent to rise, he called out from where he was sitting, "Good men of England, I could not help but overhear your talk of reform. My friend John and I are from France. My family is a product of the Revolution. Fought for the right of all men to be heard, we did. *Liberté, égalité, fraternité* was our motto. I am surprised to hear the same sentiments from Englishmen."

Oliver studied him and John where they reclined insouciantly in their chairs. For a moment Martin was uncertain of how his comments had been received, but he forced himself to remain calm as the men with Oliver took in his common attire and John's artfully shabby clothes. He waited, as if he cared not whether the men would offer up an invitation to join them.

"If yer seeking reform here in England like yer family brought to France," Oliver said at last, "we've the opportunity. Yer welcome to join us."

"If you would find that to your liking," Martin replied, "we might do just that."

The half-dozen men around him relaxed at hearing Oliver's words, so Martin nodded to John and the two slowly rose and walked across the room to sit with them. Martin introduced them as Messieurs Martin Donet and Jean Fournier.

"We're all patriots here," announced Oliver, "tired of living under the thumb of fat Prince George and his decadent friends. Spending the country's money on his pleasure palace in Brighton while the hardworking men of the country starve. 'Tis a travesty, I say."

"And what would you do to change that?" asked Martin.

"Did ye hear about the rocks thrown at the Prince's carriage?"

"All of London has heard," said Martin.

"Well, ye see now, I was there." Tapping his thumb to his chest, Oliver continued proudly. "'Twas me who told the crowd to show the princeling just how they felt. I say we need more of that kind of demonstration. Petitions like the one the weavers of Manchester planned to deliver will get us nowhere. A long list of names is too easy to ignore. And did ye see how their march to London ended? The King's Dragoons wounded some and arrested others. Now the military laughs and calls them Blanketeers. 'Twas only a joke to them!"

"So you advocate a challenge to the government?" Martin was surprised that Oliver would be so brazen, but perhaps with the backing of Sidmouth he felt free to openly recruit revolutionaries, urging them to violent protest. That would certainly provide Parliament justification for more drastic laws.

"The whole country is about to rise," Oliver said, looking at the men around him glazed with drink and taking in his every word. "There be thousands in London who will join the workers in the north when the time comes. I'll be traveling to Derbyshire soon meself to see how their efforts are coming and to tell them about the London folks, as I am their delegate."

"Would you mind if Jean and I join you?" asked Martin, indicating himself and John. "We've several weeks free just now, and I'd like to meet the workers. Though the revolution has long faded in France, perhaps I can help the men of the English countryside see the good that came from what happened there." He was testing the waters to see how badly Oliver wanted an ally. As Sidmouth's lackey, the man might be leery, but perhaps his enthusiasm would override his caution.

"'Tis your decision, Monsieur Donet. I'll be at the Talbot Inn in Derbyshire. Ye can join me if ye like."

Pleased beyond words, Martin stood and shook all the men's hands. His task had officially begun. He would meet Oliver in Derbyshire.

Chapter 10

"See that man leaning against the lamppost?" Mary whispered in Kit's ear as they stood behind a tree in the West End residential area just off St. James Square where the de Courtenays lived.

Kit's eyes followed Mary's to a man slumped against the post. "Yes, I see him. Not very subtle, is he?"

"No, he is not. His eyes never leave the de Courtenay home. No doubt he is watching for you. Do you recognize him?"

"No," Kit said, "but Rutledge has several men in his service that come and go at all hours of the day and night. They carry knives and pistols, no doubt to assist some evil purpose. This man may be one of them."

"Come, then, let us not dally."

Dressed in the plain brown gown of a shop worker, Mary handed Kit the package she carried and briskly set forth, making her way to the servants' entrance at the rear of the de Courtenay townhouse. Kit followed, head down, praying her stable boy disguise fooled the man posted to watch. Her auburn hair was tucked into a large cap that fell to her eyebrows, so she thought herself a passable shop worker's assistant.

The door was answered shortly after Mary's knock, opened by the cook. Mary immediately introduced herself. "The Marchioness of Ormond to see Madame de Courtenay."

The plump cook peered at her and Kit from under her muslin mobcap before her face screwed up in a frown. But Kit knew the cook couldn't ignore the voice of command, even if she was reluctant to trust the woman before her based on dress and an appearance at the rear door.

"I am who I said I am, good woman," Mary promised, and handed over her calling card.

Reading it, the cook immediately relented and flung the door wide. "Follow me, please."

Once in the kitchen, Kit took off her cap. "Cook, it's me."

The plump woman swung around. "Miss Endicott?"

"I had to come in disguise, Betty, but it is me."

"Miss Endicott! Why, child, where have you been? The mistress is plumb worn out from worry about you, and Gertie is fit to be tied. The twins miss you something awful."

"I am sorry, Betty, but I had to leave the ball suddenly. I was being pursued."

The cook chose that moment to remember Mary, and her eyes darted to the marchioness who said, "Can you direct us to Madame de Courtenay?"

The cook was immediately apologetic. "Fergive me, yer ladyship." She dipped a deep curtsey and escorted them into the parlour.

Mrs. de Courtenay joined them a few minutes later. She paused only a moment to consider Kit, then threw her arms about her. "Miss Endicott! It *is* you! Oh my dear, what has happened? We were ever so worried when you left the ball so suddenly."

"It is a long story, Mrs. de Courtenay. I think it best I not try to explain it all just now." She gestured to Mary. "This is my friend, the Marchioness of Ormond. Excuse us for the way we are dressed, but we were trying to avoid the man watching your house." Then to Mary: "Allow me to present to you Mrs. de Courtenay, my employer."

Mrs. de Courtenay bade them sit and called for tea. She smiled graciously at Mary, and though looking askance at her attire expressed delight at meeting Miss Endicott's friend. "Welcome to our home, Lady Ormond!" Then, seating herself on the sofa opposite, she turned to Kit and said, "Someone is watching the house?"

"Yes," Kit said. "Someone hoping to catch me returning."

"Does it have something to do with your flight from the ballroom—and this disguise?"

"Yes." Kit stared down at her hands in her lap, embarrassed. "It does."

Mary must have seen her embarrassment, because she came to Kit's rescue. "Kit—Lady Egerton—is staying with Lord Ormond and me, Madame de Courtenay, though we would ask you to tell no one."

"Lady *Egerton*?" Mrs. de Courtenay's head jerked as she glanced back to Kit. "Not Lady Katherine Endicott?"

"That was my name before I married Lord Egerton, Mrs. de Courtenay. The use of my former name was necessary, but I am sorry. I am Lady Egerton, a dowager baroness."

"Ah, I see," the woman said, nodding, though she clearly didn't. "Well, no matter, my dear. We love you."

Kit smiled, grateful to be forgiven so quickly.

"We came today," Mary offered, "so Lady Egerton could say a proper goodbye to you and the twins, and to ask if you might in exchange for her wages allow her to keep a few of the gowns you purchased for her."

"Of course! Lady Egerton may have all of her clothes, my lady." Mrs. de Courtenay turned to Kit. "And I'll not hear another word about you giving up the wages you earned." Returning her gaze to the marchioness she added, "The twins have done very well because of Lady Egerton's expert instruction. No," she decreed, directing her comment to Kit, "the wardrobe is yours, my dear, and the wages as well."

"Oh, Mrs. de Courtenay." Kit was filled with emotion. "You are too kind."

"Nonsense, my dear. You surely deserve more than the little I can do." Her countenance saddened. "We hate to lose you, Miss Eger...that is, Lady Egerton. You know the twins and I will miss you very much."

"I will miss you, too." Kit's eyes misted over. It seemed she was always saying goodbye, and she hated losing the people she loved. "Perhaps when this is over we can renew our friendship."

"Yes, we would like that. May I keep the sketches you made of the girls? They were so very good, and Mr. de Courtenay is quite fond of them."

"Oh yes," Kit urged. "Please keep them."

"You are an artist, Lady Egerton?" Mary asked.

"I like to draw, people's faces in particular. The lines form a map of one's life, reflecting all a person has suffered or enjoyed, all they have lived through."

Mary gave Kit a smile. "A woman of many talents, I see. And much insight."

"It is but a hobby," said Kit.

Mary turned to Mrs. de Courtenay. "I would propose to send men to retrieve Lady Egerton's trunks. Those men will also come in disguise, likely as carters."

"Of course," Kit's erstwhile employer said. "You may send whomever you like."

"Before we leave, I would love to meet the twins," said Mary. "If they are at home."

Mrs. de Courtenay seemed pleased. "You most certainly will meet the twins, my lady! The girls would be disappointed if they missed seeing their governess one more time."

The tea arrived just as Mary and Mrs. de Courtenay finalized plans for recovery of Kit's clothes. And just as they began to sip from the flowered teacups, the twins burst into the room.

"Miss Endicott!" Pen shouted, running over. "We were so worried. Are you all right? Why are you dressed as a lad?"

"I am fine, Pen," Kit assured her, rising to give the girl a hug. "The disguise was necessary, I assure you." Seeing Pen's sister she added, "Hello, Pris."

Pris smiled in greeting, and Kit turned to make introductions all around.

"Lady Ormond, may I present my charges, Miss de Courtenay and Miss Penelope." To Pris and Pen she said, "The Marchioness of Ormond." At the girls' puzzled looks she added, "We are both in costume. And my real name is Katherine, Lady Egerton."

The twins curtseyed charmingly before Mary, seeming to accept easily her new name. A sense of pride welled up within Kit. They had learned well the lessons she had taught them.

"Lady Egerton has told me much about your wonderful daughters," Mary said to Mrs. de Courtenay, "and I can see she was not wrong." Addressing the twins she added, "I was eager to meet you both. Lady Egerton's descriptions of you were charming and accurate. You are both lovely."

The girls beamed at the praise and joined them for tea, easily induced by Mary to tell stories of their first Season. As Kit listened, the dynamic between the pair sent her back to a day she and Anne had walked home in the sunshine, their only thoughts the things to which young girls of ten and eleven years give their attention.

"You are a vixen, Kit," her sister had said, eyes aglow with laughter.

If a vixen was impetuous and daring, Kit agreed. She had ever been quick to rise to a challenge, sometimes without thinking. On that particular day, Kit had defended Anne from some young bullies who, while taunting her, had snatched away her most precious doll, sending Anne fleeing in tears. Though Kit had come away with scrapes and scratches, she'd sent the bullies running and recovered the doll.

Another memory floated in front of her mind's eye as the twins continued to chatter on, and she paused to consider it. "Men are drawn to your auburn hair and blue eyes," Anne had told her years later. "I am content to be the small brown mouse in your shadow. You fight our battles, and I love you for it."

Kit forced back tears as she tried to focus on the two young women sitting before her, the sweet blush of blossoming womanhood on their cheeks. God, how she missed Anne. The hole in her heart was a persistent wound that would not heal. Perhaps it would always be so.

Shaking off the memory, she returned to the present and heard Mary telling the twins how she had avoided her first Season altogether. They were shocked and delighted, which only led to more stories and reminiscences, and it was all too soon that they finally bade the de Courtenays goodbye.

* * *

Kit and Mary arrived back at the Ormond townhouse to find an angry Lord Ormond hovering like a storm cloud. The marquess was clearly displeased.

"You went *where?*" he asked his wife, incredulous.

"To the de Courtenays', darling, to arrange for Lady Egerton's clothes to be returned to her."

Mary was calm, but Kit was nervous. She stood several feet away, next to the window in the parlour, watching. She did not want to become a problem for the happily married couple.

"Dressed like *that?*"

"Yes, darling. I could not exactly go dressed as the Marchioness of Ormond now, could I? Not without attracting attention."

"I suppose not." Ormond scowled. "The question is why you went at all!"

"I wanted to meet the twins Kit spoke of, darling, the ones for whom she has been governess. And besides, she must have her gowns."

Kit could see Ormond was exasperated with his wife, but his anger seemed merely a reflection of his concern for her welfare. His love for his beautiful wife was evident on his face. On the other hand, Mary was all sweetness. Clearly this was not the first time she had dealt with her husband's powerful temper.

"And, you, my lady," Ormond said, turning dark eyes on Kit. "What will Martin say about this? You were not to leave the townhouse! It is simply too dangerous."

His stare was intimidating, a dark storm about to break, but Kit would not cower. "I am sorry for being the cause of worry, my lord, but I had to say goodbye. The de Courtenays have been very good to me. I did wear this disguise, and I have no doubt it was effective. We were not recognized."

Ormond scrutinized Kit's clothing, running his eyes over the worn breeches and muslin shirt. She had shed the coat and cap.

"That attire looks very familiar—a costume my wife has worn previously, perhaps." His gaze slid to his wife, and Mary grinned sheepishly. "My wife has a love for adventure, Lady Egerton. Did you know that?"

Kit loathed getting Mary into trouble, but she would not lie to the marquess. "She did suggest it to me, my lord."

"It was only one little adventure, darling," Mary interjected as her husband's glare returned to her. "And it was not so dangerous as you imagine. It was worth it to meet the twins. They are lovely."

Ormond grunted, clearly displeased. "Were you followed? Did you see anyone?"

"No," Mary replied matter-of-factly, "we were not followed, I made sure of that. However, there was a man watching the de Courtenay house. He was hiding not very well in plain sight," she reported. "Rather nondescript, slight build, brown hair, plain clothes."

"I am not surprised," said her husband. "We expected Rutledge to learn of Lady Egerton's time with the de Courtenays. I do not want either of you to go there again. You may leave the retrieval of Lady Egerton's things to me."

Mary walked to her husband, leaned into his broad chest and reached up to kiss him on the cheek. "Thank you, darling."

Still disgruntled, Ormond mumbled something about the mother of his child taking unacceptable risks, but Kit thought the anger was mostly an act. He clearly could not stay upset with his wife for any amount of time, and she thought it one of the sweetest things she'd ever seen.

* * *

That same afternoon, Martin followed Ormond into his study, his brain reeling from all he'd learned. William Oliver was going to stir up a hornets' nest in the Midlands, that much was clear. Now he had to determine the best plan for learning all he could and minimizing the damage Sidmouth's agent could do.

Before he could say anything, Ormond frowned. "The ladies were busy this afternoon, Martin. It seems the two rebellious chits went to the de Courtenay house alone, albeit in disguise."

"What?" Martin blurted.

"I was sorely tempted to throttle Mary. Here, have a brandy," Ormond insisted, shoving a glass into his hand. "You look like you need one as much as I."

Martin was happy to accept it. "I am certain I told Kit not to leave the townhouse," he said, taking a sip of the dark liquid and welcoming the burn down his throat. He was not fond of ale, and pretending to drink it all afternoon had not been a pleasant experience, though he had done it many times before as a spy. "I cannot believe she disobeyed me. It was only concern for her safety I had in mind. What a foolish thing to do! She could have been seen, recognized."

"Likely it was my lovely wife who led her astray. Another of Lady Ormond's many adventures. Life recently has been a bit dull for her, I fear, as I have had to rein in her love of danger. Only my wife—a new mother and with child again—would consider doing what she did. We have already had words."

Martin shook his head. "It was definitely risky for them to go there. Do you think they were observed?"

"Oh, they were definitely observed…by a man watching the house, according to Mary, though given how they were dressed, I doubt he knew what he was seeing."

How could she disobey him? Martin gazed out the window in Ormond's study to the street below. The last thing he needed was to be worrying about Kit, but he *was* worried about her. Having just found her, he did not want to lose her again. He felt very possessive of the woman. His assignment was going to require his full attention, but his concern for Kit might cause him to become careless. A spy could not afford to make mistakes.

He heard a rustling behind him as Ormond set down his paper. "What do you intend to do with her, Martin?"

"I assume by 'her' you refer to Lady Egerton?"

"Yes."

"That," Martin said, staring at the iris flowers blooming on the other side of the window, "is a daunting question. I feel responsible for her, though I do not know exactly why that should be. When first I encountered her at Willow House, I thought to make her my mistress." When Ormond grunted in protest Martin added, "But of course a dowager baroness would be resistant to the idea. I've long reconsidered that thought."

"You need a *wife*, Martin," Ormond emphatically counseled. "And she obviously needs a protector."

Martin let out a breath without turning. "I had no plans to marry again, you know that. A spy should not. The risk to the woman is too great. Any woman who is my wife would be vulnerable, a target." Yet even as he said the words, Martin was intrigued. After all, this was his last mission. He felt certain he would never find a woman better suited to making him happy.

"Lady Egerton is already in danger, Martin. Besides, you cannot blame yourself forever for what happened in the past. Kit is a real find, I daresay. Even my wife has remarked it. And that raises another matter. Mary is quite fond of her. In the short time she has been here, the two have become particular friends. She would not be pleased if you failed to do the honorable thing after your…initial interaction."

Martin turned, frustrated. "If I agree to do the deed you urge, I would only be putting her in further danger."

"You are also in the best position to protect her, are you not? Do not forget she is a dowager baroness and the daughter of an earl. And a rare beauty. What stands in your way? If you desire her, make her your wife. Certainly you want her?"

"From the first time I saw her. She fascinates me, and I can barely keep my hands off her." Martin was drawn back to the night he entered the room at Willow House to see the pale rays of moonlight on Kit's face. He'd never forget her standing in front of that window staring out into the night. Even then he could scarcely believe she was a courtesan, should have realized immediately that she was no lightskirt. But a wife was a target, and to lose a wife could mean a lifetime of pain. How well he knew.

Avoiding his friend's eyes, Martin stared into his glass of liquor. "But wanting her does not change anything."

"While we are happy to have her stay with us, Martin, I suspect you will regret it if you allow her to remain free. Perhaps you failed to note the men at the Claremont ball who eyed her with such decided interest. Once this matter with Rutledge is cleared up, even without a dowry, there will be suitors vying for her hand. I went through that with Mary, and I would spare you the unpleasantness."

Martin was adrift. He wanted Kit. He craved her like a starving man would a feast, and he did not like the idea of another man courting her, another man's hands upon her. The notion was entirely unacceptable. Then a separate thought occurred: She might be carrying his child.

Damnation, she was his kitten. If he made her his wife, he would have the lovely vixen in his bed every night. Of course, he would have to take her with him to the Midlands. She could not be left in London for more adventures with Lady Ormond, nor could he risk the possibility Rutledge might find her unprotected. Which was another reason to wed her. Perhaps Ormond was right. He *could* protect her better this way.

He looked up from his drink. "All right."

"All right what?"

"All right, I will do it. I will marry Lady Egerton."

Ormond raised a brow. "May I count upon this sudden conversion as one that will not change on the morrow?"

"You may. I will marry the lady. That is, if she will have me. She was born above me. She may refuse my suit."

"You are one of Prinny's knights, Martin, a baronet. Your family's pursuits keep the bank in business, whereas Lady Egerton may have a title but not one coin to rub against another. Given her circumstances, and your prior…acquaintance, I daresay she will have you."

Chapter 11

"Marry you!" Kit challenged. "I do not even *know* you. And you don't really know me. The very notion of a marriage between us is absurd."

Martin smiled and stepped closer, taking her shoulders in his hands and reveling in the scent of roses that always surrounded her. Now that he'd made up his mind to have her as wife, he did not intend to lose this battle. Reminded of their prior argument he said, "You keep saying we do not know each other, Kitten, but we know each other quite well, do we not?"

They stood in the parlour facing each other, the rays of the fading sun suffusing the room with light. Her auburn hair shone like burnished copper, and Martin longed to lose himself in her softness has he had those many weeks before.

Kit blushed. "One night does not give either of us true knowledge of who the other is—and I find being reminded of our first meeting a very ungentlemanly act on your part, Mr. Powell."

"That is not my intent." He stroked her arms, and his eyes fell to her lips. He wanted so badly to kiss her. "I do it because you need reminding. And the name's Martin to you."

He drew her close, losing himself in her eyes. She tried to pull away, but he gently yet firmly held her steady and lowered his mouth to hers. She leaned into him ever so slightly, which he was happy to read as an involuntary welcome, and proceeded to deepen the kiss.

His embrace tightened. Her body relaxed, a signal that her resolve to break free was slipping away, and the kiss that followed said everything Martin's words could not. It was a kiss of possession, a kiss of the full passion they shared but she tried to deny. She was his, and she would do well to remember it.

Swept away by the feel of her soft warm body, the press of her breasts against his chest and their dueling tongues, Martin was once again enthralled. His body was telling him in no uncertain terms that he wanted more than a kiss; he wanted to be deep inside her once again. And that inviting stretch of velvet cushions was just behind her.

Soon they would be lying upon it.

* * *

Slowly Kit let Martin back her toward the sofa, but at the last moment she wrenched her mouth away. "No," she insisted, pushing against his chest. She would not be taken again so easily. Nor would she be taken against her better judgment even though she desired Martin Powell. There was little question of that.

She could see his determination and his desire. "Marry me, Kit. I will take care of you. I will protect you. I will never hurt you. The passion we share is unusual. Few marriages begin with as much."

Kit turned away and went to stand at the window. Her body burned with desire, but that desire did not change her concerns. Yet, were her concerns greater than the benefits? Objectively considering his offer seemed only fair.

She cared little for meaningless titles that gave excuse for old men to claim young brides or the kind of abuse her sister had suffered, and living with the de Courtenay family had reminded her that the dream of a family—of having her own children—was not dead. Perhaps she *should* marry this man and shed the title dowager. Ten years older than she, Martin was experienced, virile and handsome. Mary had told her he was an honorable man, that he had served England with Ormond, though the marchioness had declined to provide specifics. Many members of the *ton* had served in the Royal Army and Navy, and Martin's father and brothers were seafaring merchants. Perhaps he had served in the Navy. She could do worse. She had done worse.

She remembered their first night. Hadn't he been the most gentle of lovers? She believed, too, that he was sincere in his commitment to her wellbeing. He had rescued her from Rutledge, sparing her what would have been a dreadful encounter at that ball. He might not have known her long enough to truly love her, but then she didn't want to lose herself in a love match like her father. After her marriage to the baron, independence was her first goal, but she had no funds to secure that state. Martin wanted her and had said he would protect her. And he could give her the family she wanted. Perhaps that was enough.

He was also determined. She was certain he would be persistent. He had hunted for her all over London. Surely he must want her badly to do that. Surely he would treasure her all the more for it.

This would be a marriage of convenience, but it was also a matter of necessity. She was a member of the *ton*, yes, but impoverished and dependent upon friends. Kit hated being powerless, having no control over her future. At least this was one decision she could make. And with few options remaining, perhaps this was a good one.

"Yes, I will marry you, Martin."

"Wonderful."

She heard his steps behind her, coming close. She turned to face him, holding her hand out to slow his pace. He was more than handsome, his body slim and well-muscled body, a body she craved to touch. But if she was to marry him, before they made love again, before they consummated their marriage, she wanted to know this man, to start again their relationship. If she could only slow things down a bit. "But I've a condition."

"Condition?" he repeated, stopping suddenly. Crossing his arms, he wrinkled his brow. "What condition?"

"I want some...time, time for us to get to know each other without having to comply with my marital duty."

* * *

"My lord, there is a man to see you."

Rutledge glanced up from his desk. His butler seemed to hesitate.

"Yes?" he prompted, impatient and annoyed that his work was, once again, being interrupted. To calm himself he reached for the Spanish cat perched on the edge of his desk, his constant companion when he was in his study. The only female he had ever trusted, even she had claws.

"He is rather shabbily dressed. A rough character." The butler pursed his lips and looked down as if he'd just noticed something disgusting on his shoe. "He declined to give a name."

"Show him in, Thomas," Rutledge said, stroking the tortoiseshell feline now purring in his lap. "He is probably one of my new runners."

"Yes, my lord."

The man in plain brown clothes who entered shortly thereafter looked dusty and uncomfortable, and he pulled his rumpled hat from his head to worry it in his hands. "Milord...?"

Rutledge recognized the runner but offered no greeting. He rarely bothered with niceties when dealing with servants, and this man was little more than that. "Did she return to the house today?"

"No, milord. Only some merchant callers, and the usual messenger and servant traffic. The lady of the house and her daughters went out for a time, shopping I expect. They returned with packages. The man, Mr. de Courtenay, arrived just before dinner, as is his custom. The runner watching the house observed nothing unusual. Do you still want me and Frank to keep an eye on the house now that the bird seems to have flown?"

Rutledge clenched his teeth and pounded his fist on his desk. "Damn chit! One woman should not be so difficult to find." His cat, freed from his grasp, leapt away and hissed.

The runner backed up, alarmed, and Rutledge considered his words. The man was probably right; Katherine had likely fled to a new hiding place. But this time she would not get away. If he had to send runners to every alley in London he would find her. She should have been his, and he never let go of what was his. Soon he would have her. Oh, yes. One day soon he would have the redhead in his bed.

"Continue to watch the house. As long as it takes. She will have to return if only for her clothes and personal items." Reaching out, Rutledge stroked the cat now perched contentedly on the top of his desk licking its paw. "And have the nearby hotels checked for any woman matching Lady Egerton's description. She has to be somewhere in Town. I will be traveling, but should there be any developments, any word from other runners, contact me in all haste. Should you gain any information, send a fast rider to me *here*."

"Yes, milord," the runner said, accepting the note as Rutledge leaned over his cat to hand him a piece of paper with the name of a hotel in Derbyshire. The runner stuffed it in his pocket and returned to rolling his hat in his hands, looking nervously down at his feet.

Rutledge could feel himself frown. The runner's timidity was getting on his nerves. He hated weakness. "My butler will see you out," he said with the flick of his hand.

By the time he retired that evening, Rutledge was in a truly foul mood. The day had not gone well. Not well at all. None of his other runners had anything of substance to report, and his patience, what little there was to begin with, had grown as thin as the threadbare knees on the last runner's breeches. His meeting with Castlereagh had been delayed due to some task or other the viscount had set upon, and the long wait in a dismal office had truly soured his disposition. Worse, upon his return, another visitor was waiting to see him, one who left him quite disturbed.

The man—John Highmore, according to his card—was a solicitor. He had come to call upon "Lady Egerton." And the gray-haired man refused to tell Rutledge the nature of his business, insisting it was a private matter.

"Is Lady Egerton at home and receiving callers, my lord?"

"No. She is not here just now."

"When might she return, if I may ask?"

"I have no idea."

Trying another tack, the gray-haired solicitor politely inquired, "Do you know where I might find her?"

"I do not. What business have you with my sister-in-law?" Rutledge demanded. The very idea that some solicitor would have a meeting with Katherine was absurd, and he fingered the scar at his temple, an ever-present reminder of the mark left by the weapon she'd wielded against him. "I will give her the message when I see her."

"I am sorry, my lord, but the nature of my business is personal. I am not at liberty to share it with anyone except the lady herself. Please ask her to contact me when…if she returns."

Yes, the man had gone away leaving Rutledge unsettled and angry. What business did a solicitor have with Katherine? And what made the man suspect she might not return?

* * *

For Kit, time was suddenly moving very fast. Martin had accepted her condition to their marriage, though he had done so reluctantly and with a smirk, as if he didn't believe she was serious. She assured him she was.

"Very well," said Martin, disappointment clear on his face as his voice grew quiet. "We won't make love until you agree, but know I intend to do everything I can to make certain I have your agreement soon."

She would need all her resolve to resist him, but she was committed to doing just that.

A few days later, he obtained a special license. Then, at Mary's request, Mrs. Singleton had her leading seamstress sewing for two days to prepare the pale golden gown that would grace Kit's slender frame as she now dressed for her wedding.

Kit's auburn tresses were done up in curls with a few left loose to dangle at her nape. Around her neck was an elegant necklace of gold, pearls and amber, a most unusual gift from her betrothed. There were pearl earbobs to match. She had given Martin a pocket watch that Mary helped her select, with their initials and the date of their marriage carved inside. She'd paid for the gift with her wages as a governess and part of the proceeds from the sale of her jewelry she'd carried with her when she fled Rutledge's home. It seemed a good trade for a gift that symbolized the start of a new life.

After the maid left, Mary came to wish her good luck, placing a bouquet of white roses in her hand. "You look like a queen, Kit. Martin will be left quite speechless, I'm certain."

Never had she been so elegantly attired, and standing alone a few moments later in front of the long oval mirror Kit felt like a queen. A very nervous one. Her bright blue eyes burned with the anticipation coursing through her every vein, even though her other emotions were mixed. That she couldn't share this moment with her sister saddened her. The ache from having lost Anne never subsided, another reminder of the long list of goodbyes she had been forced to say. She was excited but wary about the man she was to wed, for she was marrying a man she did not really know. Mary had told her Martin was married before but that his young wife had died many years ago. Kit wondered if he still loved her. Their relationship felt too new for her to ask.

The wedding was to be small and held in the large stone courtyard around which the Ormond townhouse was built, which Kit had only viewed from the rows of tall windows in the upper floors. Boxwood plants shaped into cones and set into urns lined the perimeter, and a stone archway with the Albany crest carved into the lintel led into the courtyard from the ground floor. As she walked down the few stairs to join the waiting party, Kit noticed the overcast sky above. Pale gray clouds gave a brooding but romantic feeling to the early afternoon.

Martin was standing with the vicar under an arbor of ivy and white roses. Pen de Courtenay waved to Kit from where the twins stood with the other guests. Pris and Pen had been allowed to attend by their mother, but since the de Courtenay house was still being watched Martin fetched them from a carriage in Hyde Park where they agreed to rendezvous. In another wonderful surprise, he had arranged for Abby to attend, who was smiling broadly as Kit approached. Having her there was almost like having a mother present. Since Kit had no family and Martin's family was at sea, the only others attending were Hugh and Mary Ormond and Martin's assistant, John Spencer, to whom she'd been introduced the night before.

Memories of her first wedding came flooding back to Kit, when a scared, sad young woman married a kind old man who seemed more a grandfather than a bridegroom, when all her girlish dreams lay like shards of broken glass around her feet. Was that only a few years ago? This second wedding was quite different. The man waiting for her was devilishly handsome and charming, a man in his prime who wanted to be her protector—and her lover. The mere thought made her shiver with anticipation. If only Anne had lived to see this day. Would she have approved?

The guests in place, Kit joined Martin in front of the vicar. He gave her an appreciative smile and took her hand. She felt Mary's presence beside her. Ormond stood on the other side of Martin acting as best man. Kit handed her flowers to Mary and, as one, Kit and Martin turned to the clergyman who would marry them.

She peered out of the corner of her eye at her bridegroom. He was dressed in formal black attire, a white shirt, elegantly folded cravat and sapphire blue waistcoat nearly the color of his eyes. He must have felt her gaze, for he turned his head and winked at her, giving her hand a squeeze. He was enjoying himself!

The vicar began to drone on about the significance of their vows, about love and respect. Kit's mind was elsewhere. It didn't really bother her that there was no love involved. She did not expect, nor was she certain she wanted, a true heart-mate. That lesson she'd learned from her father was still a painful one. The consequences could be dire if such a love were lost. The important thing was that this had been her choice. The man who awakened her body when he merely held her hand would soon be her husband.

The vows were said quickly. Martin placed a ring on her finger. Kit looked down to see a red cabochon ruby set in a wide band of gold between two sparkling diamonds, but before she had time to admire it properly he was kissing her.

Soft, warm lips gently touched hers. How she loved his lips. He lifted his head and she thought he was finished, but then he looked into her eyes and whispered, "Oh, hell," and kissed her again, this time taking her fully into his arms. Only when the guests began to cough and chuckle did he pull back, and without letting her go he smiled.

"You are mine now, Kitten. *Lady Katherine Powell.*"

Kit felt the heat of her blush at his words and returned his smile. She knew little of him, but she would learn. Their life together would bring that knowledge. Mary had told her it would be an adventure. This marriage was rash, she knew. Foolish, perhaps. But she wanted him, and she knew he wanted her. When they finally did consummate their marriage, at least their nights would not be cold.

She was suddenly pulled from his arms and embraced by Mary and kissed on the cheek by Ormond. The marchioness handed back her bouquet and whispered in her ear, "That second kiss tells me all will be well, Kit."

"Oh, you are such a beautiful bride," gushed Pen from nearby.

"Congratulations, Martin, old man!" Ormond enthused to his friend, slapping him on the back. "You have made a wise decision—finally."

"Thank you for inviting us, Lady Egerton," said Pris, who was the next to congratulate them. "We were ever so pleased to attend. You are like an older sister, you know."

And, Abby…Abby just tilted her head to the side and smiled, tears running down her cheeks. "I am so happy for you, my darling child. And to think, the two of you met in my home." With a slight wince she added, "Well, I guess I won't be saying much about that. But it does my heart good to have played a small part."

It seemed her new friend the marchioness had gone to a great deal of trouble. Inside the townhouse there was a wonderful meal waiting, followed by a large tiered marchpane cake decorated with white roses like those Kit carried. Kit thought the cake would serve many more people than attended. Perhaps the servants would enjoy it this evening.

Champagne was passed around freely, and many toasts were uttered congratulating the newlyweds and wishing them a fruitful union, the latter causing Kit to blush, though Martin looked pleased. The toasts reminded Kit again that she had always loved children and wanted her own. Her eyes drifted to her bridegroom. What kind of father would he be? She had seen him at ease holding baby Henry. Would he one day hold their child like that? The thought of an ebony-haired boy with Martin's grin brought a smile to her face.

After the toasts, Ormond asked them to raise a glass to another event that had occurred the day before. Azor, the chestnut colt out of his favorite stallion, had won the Epsom Derby.

"Three cheers for Azor!" said Martin enthusiastically. "And three cheers for my good friends Lord and Lady Ormond!"

Kit was amused to see Mary roll her eyes and say, "Now there will be no living with my husband."

Pris and Pen giggled, each having consumed a glass of champagne, and sneaked glances at John Spencer, seated between them, who seemed delighted with the attention. Among the gifts Kit and Martin received was one from the twins, a new device called a kaleidoscope that had become all the rage in London in the last few months. The guests passed it around, remarking on the world of color it spun before the eye. Kit truly thought it a marvel, and her new husband had just picked it up when Abby turned to Mary.

"Your husband seems quite fond of horses, my lady."

"We both are, actually," the marchioness replied. "A friendly rivalry. I think my black stallion Midnight is much more the horse than my husband's chestnut that sired Azor, but Ormond will have none of it. It was the horses that brought us together, you see. It is no wonder he thought of Azor today."

Ormond chimed in, "Among our many shared interests is a love of horses." When he reached over and kissed Mary's temple, Kit smiled. The love the two had for each other shone on their faces. Would she ever share such a love with her husband? Would she want to? Such a love was dangerous. Such a love could be lost. Sighing deeply, she returned her mind to the guests.

Martin grinned at her. "We will find common interests, Kit, I am certain. Do you like the sea perhaps? Ships?"

Kit did not have to think long before answering. "I have always yearned to see faraway places." When she and Anne were young children their mother had often read to them stories of distant lands. She had dreamed of countries she had never seen, of tropical isles and exotic faces she would love to draw. Her father had been a dreamer, too. She supposed she had inherited his wanderlust.

Martin reached for her hand and grinned broadly, a lock of ebony hair falling onto his forehead. Kit thought he looked rakishly charming, indigo eyes sparkling, and she fought the urge to reach up and sweep the lock of hair from his forehead. "One day we shall see all those places together, *wife*."

The reminder of her new status made Kit's cheeks warm, and she hurriedly took another drink of champagne, certain a blush had crept into her cheeks.

Martin leaned over and whispered, "You look lovely, Kitten. Absolutely beautiful."

The afternoon was an island of celebration in what Kit knew was a sea of uncertainty, so she was determined to fully enjoy the respite. She had the feeling her life in the future would not be so tranquil.

Chapter 12

It was their wedding night, and Martin wondered what he would find as he ascended the stairs to the chamber he would share with his bride. His *wife*. How strange that word sounded after so many years. He hadn't planned to marry again, hadn't wanted to risk taking another wife with his life as it was. But then he'd made love to a bewitching auburn-haired woman who seemed not of this world, and somehow he couldn't let her go. Now, though strangers still, they were wed.

With feelings of both trepidation and anticipation, he walked to the door behind which she'd disappeared several minutes earlier. He supposed he should have given her more time to ready herself, especially since he'd agreed to her absurd demand that they have a pause before consummating their marriage. But then again, he might find her undressing, and that pleasant thought caused him to turn the handle and enter without knocking.

A young maid was helping Kit undress as he stepped into the bedchamber. "I'll take over from here. You may go."

The maid blushed and scurried out, obviously grateful to leave the newly wedded couple alone. Kit had her back to him, only partially undressed, as she glanced nervously over her shoulder. There was a moment of silence before she cleared her throat. "Did you forget our arrangement?"

"No, I did not forget," he said, quietly moving to place his hands on her warm, bare shoulders. Her gown would have fallen to the floor had she not clutched it to her breasts. "Still, this is our wedding night, Kitten, and I would be with you. It would seem strange, would it not, if the groom were to find more joy with his guests than his bride?"

Her long auburn hair hung in waves down her back, bared to his view by the unfastened gown and corset. Her pale skin glowed like a rich pearl providing the perfect contrast to those fiery tresses, and despite his resolve his body responded. He wanted to touch her, to slide his hands under that loose gown and cup her warm, full breasts. He grew hard just thinking about the prospect.

"Ah, Kitten." He pressed a kiss to the juncture of her neck and shoulder. "Can I help you finish undressing? You smell wonderful." The scent of roses mixed with her own scent, sweet and exotic, swirling around his head as he nuzzled her neck with his mouth.

"I can finish, myself. Just give me a moment." She pulled away, but not before he heard a soft moan. He was not alone in having trouble with the arrangement they'd reached. He took some pleasure in that.

It was obvious she wanted privacy, but he had no intention of leaving or rendering this forced distance easy when what he really desired was to make love to her. "I'll just turn around, shall I?"

He did so. Behind him, Martin heard the sound of her clothing falling to the floor, and his mind conjured a picture of her naked, clothed only in moonlight. He had a vague fear he would be walking around in a perpetual state of arousal as long as this introductory phase lasted. It had best be short.

He turned to face her. Dressed in a sheer nightgown that did nothing to disguise her curves, she reached for a silk wrapper. Martin took a deep breath and forced his gaze back to her eyes, but it seemed as if he glided toward her, no longer feeling the floor beneath his feet. He gave her the gentlest of kisses and his hand cupped her shoulder, afraid if he put his hand anywhere else their agreement would come to an abrupt end.

A quick intake of her breath confirmed she was not indifferent to his touch. "You gave your word."

"Oh, all right. So you are serious about this—?"

"I am." Her insistent blue eyes and a raised brow told him she wouldn't change her mind, not even when she had to deny her own desire, at least not tonight.

"Then let us have a toast to our marriage," Martin said, resigned.

"But we've had many toasts."

"None by ourselves."

Taking off his coat, he reached for the champagne he'd had delivered to their room. Pouring the sparkling wine into two glasses, he handed one to her. "To us," he said, raising his glass, "and to a strange beginning come right."

"To us," his wife echoed, and she took a sip, a faint smile on her lips, those luscious lips.

The memory of another night and a toast long ago crept unbidden into his mind, the night he'd lost Elise. But he was able to shake it off. Ignoring the brief feeling of foreboding, he focused his gaze on the woman before him. Somehow he would get through this night. And he would be patient with his lovely wife, though he could not be patient for long.

* * *

Kit stretched and yawned as sunlight streamed into the room from the two tall windows, and twisted her head to see the empty pillow next to her. Martin was gone.

How had he managed to wake so early? He had insisted on sleeping next to her, though he'd kept his promise and not exercised his husbandly rights. For that she was grateful, though it had been torture lying so close to his warmth and being unable to reach out and touch him. At one point she had awakened to find her head nestled against his shoulder. She had moved away quickly, but his arm had snaked out and pulled her back.

"No, Kitten. I like you close," he'd whispered in a gravelly voice. For a long time she had lain awake, trying to still her restless heart. Finally she'd fallen back to sleep.

She'd best rise and dress. He had told her last night it would be a busy day.

At breakfast, over warm, crusty rolls and coffee, Mary told her Martin was attending to an errand at the docks, something to do with his family's business, and would return by noon. Last night he'd informed her they would leave this afternoon for Derbyshire in the Midlands. Why, Kit wondered? It was certainly no wedding trip. She asked Mary, but the marchioness was vague, explaining only that Martin's work required him to be there and that he would not leave his new bride behind.

"You look happy if tired, Kit. I told you all would be well."

Kit fought a blush and knew she lost when Mary smiled. "That good, was it?"

She did not want to admit to her friend that the marriage was not yet consummated, but she could speak a truth that would satisfy her hostess. "We seem to be well matched in one way, at least."

"I think you are well matched in more ways than that, Kit. He may not realize it yet, but I believe Martin is quite smitten. He is just what you need, ever the protector, and you are a woman worthy of his many talents."

"No," Kit said, looking down at her coffee and toying with her roll. "Martin is not smitten, but I am glad I made the decision to marry him all the same."

The marchioness gave her a knowing smile and offered to help her pack. "Just allow me to feed little Henry, and I will be with you."

Martin returned with John a few hours later, and Ormond arrived shortly thereafter. Kit was in the parlor talking to Mary when the trio joined them. Martin strode over to kiss her temple.

"Hello, Kitten. I missed you this morning."

She gave him her sweetest smile, relieved he was not holding a grudge for their bargain.

The butler announced the luncheon would soon be ready. Mary had told them the cook was creating a feast, aware they might not encounter the same food at coaching inns on the carriage ride north, and a feast it was. A salad of oranges followed a wonderful fish soup. A magnificent roast chicken followed, and a baked ham with sauce, and side dishes of roasted carrots and a ragout of celery. Dessert was a wonderful confection of poached pears in honey and a pudding with cinnamon and raisins.

As the last bit of pudding was consumed, Ormond, who had come home for the meal, herded Martin and John into his library "for port and a few words" as he put it, while Kit and Mary lingered over tea. Having eaten everything, Kit was quite sated when she went upstairs to don her traveling dress of fine green wool. Later, she and Mary rejoined the men who were discussing the trip north.

"You might catch my friend Hart at home in Derbyshire," Ormond said to Martin. "Your destination of Pentridge is a part of his lands lying south of Chatsworth, his home. If you can call nearly a hundred thousand acres and a house as grand as a palace merely 'a home.'"

"Hart?" repeated Martin.

"Ah, yes. You might have heard of him as the Sixth Duke of Devonshire," said Ormond. "But since he was born the Marquess of Hartington, his family and friends have always called him Hart. He's still a young man, only in his middle twenties."

"Something tells me we may not be moving in those circles on this trip," said Martin.

"Well, he is a good friend of the Prince Regent and a good friend of mine, should you have need of assistance. I've sent him a note to expect you without notice. Hart doesn't stand on ceremony."

"Now, that I will remember. One can always use a friend if things get sticky."

"I've never seen the Midlands," said John wistfully.

"That part of England is very different, very rural and not at all like London," Martin announced. "You'll find life much slower there." He turned and squeezed Kit's hand. "We had better depart if we are to put some distance between us and London this day."

"I do wish you would wait until tomorrow to depart," said Mary, looking concerned. "Traveling at night can be dangerous. The roads are still plagued by robbers."

"Much as I'd like to spend another night with my new bride beneath your roof, my lady, we must away. I am anxious to get to Pentridge. Things are happening too fast for me to delay any longer...and you know I am always prepared should we encounter any difficulty."

Mary replied, "I should have realized. How silly of me."

"Perhaps," Kit suggested, "I should tend to the last few things I want to take with me."

Martin nodded. "Yes, it's time." Then he faced Kit, took an item from his waistcoat pocket and placed it in her hand. When she looked up at him in question, he said of the plain gold ring, "Wear it in the Midlands, Kitten. Leave your other jewelry behind."

She nodded, wondering why, but upon reflection decided he was being wise. The gowns she would take were simple, apart from a lovely riding habit upon which Mary insisted, but none were like the finery she would leave behind.

Accepting a kiss on the cheek from her husband, Kit followed Mary upstairs. There she folded the last of her things into her small trunk and a valise, while Mary left the room for a moment, returning with the stable boy clothes Kit had worn on their one adventure.

"These might prove useful where you are traveling, Kit. I myself prefer to ride dressed as a man, though I have to be careful I am not observed by any in the *ton* save a few close friends. I'm already considered a hoyden. These are clothes I brought back from France. You are welcome to them."

Kit wondered what circumstances might cause her to want to dress as a lad again, but she took the clothes all the same. "I suppose it will not hurt."

Like John, Kit had never been to the Midlands before, but she knew of its beauty from friends who had traveled north. She was looking forward to seeing what she had heard were beautiful rolling green hills, but she was definitely not looking forward to a long carriage ride. The roads were dusty, often muddy, and returning passengers she'd spoken with complained of being tossed to and fro. Still, she would happily endure the rough ride for the sheer delight of seeing someplace new. Besides, the farther she was from Rutledge the better. Perhaps in the country, with fewer demands, there would be time for Martin and her to get to know each other.

It was late afternoon by the time the traveling coach was loaded. Mary kissed her on the cheek and bade her a safe journey. Martin handed her into the sleek black carriage pulled by four black horses, and he climbed in to sit beside her on the green velvet seat. John followed, taking the seat across from them. In a tender manner, Martin settled a lap robe over Kit's knees then signaled the coachman to depart.

At first all she saw was the city as they left the West End to take the main road north. They traveled for several hours. Kit watched the buildings and homes grow sparser until they were finally passing only countryside, and twilight overtook them. Sitting close, Martin held her hand, leaned his head back onto the seat and closed his eyes, not saying much. John entertained her with stories of his unusual family, all girls save for him.

"'Tis like having six mothers to have a mother and five older sisters. Even though they are all married now, they still treat me like I was one of their babes."

"I don't think you mind overmuch, John," Kit said, not able to help the smile that crept over her face. It was easy to like him. With all those sisters, no wonder he was comfortable with women.

"No, m'lady, 'tis the truth I do not mind, not much. Besides, my sisters' coddling of me is all I've ever known. I had to get away to France to become a man."

They bumped along in the fast-moving coach, Kit feeling every mile once they left the town behind and encountered the rutted rural roads. And the day was cold. They passed beautiful rolling hills on which sheep grazed like small white clouds painted on a vast green canvas, but by then she was longing for a steaming bath. An hour later, night had fallen as the carriage slowed to take a knoll. Suddenly, Kit heard the horses make a sharp snorting noise as if in alarm. The carriage stopped abruptly and the coachman shouted, "Whoa!" as she heard him trying to rein in the frightened steeds.

"Merde," Martin growled under his breath, coming to life at her side. Then he shoved her to the floor with an urgent whisper. "Stay down!"

Men talked outside the carriage. A deep voice ordered the coachman to leave his hands on the reins, and Martin whispered to

John, "Cover your side. Wait until they are close. Then, at my signal, shoot through the door."

Without a sound, John crouched and drew his pistol, aiming it just below the curtain-covered window.

Highwaymen! Cold fear cut through Kit like a knife. She'd heard stories of the bandits who frequented these lonely roads north of London, particularly on a night bathed in moonlight such as this.

Sitting on the edge of the seat, pistol aimed at his carriage door, Martin pulled back the window curtain and peered out. John did the same on his side. As he did, Kit heard a man shout, "Step out of the carriage with yer valuables, sar."

It sounded as if that voice was very close. Another man outside John's door added, "Ye also, laddie. I want ta see what sweet baggage lies within." Kit couldn't tell if he was talking about her or any goods they might carry. Either way was a terror.

The man began to open the door, and Martin whispered, "Now!"

Gunfire exploded from the two pistols simultaneously. Kit covered her ears, but the sound was deafening even so. Smoke and the sharp bitter smell of gunpowder filled the coach and her nostrils, nearly causing her to gag.

Martin flung open his door and jumped out, holding ready a knife he had pulled from his boot. John scrambled out his side, and Kit rose from the floor to peer through the door Martin exited. One highwayman lay on the ground; another sat atop a dark horse flailing with a pistol as he tried to control the rearing, screaming animal. A knife sailed through the air and the rider fell, his pistol firing wildly and dropping from his hand. Martin's knife was lodged deep in his chest.

Kit could hear the carriage horses snorting as they strained restlessly against their traces and the coachman's soothing words as he attempted to calm them. Martin encouraged the driver to hold steady. Through the open door, Kit looked again at the man Martin had shot. He lay on the ground, a dark liquid seeping from his chest.

My God. Kit's heart pounded at the carnage in front of her, every nerve on end. Martin helped her down just as John asked the coachman, "Did you see any others?"

"Nay, only the three. Ye dispatched them most remarkably. I am grateful."

Holding her close to his side, Martin studied Kit, concern in his eyes. "Are you all right, Kitten?"

"Yes, just a little shaken. I think my ears are still ringing from those pistols firing so close."

"I'm sorry, love, but there was no other choice." Then Martin turned to the coachman and his outrider, a young man sitting very still. "You have some damage to your carriage you did not have before. You must forgive us for that, but it was necessary. I was taking no chances the bandits would see our pistols."

"Not to worry, sir," the coachman said. "You saved me life. 'Tis in your debt I am."

Martin addressed John. "Help pull the bodies into the brush, and tie the rider's horse behind the carriage. The two other horses are likely close."

The outrider climbed down from the carriage to join John as the two hurried off to complete the tasks. Martin turned back to Kit and drew her more tightly into his arms and kissed her hard. Even in the moonlight she could see worry in his furrowed brow as he broke away. "Truly, you are fine?"

Breathless, she said, "Yes." Staring at him with disbelieving eyes in the light of the moon she added, "You were…amazing! I still cannot believe you fired at the robbers through the coach doors."

"Well, I expected we could encounter a highwayman or two, and I might have preferred not to kill them, but with you along I was taking no chances."

"You killed them because of *me*?"

"Do not fret, Kitten. They would have hanged if I had brought them to a magistrate, but they might have wounded us before I accomplished that bit of work. I refused to risk your life."

"I am…thankful." She was also in awe. What kind of a man had she married? Skilled with both pistol and knife and prepared for highwaymen? He had reminded her of a general in command of his troops as he dealt with the sudden attack, both fierce and calm. In fact, she realized, staring at him, he still appeared calm, his only worry seeming to be her welfare.

The outrider and John returned, leading two more black horses. "I'll tie these two and the other to the carriage, sir," John said. "We can use them in Derbyshire." He headed to the back of the conveyance, reins in hand.

"A splendid idea, John. Oh, and I'd like you to ride alongside on one of the horses or on top of the coach for the rest of the trip."

"Aye, seems best," the young man agreed. "I think tonight I'll sit atop. Tomorrow I'll ride alongside."

"Fine," Martin allowed. "As soon as you have the horses secured, we'd best leave. I shouldn't want to linger long under the full moon. The devils might have comrades lurking about."

The coachman was ready to depart, hands on the reins, and Martin turned to him. "I am anxious to stop at the next coaching inn as soon as you can get us there." Returning his gaze to Kit he explained, "We can change horses and get a bite to eat."

The coachman tipped his hat, John climbed up top alongside the outrider, and Martin helped Kit into the carriage, now even colder for the holes blasted in the doors. Shivering, she pulled the lap robe up to her chin, but Martin joined her, drawing her close and whispering, "I'll get some heated bricks for tomorrow, and once we're at the inn, Kitten, I have ways to warm you."

Chapter 13

"Ahhh," Kit sighed, letting out a long breath as the heat from the bath permeated her weary bones and soothed away the knots in her muscles. The entire journey had been cold, and though they'd made frequent stops to change horses, no stop brought the relief she now felt. For the last leg of the trip, even with Martin's warm body beside her, she had felt iced over. The air blowing through the blast holes was almost intolerable. When she'd seen the name of the public house Martin chose for the night, the Sun Inn, she thought it might be a good omen. As it turned out, she was right.

Wiggling her toes, she sank contentedly into the hot water in front of a fire in a clean if sparely decorated upstairs room. Martin had gone to see the local magistrate about the highwaymen, and John was making arrangements for the horses. Because of that, Kit's mind wandered to the man she'd married. How mysterious he sometimes appeared, like she was only seeing a costume he chose to wear. He could be very British, with a gentleman's manners and speech, then in an instant change into the seductive Frenchman. She liked both, but which was the real Martin?

When the highwaymen attacked, he had taken control in a way that surprised her. She could still see the dead men lying on the side of the road, their blood glistening in the light of the moon, and she shuddered. Their faces were not ones she would be sketching. Three men dead because of their own avarice? What wasted lives. Did the men have families? She wondered.

Her new husband was obviously comfortable with violence. There had been no panic in his voice, only calm words and well-laid plans when the highwaymen stopped the carriage. And then it struck her: He had been prepared for the highwaymen, prepared to fight. Surely he had some military training, and yet she continued to believe he had never worn a uniform. She had never met a soldier who did not mention his regiment.

John followed his lead as if they'd fought together before as a team. Martin had called the younger man his assistant, but surely Mr. Spencer was more than that. The calm both men displayed was unlike other men. Her father had told Kit of the composure some had before battle, a control others did not share. Not for the first time, she wondered at her husband with his almost beautiful face and indigo eyes, the charm of an English rake, the sensuality of a French lover, and the skills of a trained warrior.

What were they doing here? It seemed to Kit that Mary had been purposefully vague when explaining this trip to the Midlands, and the young lad who'd brought up her bath when they first arrived and the woman who followed with the tray of food now sitting on the table next to her had called her ma'am not m'lady. Not that she was offended. She had, after all, been just Miss Endicott to Pen and Pris, but the address suggested Martin had not properly explained their identities to the proprietor. Ah well, she was too tired right now to ponder all that could mean.

Rising from the tub, she reached for a drying cloth and wiped away the water from her body and freshly washed hair. It felt good to be clean, free of the road dust and the smell of gunpowder and a body too long in a carriage. Donning her nightgown, she sat by the fire eating the lukewarm stew, which was hearty and tasty, and she was so hungry that the temperature was of little concern. She hurriedly drank from the tankard of ale, combed out her long tresses, slipped into bed and thought no more.

* * *

Aware of the possibility of highwaymen on the road, Martin and John had discussed what measures they might employ, though Martin had of course hoped none would be needed. Though he was prepared he had still been shaken by the danger to Kit. Once again, he was protecting a wife while acting the spy. At least this time he had been successful.

Mulling over both his past and their future, he'd left Kit to her bath and joined John in the common room of the inn for a late supper of mutton stew and ale, good country fare though it would not have been his preference. Living in France had taught him the value of well-prepared food and good Bordeaux, but he accepted that it was ale not wine that was the staple of the local English farmers, and he appreciated it for that reason.

Having finished his meal, Martin ascended the steps to his room, thankful for an understanding magistrate. Of course he'd had to present himself as Sir Martin Powell and accept the official's gratitude for ridding the countryside of the bandits who'd been plaguing it, but soon thereafter he was three horses richer and free of any suspicion.

He was unsurprised to open the door and find a dying fire and Kit curled up in bed, her hair streaming across the pillow like dark red ribbons. His groin tightened at the prospect of stripping naked and sliding into that bed; it had been too long since he'd shared anything more with her than a comforting hug and a quick kiss, and he was desperate to take her in his arms, to lose his body in hers. As long as Ormond had talked him into this marriage, he might as well have the pleasure of it. But he'd made a bargain, one he was coming to hate. Then, too, she was surely exhausted and emotionally spent.

Standing at the edge of the bed, watching her sleep, he felt another surge of worry. What he had heard in the common room proved that unrest was rising in Derbyshire. The prior year had seen a hard winter with snow lingering into late spring. Many crops failed and families faced starvation. Men at the large ironworks in Ripley had lost their jobs now that the war with France was ended, and some were openly speaking of rebellion against the new laws, some urging another march on London in protest. The Midlands had become a powder keg waiting to explode, and he wondered if Oliver might just be the match that lit the fuse. He was taking his new wife into the center of that storm.

Wife. The prospect of having one made him feel vulnerable, but now that Kit was his he had to admit he wanted to keep her. Every night in his bed. But not in the middle of a revolution being purposefully fueled by a government spy. Since Oliver had said he could be found at the Talbot Inn in the town of Belper, north of Derby, Martin would keep Kit far from there. It was too close to the flame, too dangerous. Instead, they would stay a few miles farther north in Pentridge. Perhaps he could protect her by confining her to the inn and the village. He and Ormond had discussed it.

He washed, doffed his clothes and pulled back the cover, and had to restrain his hand from lifting the nightgown that covered Kit. Her beauty tempted him beyond reason. Naked, Martin crawled into bed and curled his body around her warmth, drawing her close. She was soft and her hair smelled of roses. A part of his anatomy longed to join them together, but his drooping eyelids told him he needed rest as much as she, and then there was that silly promise.

As he drifted to sleep, a thought crossed his mind. He had not even told her they were registered as Martin and Katherine Donet.

* * *

Kit woke early to find Martin again gone from their room. She was certain he'd come in last night, as she recalled his warm chest at her back and his arm draped around her. The thought made her smile. His presence brought not only the desire she had tried to suppress but comfort, for while their marriage had a strange beginning, she was pleased with the tenderness he had shown her. Given their passionate first night and his words since, she knew such restraint came dear.

With a smile on her face, Kit washed and quickly dressed in a cerulean day gown, pulling her hair back into a knot at her nape. Someone had left her a tray of food, and she greedily ate the coddled eggs as she looked forward to a last day of travel and to finally being settled in one place for a while. Packing her things in the small valise and taking up her cloak, she went in search of her husband.

Not seeing Martin in the main room of the inn, she stepped outside to find him talking to the coachman. As she approached the carriage, he greeted her with a broad smile.

"Sleep well, Kitten?" He took her valise and handed it to the waiting coachman.

She could feel herself blush. "Yes, thank you." The name always reminded her of the intimacy they once shared, an intimacy she knew he was anxious to share again. But she supposed she was his kitten now, and the thought made her smile. "Are we to leave soon?"

"Almost ready," said Martin. "I was letting you sleep, but I would have been up to check on you in a moment. You will be happy to see the carriage doors have been repaired and I've added some warm bricks to the floor. It should be much warmer inside."

It wasn't yet very cold out, but the day was damp and she was grateful. "My toes thank you," she said, smiling just as John approached the back of the carriage with the horses. "Will one of these three be mine?"

Martin raised a brow. "You ride?"

"I do. Perhaps not like Lady Ormond, but yes, I love to ride."

"All right, but I don't want you riding around the Midlands alone, not without one of us along. Promise me."

A ride through the countryside each day was something she'd look forward to, but she would expect to be accompanied. "Of course."

While the rest of their baggage and the food they would carry with them was loaded, Martin went into the inn to settle their account. This left Kit with the coachman, who was from Derbyshire and happy to share his knowledge of the area in response to her questions.

"Aye, the gentle hills of Pentridge could tell you a story if they could talk, ma'am. 'Twas the site of an old hill fort at one time. The village has been there as far back as the Romans. On the steeper slopes, there are even remains of Celtic fields. Why, the very name Pentridge was borrowed from the Celts. Some say it means the Boar's Hill. There's an old church ye might want to visit—St. Matthew's. It goes back to the time of the knights. O' course, the coming of the turnpike and the Butterley Ironworks in nearby Ripley changed many things."

"Ironworks?"

"Aye, since the Conquest the land around Pentridge has been known for its coal and iron veins. Though farming is still much a part of the village life, many of the men have taken up the job of colliers or miners."

Perhaps the village of Pentridge had much to teach her. With somewhat more optimism than before, Kit looked forward to their arrival. She thanked the coachman just as Martin, finished with his tasks, came to help her into the carriage. John mounted one of the horses and tipped his hat to her in greeting.

The day proved long and the ride bumpy. Still, she found the passing hills and cloudless blue sky beautiful. The late spring sun lit the green valleys dotted with small farms and sheep, and the country road was such a contrast to the congested and dirty streets of London that to Kit her surroundings appeared something out of a dream.

She turned to watch Martin stare out the window at the lands bordering the narrow road they traveled. His hand held hers, so perhaps now was a good time.

"Can you tell me something about your family?"

Martin took a deep breath and turned to face her. "Must I? Speaking of one's beginnings can be so tedious." But he offered that rakish grin which implied he was not truly averse to sharing with her.

"Are you are flirting with me, husband?" she whispered.

"Yes, and I'd like to do more." Pulling her into his arms he said, "I'd rather kiss you."

He did, gently at first and then more forcefully, entwining his tongue with hers. She was swept into the feel of his masculine body wrapped around her. It seemed she had little resistance to his charm. "Kitten," he murmured, trailing kisses down her throat. "I want you."

Her body responded to him as it always did. Tempted to let him have her right there in the coach, she nonetheless resisted, wanting to know him in more ways than just this.

"Martin," she said in a breathless whisper, "can we just talk for a moment? It's part of the reason I wanted to slow our…coming together."

He sighed and released her, but he kept her hand and pressed a kiss to her knuckles. "Besides," she continued, "how am I ever to know you if you do not enlighten me?"

He quirked a smile and let their joined hands fall to his side. "Just living with me would tell you much, Kitten." He peered at her out of the corner of his eye and let out a breath. "Ah, well, I can see you're determined."

"I am."

"Let me see. You met my brother Nick. Jean Nicholas."

"The sea captain."

"Always and forever. Only one year older than me, he takes after our father more than the rest of us. Quite the adventurer. He's named after our grandfather, the French pirate Jean Donet."

"A pirate! He reminded me of such when I met him."

"I doubt it not. There have been times in the past when he appeared the pirate to me as well. He certainly lived like one for a while. Our grandfather was the younger son of a French count. Nick has stayed on the right side of things, but privateering, even in the Crown's name, can be a fearsome endeavor."

"I daresay it is. And…you have other brothers?"

"Yes, two younger, the twins Robbie and Charlie. They are the jokers of the family, and they compete for everything. Both are good sailors."

"And so were you?"

"Perhaps at one time," he admitted.

"Why did you leave the sea?"

Martin stared out the window at the passing countryside. "It was a long time ago." He turned back and added, "I had just become captain of my first vessel. I enjoyed command, but unlike Nick I preferred our business on land to the sea, a fact my father considered unacceptable and tried to ignore. Ever the rebel, I thought to have my own way, and after one rather strident disagreement I left for…other pursuits." He stared into the distance again, and she sensed a sadness when he spoke of that time. "It caused quite the rift in the family. It was Mother who held us together."

"Is your father still angry with you?"

"Not any longer. I have since seen the wisdom in what he wanted. He believed I could only understand the business if I was first responsible for the lives of our men. He was right, of course, but it took me several years to admit it—to myself and to him." Martin crossed his arms and smiled. "Now it's my turn. Tell me something of you and your family."

Except for Anne, who was ever on her mind, Kit hadn't thought about her family overmuch since she lost them; it was a sadness long locked away. "My mother and sister were two of a kind, both gentle souls accepting of a woman's place. They stayed about the home, engaged in the usual activities allocated to our sex, like embroidery and music. My father loved and understood them. While I believe he loved me, he didn't understand me. Not really. I was always the cause of his worry. I pursued my art with a passion, even as a child, refusing to confine myself to the usual watercolors. My sketching took me far afield. It was not uncommon for me to lose track of time while pursuing some unusual face."

"You really are passionate about your art, aren't you?"

"I was. I suppose I still am." She glanced at him. "Do you mind it so much?"

"I do not mind it at all."

Kit was relieved to see his grin. Most men were amused by how seriously she took her art, and her family had been concerned by her unladylike behavior. But Martin did not mind at all. The thought gave her great peace.

Changing the subject she said, "My mother's strength was her love for her family. She was not strong physically. It was the same for Anne." Kit had tried to be her father's strength after her mother died but, as with Anne, she had toiled in vain. Her eyes threatened to overflow with tears as she recalled the last time she saw her parents; their deaths had left an emptiness in her life that only

Anne filled, and Anne only until her demise. Oddly, however, Kit felt slightly less bereft considering them. Was it because of Martin?

"You miss them, I'm sure," her husband said, giving her a sympathetic look.

"Very much." Then, after a short consideration, she decided to ask the next question that burned inside her. "Mary told me you'd been married before. That your wife died."

"Yes." Martin looked out the carriage window. "It happened many years ago in France."

"Am I anything like her?" Kit felt her cheeks warm at the intimacy of the question. She had wondered about the woman who once held Martin's heart. Though she had not wanted a love that could leave her despairing of life if it were lost, Kit had no desire to compete with a ghost. Elise had been French, and perhaps young. Kit was sure now he'd loved her. A younger Martin would have most certainly married for love.

"No, you are nothing like her. And, it was a long time ago, Kitten." Drawing her into his arms, he kissed her, and she forgot to ask the next question.

Chapter 14

They arrived in Pentridge just before twilight, and Kit felt every stone in the road as the carriage bounced along a narrow lane flanked by earthen banks topped with hedgerows. As they approached the village, the road descended and the earthen banks fell away to reveal small white cottages set at right angles to the road. A ways on, she saw a sandstone inn. A simple sign with dark brown letters hanging just under the roof declared it to be the Dog Inn.

A short distance more, they passed the crenellated tower of a medieval church surrounded by yew hedges. It must be the one the coachman spoke of, for it appeared ancient, reminding Kit of a small castle set upon a hill. A line of tall Scots pine trees stood in the distance stretching up to the sky and forming a wall of dark green.

The carriage slowed to a stop in front of a large two-story building constructed of the same buff-colored stone as the Dog Inn. The slanting gray slate roof contrasted with the faded brown of the stone, though equally rocklike, and the sign for the White Horse Inn featured a prancing white palfrey painted on a black background. The addition of lace curtains on the two rows of windows softened the hard appearance and provided a much-needed feminine touch.

Martin, who before seemed lost in his thoughts, spoke and gestured out the carriage window. "We've arrived. This will be our home for the time we are in the Midlands, Kitten."

The inn was a welcome sight, and she smiled in relief.

Martin opened the door and stepped out. "You will find the accommodations quite adequate, I believe. Though not London, certainly, we'll have two rooms and I've been told the establishment is well cared for. It's fine for you to take a meal in the common room during the day, you'll be safe here. It's important to me, Kit, that you confine yourself to the inn and the village. If you wish to go farther afield and I'm not available, you must take John."

"Where will you be?" she asked as he handed her down from the carriage.

John dismounted to join them, and she didn't miss the glance her husband gave the young man. "John and I have business in the surrounding towns. I expect to be away often during the day, though I should return in time to take dinner with you."

Kit felt keenly disappointed. She didn't want to be confined to their rooms, or the inn, or even to the village if there were things to see and sketch around the countryside. It was unusual, she knew, for women to be included in matters of business, but she had hopes for their marriage to be a partnership in more than matters of the home. Perhaps she could eventually assist in his work.

In their rooms, she raised the issue again. "I cannot accept being confined to these chambers, Martin, however comfortable they may be. Though I know some women are content to do so, I am not a plant you can set in a corner and forget."

"No, I suspect not," he said with a small chuckle and took off his coat. Apparently he found her ire amusing, which further irritated her. "Still, you will do as I say. It is only for your protection I ask this, Kit. Oh, and we are registered as Mr. and Mrs. Donet."

"Why is that? Are we hiding from someone?"

"No, not hiding. But my work here requires the…er, fiction."

"I do not understand."

"No, I expect you do not. You need not be aware of all I am doing here, you need only trust me. The deception is necessary."

Kit was frustrated and angry. Her new husband was a man of many talents it seemed, and not a few disguises. And he wanted her to trust him? "The last time you asked me to trust you I found myself in your bedchamber—a room you thought we'd be sharing for the night."

"And didn't that work out well?" he asked with a wry smile.

Kit's eyes narrowed. He thought to play the charming rogue once again, but it was not to be borne. Still, she found it difficult to stay angry with him when his blue eyes were smiling and his white teeth displayed that rakish grin. The man was handsome and mysterious, a dangerous combination to be sure.

"Hmm," was all she could manage.

More seriously he said, "You will do as I say, Kit. I do not want to be worrying about you while I'm away from our lodgings. Perhaps you will find something to draw in the village."

Mary had given Kit a new sketchbook and pencils as they left London, and that was a welcome gift. Still, Martin's dismissal and unbending stance left her annoyed. She wasn't a wife to be put away, and why was he so concerned about her protection? Rutledge was surely back in London, so what trouble could she get into in a small country village—unless one considered the danger of being surrounded by a herd of sheep congregating on the road? Surely he was being overprotective. But she was too tired to argue, so she reclined on the settee in the sitting room and let out a sigh.

"Come, Kitten. Some dinner is in order and then to bed. Perhaps tomorrow I'll take you riding." He smiled again with those dark blue eyes, and she wondered if the hunger she saw in them was for food or for her. Probably a little of both.

* * *

The heavy weight of a body pressed down on her. Cruel, hard lips crushed hers, and Lord Rutledge rose above her, a twisted, evil sneer sweeping across his face. "I'll have you now, Katherine."

He forced his body between her thighs, letting his hard shaft settle against her. No! This could not be happening, she would not let him have her. Pressing her hands to his chest, she shouted, "I don't want this...take your hands off me...stop!" Balling her fists, she pounded against his shoulders. Using every bit of force she had, she twisted away, trying to pull free, but his strength was too great.

"Kit! Kit, wake up!"

Through the lifting fog of the nightmare, Kit recognized Martin's deep voice. Slowly the fog receded as she woke to her surroundings. Their room lay in darkness, and Martin sat next to her, holding her and whispering words of comfort. Her skin glistened with sweat from her struggles, her breath came in pants. She could feel her heart racing.

"Martin?"

"Yes, Kitten, it's me. You were dreaming. From the way you were fighting, I'd say you were having a terrible nightmare."

"I was...about Rutledge. He was attacking me."

Holding her tight, Martin whispered soothing words. "Shhh...*ma cherie.* You're all right now. He'll never hurt you again."

Still, she trembled. "Do you think he is searching for me?"

"I suspect so." He drew Kit to his side, lying back on his pillow. "The man is obsessed, and his type never accepts defeat easily. Even if he isn't deranged, which I suspect he is, his ego won't allow him to leave off. Eventually I will have to deal with him. But you need not worry about that now. Try and get some rest."

He kissed her, and Kit clung to the comfort he offered, his whispered words between kisses calming her. His lips were so gentle, she could feel herself relaxing. The man had magic hands and fingers that made her tingle. She wanted his hard body next to hers.

Her hands drifted to his broad shoulders and into the ebony locks of his wavy hair. His kiss turned more insistent, his tongue moving in slow seduction.

"Wait!" She wrenched back, though her body protested. "You promised."

"I was hoping you'd changed your mind, Kitten. I am finding you nearly impossible to resist."

"And I want us to share more than a bed. I need some time together before we resume our...before we consummate the marriage. I've never been courted, Martin. Not really. I rather like the idea."

She could feel the tension in his body as he rose. "If courting is what you desire, you shall have it. But I don't think we can sleep in the same bed, at least not for the time being. It's too difficult to be so close to you. I fear I may not always act the gentleman."

Kit watched him pull on breeches and boots. He was firm and lithe and compelling, his back muscles flexing in the pale light from the window as he reached for his shirt. She wanted to reach out and draw him back under the warm covers, but she'd made this commitment to herself so she refrained. She needed some control over her life, and it seemed this was one way she could have it.

"I'll be back," Martin said. He spoke in a low voice she barely heard. Then he left the bedchamber.

* * *

He woke on the settee in the parlor where he'd spent the remainder of the night after returning to their rooms.

Uncoiling from his position on the small piece of furniture, Martin shook off the memory of holding Kit after her nightmare. Just thinking about her warm body caused his morning erection to stiffen. The walk in the cold night air had helped slacken his craving, but he had not returned to their bed. The vixen was too great a temptation. The more time he spent with her, the more he wanted her, so for the time being he would sleep alone.

Entering the bedchamber, he nuzzled Kit from sleep. "How about breakfast and a ride around Pentridge?" Before he met with the duplicitous William Oliver he would dispatch John with a message seeking approval from the Prince Regent to intervene and expose the man should it become necessary to prevent violence. While John was busy with that task, he would ascertain the lay of the land.

She slowly opened her eyes and stretched. "Sounds perfectly wonderful."

"Or"—he pulled her into his arms—"we could stay in this morning and spend some time in bed." He was teasing of course, but there was always the slight hope she would recant her request for more time. His hope became enthusiasm when she responded with a shiver to the kisses he spread along her soft, warm throat.

"Martin," she murmured. "You are distracting me."

"I fervently hope so," he said.

"Breakfast and a morning ride would be most welcome," she said before he could begin kissing her again.

"Well, I promised you a ride, so you shall have one, though I'm tiring of this arrangement, Kitten," he grumbled. He took her earlobe between his lips and gently pulled, and when she pushed at his chest confessed, "Waiting for you does not come easy."

She trembled in his arms. "It won't be long, Martin."

Encouraged, he sat up and touched her nose with the tip of his index finger. "While you change, I'll see about our horses."

* * *

If Oliver was to stir the men of the Midlands to an uprising—and Martin sincerely hoped he would not—he had best know the land they'd be fighting on. For that reason Martin was soon taking a tour of the countryside, and he gazed in quiet awe at the woman riding next to him. In her Turkey red riding habit, she looked more a lady than ever. *Wife.* His wife. He could scarcely believe the auburn-haired vixen was his. There were times, like now, as they reined in their horses to absorb the wide expanse of green hills before them, when he saw more than a beautiful woman. He saw his heart reflected in that enchanting smile and wondered if he wasn't actually falling in love with her. Perhaps it had even begun that night he first glimpsed her in the moonlight.

It had been over a month since he first made love to her at Willow House, and he wondered how long he could keep his promise. If it had not been for this assignment, this troublesome adventure in folly, he would have swept her away on a wedding trip to grant her wish to see faraway places. A wayward strand of lovely hair caused him to nudge his horse closer, and he reached over to smooth the auburn tendril away from her forehead and wrap it around her ear. The contact sent waves of desire coursing through him, but her smile was all the reward he needed—for now.

They spent the morning riding around the small towns near Pentridge: South Wingfield, Belper and Ripley, the closest town. The sky joined gray clouds with patches of blue, and there were green tree-covered hills all around. Bucolic calm belied the rebellion Martin knew brewed just below the surface.

As they approached Ripley, he could see in the distance the sprawling Butterley Ironworks. There, he had learned, hundreds of men worked, men that Oliver would try to enlist to his cause. Martin felt a foreboding sense of what could happen in this tinderbox, and he was torn again by the competing desires of wanting to have Kit with him always and wanting to send her away in fear for her safety. But London carried its own threat he knew. His mood grew dim, matching the darkening sky overhead.

From atop her horse Kit asked, "Would it be all right if we stopped here so I could draw the ironworks? I brought my sketchbook and pencils."

"Certainly," Martin said. "We've time, as long as the rain holds off." He dismounted and led his horse to the side of the clearing in front of the factory near a small copse of trees. "You can sit over here where it's more sheltered."

Kit followed, and he helped her down from her horse. Spotting a fallen tree that provided a rugged bench to sit upon, he let her retrieve her sketchbook from her saddlebag and helped her settle onto the log.

Martin studied the factory in the distance and then turned to see Kit concentrating on the large structure, her bottom lip held firmly between her teeth as she drew. The pose was endearing, reminiscent of what he imagined she'd looked like as a young girl set upon an arduous task. Perhaps as a youth she had tried to please her father but her spirit kept her from being a compliant child. He loved her all the more for that spirit.

Unable to resist, he came up behind her, placed his hands on her shoulders and kissed the top of her head. She turned away from her drawing to give him a small smile, and then returned to her work. She looked happy. He drew pleasure from seeing that, and peeking over her shoulder he saw the large ironworks take form on her paper. Her talent was impressive.

Martin returned his gaze to the factory, but this time with the informed eyes of a spy. Plumes of black smoke belched from the large blast furnaces set against a grassy knoll. This place would be important. Not only did it hold the largest group of men to be levied, but also the largest source of weapons. His eye fell on the cannon standing in front of the ironworks. God save them all if Oliver planned to use it.

"The factory is much larger than I would have thought," Kit said, pausing in her sketch to survey the looming brick buildings and the tall chimneys releasing smoke to the breeze.

Martin watched some workers trickle out of the large open gates and wondered how many who worked here had lost their livelihood in the last few years. He would have to speak with the man in charge to warn him of what was coming.

"Before it was the ironworks it was the Butterley Estate," he said to Kit as he took in the sprawling site. "Many of these are original buildings, adapted for the making of iron tools and machines. It was when they dug the Butterley Tunnel for the Cromford Canal, just there alongside the compound, they discovered veins of coal and iron."

"Why, Martin, you sound like a professor of local history. Wherever did you gain that knowledge?"

"From our coachman. He was a wealth of information on Pentridge and the towns surrounding it."

"Yes, he was," she agreed.

Martin stared off into the distance, wondering what kinds of weapons and men could be mustered at such a factory. The coachman had offered little with sureness, but he'd used the word *hundreds.*

Chapter 15

What a strange journey she'd been on, Kit reflected as she continued to sketch the ironworks. The White Horse Inn was her seventh home in only a few months, if she counted those where she'd spent only one night, and Pentridge was a far cry from the parlours of London. Yet here she was with a new husband who was charming, intelligent and handsome—and proficient with a pistol and knife. He was more than she'd ever thought to have, and she was becoming very attached to him. Still, he remained mysterious; now even more so. This morning and here at the ironworks she had sensed some tension hidden beneath his otherwise calm surface. He was worried, but about what?

As she watched him staring at the ironworks, his ebony hair blown by the breeze in casual abandon, her heart warmed. She would have to remember that pose to sketch him when they returned to the inn.

"Come, Kit," he said as she finished her picture of the ironworks. "Let us return. I must see to a few things with John this afternoon. Perhaps tonight our proprietress can find us some wine for our dinner. I'm already weary of English ale."

They returned to the White Horse, where John was waiting. He had news, and once she and Martin dismounted the two men started off with the horses toward the stables, their heads bent and speaking in whispered words to each other.

As she watched, Martin's head jerked up and he turned from John to look down the road into the distance. Then Kit heard the shrieks and screams, and she followed Martin's searching gaze to the end of the village.

Martin returned to her side and commanded, "Stay here, Kit." Then he and John mounted the two horses and kicked them into a gallop.

Something of great magnitude was obviously happening, and Kit would not be left behind. She hurried down the road after them and arrived to see villagers gathered around a fenced paddock. Martin and John had left their horses and were at the fence surrounding the large enclosure, watching as a drama unfolded before them.

A crying woman stood at the railing, her eyes focused on a large red-brown bull with pointed horns standing in the middle of the pen, shaking its head up and down and pawing at the ground. Several feet in front of the agitated beast was a small child, whom Kit thought could not be more than two, walking on wobbly legs.

The village men stood debating what to do. "I ain't going in there," said one. "That bull already skewered young Harry this week."

Martin didn't hesitate. He shouted an order to John, and both leapt the railing and dropped into the enclosure. The village men took a step back, expressing amazement, and the bull raised his head. Kit rushed the fence to watch.

The child stopped walking and sat roughly on his bottom, only now aware of the two approaching men and the bull. He began to wail. The woman next to Kit gripped the rough wooden railing with white-knuckled hands, sobbing as she stared intently at the child; then she made as if to climb the fence.

Kit put her hand on the woman's arm, stilling her movement. "Let the men try first."

Martin cautiously approached the bull while speaking to John. "Let's circle him. I'll draw him off then you grab the child."

Working in tandem, the pair wove a path in front of and to the side of the bull, distracting it from the child. The beast dug one hoof in the ground and growled its displeasure at the invasion of its enclosure, darting its head from side to side and all the while keeping its eyes on the men. Then, suddenly, the beast dropped its head and charged.

Kit held her breath, her fist pressed against her clenched teeth as she anxiously watched the now aggressive and snorting bull aimed full tilt at her husband. She was shocked at how fast the large animal moved, but Martin must have expected it, or perhaps even encouraged it, for he made a sharp turn to the left. The bull, undoubtedly wanting him gone, tried to follow.

Having lured the bull half the pen's distance from the child, Martin called out to John, "Now!" John dove to the ground, swept the crying child into his arms, and raced back to the fence where Kit stood next to the terrified mother. He handed the child over the railing, into the eager arms of the waiting woman, and scaled the fence himself. In the distance Martin jumped, but the bull's horn caught his forearm as he cleared the far rail. Kit gasped, seeing the red on his torn sleeve.

"Martin!" She rushed around the side of the pen toward him, but he was already striding around the paddock to join her. "You're hurt," she said as he closed the distance. His left forearm was bleeding.

"Fortunately only a scratch," he said, holding his hand over the place where the bull had marked him, indicating they should join the mother and her child beside John.

Kit wrapped his wound with a handkerchief she took from her pocket. "This will hold the cut until we can return to the inn."

They arrived at front of the enclosure to the cheers of the men who had done nothing but watch. The mother of the child was running her fingers over her son in careful examination, but by this time the child had stopped crying, happy to be in his mother's arms.

The woman faced Martin and John, surrounded on all sides by her neighbors. "Oh thank ye, good sirs, thank ye." She held her child close to her chest as tears ran down her cheeks. "I was so afraid."

"We were pleased to help, ma'am," Martin said.

John smiled in agreement and asked, "Is the child unharmed?"

"Aye, he is well," the mother said. She stared at Martin in awe. "He's nae hurt, Mr.—"

"Donet," Martin supplied, "and this is my wife Mrs. Donet and my assistant Mr. Fournier."

Kit wondered at that. Wasn't John's surname Spencer? That was how he'd been introduced in London.

"I am much in yer debt, all of ye. And I'm very sorry for yer wound, Mr. Donet. Is it bad?"

"No, ma'am. I've suffered much worse," Martin said, making light of the injury that, to Kit's dismay, still seeped blood.

"I've quite forgot my manners, Mr. Donet. I am Mrs. Moore. My husband Edward is the cobbler. And this little one you and yer friend rescued is my precious Johnnie."

"He's a beautiful boy," said Kit, happy to bring a smile to the woman's face, though she wanted to leave and get Martin to a place where she could properly tend the gash in his arm.

"'Twas a splendid quick move, sir," John remarked.

Kit couldn't help smiling at the pair, so quickly heroes in the eyes of the villagers. Heroes in her eyes as well. She wasn't surprised Martin had rushed into danger to save a child; somehow she knew he would always be the first into the path of harm to rescue someone in need. He had rescued her more than once. But the knowledge both comforted and frightened her. While proud of his bravery, she suspected this would not be the last time he put himself at risk. That he might be put in danger—that she could lose him—was not something she wanted to think upon.

Accepting the congratulations of the villagers and ordering John to take the horses back to the stable, Martin turned his attention to Kit, a frown on his face. "It was less serious than I'd thought, Kit, but I see you did not see fit to stay where I left you."

"I could not allow you to go into danger alone, not without knowing what was happening. I just could not, Martin."

Holding her gaze for a moment, he finally shook his head as one might at the antics of an errant child, and taking her hand he led her back to the inn. "It was for your own good."

"Yes, but—"

"I meant my words, Kit. I don't deal lightly where your safety is concerned. You are precious to me."

She was precious to him? Her anger disappeared as joy leapt in her heart. With a pleased smile on her face she said, "I must tend your wound."

He shook her off. "You need not bother with my arm, Kit. It's only a small nick. Why don't you have a bath before dinner and, as soon as I speak with John, I'll meet you in our rooms?"

* * *

Martin hoped to be alone with his rebellious bride before dinner, and it was with that thought in mind, after he'd seen to the cut on his forearm, that he asked the proprietress of the inn to scour the cellar for some red wine. A young man returned dust-covered but victorious, and Martin was delighted. It might not be the finest Bordeaux, but it would suffice.

Carrying two glasses and the decanter of the rich red liquid upstairs, Martin was not disappointed when he opened the door and his eyes reached past the sitting room to their bedchamber. Kit was rising from her bath like Aphrodite rising from the sea, her auburn hair piled atop her head with a few tendrils loose around her neck. Water dripped enticingly from her alabaster skin.

He set down the wine and glasses and strode to her, reaching for the drying cloth. "Can I help?" he asked, his eyes feasting on her lush curves.

She gasped and turned, grabbing the linen from him, wrapping it around her and depriving him of the view. "You frightened me. I didn't hear you come in."

He couldn't resist the pull of her. While she turned her back to him to wrap the cloth more tightly around her, he pulled the pins from her hair and ran his lips across her damp shoulder. The now familiar scent of roses intoxicated him, and kissing the base of her neck he pulled her against his chest.

"How is your arm?" she asked.

"I've cleaned it; it is fine."

She looked at his forearm now in front of her and peeled back his coat. The shirt had been cut away. She placed a kiss on his hand and said, "I was worried."

"Ah…Kitten." Her lips were warm on his skin. "You worry about my meager cut, while I have thought of little else all afternoon but this beautiful body of yours. Surely we know each other well enough now. The young man who works here managed to find some wine, and we've time to enjoy both it and each other before dinner." He leaned down and nuzzled her neck. "I *want* you."

* * *

As Martin's hands caressed her breasts, Kit realized she very much wanted him, too. He had played the overprotective but sensitive husband, become a hero to a village child. How could she deny him what she wanted herself? Doing so would be cruel to the both of them.

She turned in his arms, her heart beating a fierce tattoo. The smells of horse and man were strangely titillating, and the thin cloth did nothing to prevent her every nerve from coming alive. Drawn into his heat, she felt her nipples harden into tight buds. She had only to cast aside the towel and give him his way.

She gazed into his eyes so dark with desire. "I think it's time."

"Time?" he said, wrinkling his brow.

"I want to be with you again. To make love with you." To become his wife in truth.

A slow smile spread across his face, and he came alive at her words. "Kitten, are you sure? I'll not ask twice."

"Yes, quite sure." And she was. They had said the vows that bound them, but that had been a marriage of necessity. This was now a marriage of love, for she had fallen for this man to whom she had given herself that night at Willow House. Mary predicted it, and her fear for his safety as he confronted the bull convinced Kit. She would no longer deny him.

"I must be the happiest man in England tonight," he said.

He gathered her up in his arms, and she embraced him eagerly as he kissed her, a deep penetrating kiss that foretold all that would follow. Then he pulled the towel from her body and cupped her breasts with his palms. He bent to kiss the base of her neck while he slid his warm hands to her buttocks.

"You smell of roses. So warm, so lush. So beautiful. You've driven me half mad waiting for you, Kitten."

She nearly purred when he ran his lips over the sensitive skin of her ear then kissed her neck. His hands, still on her bottom, drew her tightly against him. She shivered and felt her whole body respond as he carried her to the bed and laid her down.

That look in his eyes. She had never felt so powerful. Staring at him she commanded, "Now it's your turn to undress."

* * *

He cast aside his clothes quickly, Kit watching him with rapt fascination, her blue eyes already glazed with beginning passion fixed on a particular part of his anatomy.

"I have been in this condition since we married, Kitten," he said, unable to resist a smile. "It only takes seeing you."

She blushed. "I know after our…beginning, Martin…you may find this hard to accept, but I am still new to lovemaking." Her words were a nervous whisper.

"You need have no worry, Kitten. I am looking forward to teaching you everything you need to know."

To be honest, he was delighted that she was still new to what lay before them. That innocence was something he noticed the first night they came together.

He moved to the bed and in one fluid movement slipped in next to her, taking her into his arms. She was all softness, skin like the smoothest silk, hair a long fiery stream on the pillow. He pressed his full length against her. For a moment he just held her, stroking the round softness of the side of a breast, then her ribs and the curve of her hip. He was hard as a rock and he murmured, "I am so hungry for you."

Letting her settle on her back, he rolled atop her, kissing her deeply. Purposely he slowed his movements, relishing the feel of her body, trying to take his time. They had all night. They had the rest of their lives.

She threaded her fingers through his hair. He loved the touch of her hands and he said so, pressing his body closer to hers.

"I like touching you," she responded.

"I had hoped to go slowly, but—"

"Perhaps another night," she whispered. Her voice was breathy, and she dropped her hands to his shoulders pulling him more tightly against her.

Martin swept his hand the length of her body. It was perfect, though he already knew that. He had an exceptional memory where she was concerned. He bent his head to the base of her neck and kissed her there, his hands gliding over her belly to her woman's mound where warm, willing flesh greeted his fingers. She responded as she had before, with a soft moan and an eager kiss on his ear.

He brought his mouth to her full breasts and could not resist licking them. Her skin tasted like salted honey. Taking a warm nipple into his mouth, he slid his hand down her body and back to the wet folds at the apex of her thighs, and there he slipped a finger inside. She pressed her body against his hand, writhing in response to him teasing that tender bud.

She was ready, and he was beyond restraint. Unable to wait any longer he raised his body over hers and, in one thrust, claimed her. His bride gasped as he did, but she soon began to move with him.

"Oooooh," she moaned as her tight, hot flesh gripped him, nearly causing him to lose his seed. Only years of self-control and his desire to see her satisfied allowed him to stave off the overwhelming urge.

She threaded her fingers through his hair as he drove into her. His heart beat rapidly, and they were both panting. They moved together, lost to passion. Kit's breasts rubbed the hair on his chest, teasing him into a frenzy as they neared the precipice of their pleasure, and as she writhed beneath him his control was lost. He took her mouth in a deep kiss before lifting his head. "Now, my love, now."

Her muscles spasmed in release and she whispered, "I love you, Martin."

Those words sent him over the cliff. "Ah, *Kitten.*" His release came fast, and he collapsed into her embrace. Nothing had ever felt so sweet, so right. Was it possible he had found love twice in his life? His love for Elise was lost to the past, but this woman he held in his arms, she was his future. And, she loved him!

It was more than he'd hoped for yet all he desired.

* * *

Kit woke in darkness to Martin's hands roaming her breasts, his fingers gently teasing her nipples. His erection pressed against her bottom, hard and demanding, and she found herself already aroused though still rising from a deep sleep. Eager for what she knew was coming, she turned in his arms and pressed her lips to his.

"The feel of you is too great a temptation. Sleep has eluded me."

His chest hair tickled her breasts. Kit had no desire for sleep either.

He began with a teasing rain of kisses on her breasts and then slid down to her belly. Spreading her legs with his hands, he ran his lips over her inner thighs and finally settled his mouth on the dark red curls between her legs.

What was he about?

"Don't be alarmed, Kitten," he said as she stiffened. "I want to love you this way."

His tongue dipped into her, and she melted at the slow erotic torture as he circled the sensitive place that brought her pleasure.

"Martin, Martin." She shivered, wanting more.

"Yes, I know." Crawling up her body like a predatory cat, he kissed her. Then she felt him enter her. Joined together they began to move, her hips rising to meet his thrusts. Whatever they'd shared, whatever they would share, even if he never returned the love she'd admitted earlier, they had this passion between them.

In only a moment she reached her peak, and with another thrust, he joined her.

Chapter 16

Martin awoke more content even than that morning at Willow House. A great sense of peace flooded him. He had his kitten. All was right with the world.

Donning his clothes, he watched his wife sleep, beautiful and tousled, her auburn hair scattered on the pillow. Best to let her rest after that night. That magnificent night. It was past time he caught up with Sidmouth's spy, Oliver. Time to turn to the business that had brought him to the Midlands.

After a brief breakfast with John the pair set off for the Talbot Inn in the town of Belper, just south of Pentridge. Drawing up in front of the building, he noticed it was not unlike the White Horse: tan sandstone with small-paned windows and a slanted gray roof. This seemed the common construction for inns in Derbyshire. There must be a quarry nearby.

The innkeeper was a swarthy man with dark hair and eyes, and, Martin was certain, a wariness of the two strangers approaching him where he stood wiping down a counter.

Martin spoke, allowing his French accent to rise and resuming the disguise to which Sidmouth's spy had responded so favorably. "Can you direct us to a person who is, I believe, lodging with you? One William Oliver."

The innkeeper eyed them silently for a moment. "And, if'n I know such a man, why would ye be wantin' to see him?" The Talbot Inn was where many of Oliver's meetings with unhappy workers had taken place, and likely the innkeeper welcomed the business that brought but was consequently wary of strangers, particularly those with odd accents.

"Mr. Oliver is expecting us," Martin explained, maintaining his accent. "We met with him in London when he was speaking with his representatives. I am Mr. Donet, and this is my friend Mr. Fournier. We have business with Mr. Oliver, good sir. He will want to see us."

The innkeeper's shoulders visibly relaxed. Pausing in his work, he gave the two of them another slow perusal. "Oliver is staying here, yer right, but just now ye can probably find him in Pentridge at the Dog Inn."

Martin was not pleased to learn Oliver was holding meetings in Pentridge, so close to his own lodgings, where his new bride was even now. He hoped it was not to be repeated, but short of moving to another town, which he dismissed as too disruptive at this early point, there was little he could do.

Thanking the innkeeper, he jerked his head to John in a signal to leave. A moment later they departed.

* * *

Kit descended the stairs of the White Horse Inn to the common room where a few lodgers were still eating breakfast. As she sat down at an empty table, a handsome young man perhaps a few years older than she, with the shoulders and muscled arms of a sawyer, brought her a bowl of porridge, warm bread and butter and a pot of tea.

"Good day, ma'am," he said with an eager grin. "If'n ye need anything else, just let me know. My name's George Weightman."

Ah, the son of the proprietress, no doubt. Kit had met Nanny Weightman the day before. "No, this will be fine, thank you." But she couldn't resist staring at the young man's face.

She ate her porridge and then took up her sketchbook. George Weightman went about checking on the other guests, and Kit proceeded to draw the comely youth as he cleaned off several tables. From time to time he would glance at her, obviously fascinated by the quick movements of her pencil across the paper.

"What are you drawing, if'n you don't mind my asking?"

Kit smiled. "I'm drawing you. Your face. Is that all right? I like to draw the faces of people, and you've the face of an angel."

The description did not please him, for he frowned. "Ye don't mean I have the face of a woman!"

"Oh, no," she said with a small laugh. "The angels are males, you know. Gabriel, Michael…even Lucifer." She trailed off as she concentrated on getting his jaw right.

"Well, I suppose when you put it like that it'd be all right." She recognized a male's approving assessment in the smile he gave her. "Are you in Pentridge for long? Yer wondrous fair, ma'am, if you don't mind my saying so."

"Why, that's very kind of you," she acknowledged. "As to how long my husband and I will be guests of the inn, I cannot say. But for a while, I think." She noticed his look of disappointment when she mentioned being married, then returned to her sketchpad and carefully refined his features in her drawing.

Her subject left Kit as Nanny Weightman's commanding voice echoed into the room, ordering her son to finish his chores and get along to a meeting. Kit ate the last of her porridge and drank the last of her tea, anxious to have a walk in the morning sun. But just as she was about to leave, the young man returned to hurriedly dust a cabinet near her table.

"Did your mother make the porridge?" she asked, setting down her sketchbook. "It was very tasty with the dried fruits and nuts."

"Aye. The morning fare is one of her specialties. She bakes the bread, too," he said with a smile. He was staring at Kit's hair, something she'd grown used to from men over the years. "Yer hair is the color of a sunset. 'Tis wonderful."

Having already thanked him for his first compliment, Kit just smiled in return. She didn't see what harm there could be in allowing this county lad his small crush on a visitor, but she would not encourage him. And she doubted the *ton* would agree with his assessment of her hair. "Would you like to see my sketch of you? At least the beginning of it."

The young man came around to stand behind her and studied the partially completed portrait. "Do I really look like that?"

"You do to me, but then I see you though an artist's eyes." Not that anyone could fail to see how good-looking he was.

"I like it."

"I can do one for your mother if you think she would want it."

"I think she'd like that. Mothers, ye know. When she sees it, she may ask ye to do one of my brothers as well."

"I'd be willing to do that if it would please her," offered Kit.

George said, "I'll ask."

Taking away her empty dishes, he retreated to the kitchen. She heard him talking to his mother in muted conversation, and then his voice rose. "I've only a few more things to see to, and then I'll be off."

"See that ye hurry or they will be having the revolution without you," Mrs. Weightman replied.

His shoulders were slumped resignedly as he returned to finish his work, and he didn't say another word to Kit but hurriedly attended his mother's bidding. Kit picked up her sketchbook and turned toward the door, but the woman's words came back as she did. *Revolution?* What revolution was it that George's mother wanted him to be part of?

For her morning walk Kit decided she would see the old church the coachman told her about. As she strolled across the road the beauty of the surrounding country overwhelmed her senses. Raised in London, she found the roads here a pleasant change, bordered by flowers in many places and flanked by trees. All was surrounded by expanses of green rolling hills and small white cottages. She reveled in the peace not found in the city, and the sweet chirping of birds, an occasional chicken pecking at the ground in a yard facing a cottage, the sounds of horse-drawn carts and the smiles of the folks passing her were welcome additions.

The Church of St. Matthew was the most imposing structure in Pentridge. It stood on a hill above the village, a monument to a time long past. It wasn't hard to imagine knights and their ladies worshipping there. The ancient sanctuary drew her, so incongruous was it to the otherwise simple village. Rising above the gray stone of the main structure was a tall square tower with a crenellated top that, when she'd first seen it, reminded her of the sawtooth battlement of a castle. The main building had the same crenellated roof. It was a most impressive sight, and so different from the village's otherwise simple inns, taverns, shops and cottages.

Kit walked to the top of the hill, determined to see inside the formidable structure. On her way she passed tall stone grave markers, some obviously very old as the writing was weathered by time and the elements.

Entering through the church's arched wooden door, she noticed the stone beneath her feet. Like the rest of the building it appeared worn and ancient. Two aisles separated the simple wooden benches facing the nave, and between the main part of the church and the nave were five tall arches. Colored-glass windows depicted scenes from the Bible. The morning sun shone through these, scattering beautiful hues around the church like the kaleidoscope she and Martin had received as a wedding present.

As she was absorbing this stately place of worship, thinking how she might draw it, a man dressed as a gentleman approached from the other side of the arches.

"Good day, miss. Are you visiting Pentridge?"

Kit supposed the vicar would know everyone in such a small village, so she was not surprised he took her to be the stranger she was. "Yes, I am. My husband and I are here just for a short time. I was admiring the church."

Rather thin but with strong features and a welcoming presence, the older man came to stand in front of her. "I am Hugh Wolstenholme, the new curate of Pentridge. The vicar is away for some weeks. Welcome to our parish."

"Thank you, Mr. Wolstenholme," Kit said. "I am…Mrs. Donet." Hating to lie to a man of the church and not wishing to dwell on her name or her reason for being in the village, she gestured to the nave and the windows. "Your church is very grand and so…ancient."

He looked around as if trying to see it through her eyes. "I have always thought St. Matthew's quite special, and it is indeed ancient. I have a few minutes. Would you like me to show you around?"

"Yes, if you have the time. I was just noticing the tiles we are standing on. Are they original?"

"No, not original, but still very old. They date to the fourteenth century. Normans built the church eleven hundred years after our Lord walked the earth. Of course, it has been added to down through the centuries, but there is much that harkens back to the original construction."

"In the churchyard…the gravestones. Some seem very old."

"They are. Did you see the Saxon cross?" At her nod the curate added, "Perhaps that would be a good place to begin."

They walked out the door and onto the green grass from which rose the large flat standing gravestones. "Some are Saxon," the curate said, pointing to a tall, tilting, sand-colored marker. "Though the stones still mark the graves, the writing has long since worn away." Gesturing to the tallest he added, "These are as old as the church, perhaps older, but some of our headstones are quite new. And I fear there soon will be more."

Kit looked up at the frowning cleric. "Oh?"

"I suppose you'd not know, being as you're not from this part of the country. Times have been hard in the Midlands. Some of the parishioners were lost to hunger in recent years and four young men are currently awaiting hanging for setting fire to Colonel Hatton's haystacks in South Wingfield."

"Why would they set fire to a colonel's haystacks?" Apparently the countryside was not as peaceful as she thought.

"Colonel Hatton is the local magistrate and squire. People in the countryside are frustrated because they cannot gain the attention of the authorities to help them in their hour of need. Likely it was a way of getting his attention. Not a very good one to be sure. On the other side of it, the prosecutors are overzealous and looking for anyone to hang as a warning to others. The young men have protested their innocence, and I for one agree they may very well be falsely accused. But it does not seem to matter what the church believes."

Kit was surprised by what some would consider a radical view for a member of the clergy more typically aligned with the gentry. Perhaps the curate was closely tied to these men and their families, his flock. But he had said he was a new curate. How strange.

"It sounds like a rather dire situation," she offered, sad for any people who struggled so.

"It is. Even the Prince Regent has recognized the severe trials the people have undergone, I daresay made worse by the heavy tax burden caused by the war with France. But the war is over and the justification for such taxes no longer exists."

"Have you heard the Prince Regent speak of such matters, Mr. Wolstenholme?" Kit asked.

"Nay, but I read Cobbett's *Political Register*, and many a time it has printed His Majesty's speeches. Cobbett recognizes how easy it is to suspend the Act of Habeas Corpus, easy to enact the Sedition bills and easy to muzzle the press, but it is not so easy to quiet the cries of the paupers among us. As Mr. Cobbett says, 'A country filled with paupers is not easily restored to happiness.'"

"I see. I did not realize how badly the people in the countryside were faring." She'd been so occupied with tending her sister that she'd seen little of the news. Still, she was aware of the publication all England seemed to be reading now that newspapers were so expensive, though she hadn't realized there were men in the countryside who followed Cobbett's persuasive rhetoric.

The lines in the curate's face told her he bore the worries of his flock. How unusual he was, so vehemently taking up their cause. She admired the man all the more for it. He could easily confine his concerns to their souls, but he cared about their lives on earth as well.

"Whole parishes have been rendered destitute from feeding so many poor. You can read about it yourself. They keep a copy of the *Register* at the inns," Wolstenholme said as he gestured back down the road.

"I will, and thank you for telling me."

Kit followed the curate into the church where he told her of its history, now describing the stained-glass windows. Though created by man, the windows cast a waterfall of color over the hard stone sanctuary, softening its appearance and reflecting the beauty of nature as well as speaking to man's love of his Creator.

Kit spent several minutes talking with the Reverend and learning more about the church. She even began some sketches of the place and the politically minded curate, but just before noon she took her leave. She intended to return later to finish the drawings, after she'd searched out a bite to eat.

In response to her inquiry, the curate recommended the Dog Inn.

* * *

The Dog Inn was just down the road from the White Horse, and Martin and John shook the dust off their boots before entering. A servant approached and, after questioning, advised them that Oliver was keeping company with several men in a private room upstairs. Thanking him, Martin and John climbed the stairs.

Trying the handle of the door at the top, Martin found it wasn't locked. He opened it to see Oliver again holding court, this time around a rectangular table surrounded by a half dozen men.

Sidmouth's spy immediately recognized them. "It's Monsieur Donet, is it not?"

Martin was relieved, since the other men were giving him and John hostile looks, born, Martin suspected, of a fear of discovery.

"Come in, come in!" Oliver beckoned them forward.

"*C'est bien.* You remembered," Martin said. Beside him, John tipped his head in greeting but said nothing.

With a sweeping gesture of his arm, Oliver urged them join his group of followers. "Why o'course I recall ye. I recall all those in the London group of gentlemen anxious to join the uprising."

They were no part of Oliver's imaginary London cohort, but he would let that pass. He and John found two chairs at the side of the room and pulled them up to join the others. The men around the table studied the newcomers with curious stares.

"Meet some of my country friends," Oliver said, employing the term he had used in London for his contacts in the north.

Going around the table, Martin was first introduced to a man in his fifties, Isaac Ludlam, a brown-haired stonecutter who looked as if he had once been a man of means. His clothes were of good cloth, though noticeably worn. Next to him was William Turner, a stonemason, an average-looking man, thin but of wiry strength, whom Martin judged to be in his forties. Both said they were from the Derbyshire town of South Wingfield to the north. There were three from Pentridge: John Onion, a husky ironworker with powerful hands, and George Brassington, a dark-haired miner, both of whom seemed to be in their early forties; and the shoemaker, Edward Moore, who was perhaps a bit younger and obviously shy, dressed more for the town than the field.

Before they could introduce the last man Moore exclaimed, "Oliver, these are the men who saved my young Johnnie!"

"Well, now," said Sidmouth's spy. "'Tis two celebrated heroes who have joined our ranks, men. I heard of the rescue, how the man who saved little Johnnie faced the bull." He eyed Martin. "Not many men would have done that." The rest of the men smiled and mumbled their appreciation.

Oliver finally returned to his introductions. Draping his arm around the shoulders of the young man sitting next to him he said, "Meet my good friend Jeremiah Brandreth," a man whom he thereafter referred to as their "Nottingham Captain." Brandreth was young, maybe in his late twenties, with curly brown hair not unlike John's, but his piercing black eyes now glaring at Martin over that tankard of ale reminded Martin of a cornered animal. Though his complexion was sallow and his shoulders slight, there was something of the air of command about him. From his bearing and manner, Martin thought perhaps he had been in the militia. The designation of captain, though clearly unofficial, suggested as much.

Martin and John shook each man's hand, Martin telling them how glad they were to have the opportunity to meet those seeking reform, especially since he was the product of a family that advocated *liberté, égalité, et fraternité* in France. That he was glad of the opportunity was no lie. What better way to spy on Sidmouth's conspirator than appear to be joining him?

When the introductions were complete, the door opened and a young man in his twenties entered with a tray carrying more tankards of ale.

"Ah," said Oliver, "'tis our young friend George Weightman, son of the proprietress of the White Horse and a supporter of our revolution. Come in, lad! Are ye serving here, now?"

"Nay, I just offered to bring up these drinks for Mrs. Onion who is busy waiting on patrons below. I cannot stay for long. Me mother requires me services today but she wanted to be sure I was here to at least meet with ye."

Martin recognized the strapping blond man as the one who'd fetched him wine at the White Horse. He could see by his face that George was uneager to follow the older men into a losing cause, and a sudden pang of regret seized him. How many would Oliver lead to destruction if this absurd venture were not stopped before it began?

The other men welcomed George warmly, and the young man, nodding a greeting to Martin, said to Oliver, "Have I missed much, sir?"

"Not at all. I've just been saying that everyone in the south is ready to rise, but the folks in London I represent will not be satisfied unless Nottingham is secure, for there can be no denying that it is the rallying point for Nottinghamshire, Derbyshire and Leicestershire, essential to our cause."

Jeremiah Brandreth was quick to give assurance. "Aye, and the men of Nottingham are with us, Oliver."

"'Tis good they are," replied Sidmouth's spy. "In my travels around the Midlands, I see thousands of men ready to join us in demanding Parliamentary reform. Why, the lads of Yorkshire and Lancashire can hardly be kept down they're so anxious to begin.

From Nottingham we must press on to London, joining with those in the south who are ready to fight. Ye'll find London ripe for revolution. I am only here to see that all is ready before I meself return."

Martin and John exchanged a look. Neither was surprised to learn Oliver would soon leave for London. Having stirred the embers of rebellion in the Midlands, he would want to be gone when they finally caught and flamed into a full-scale insurrection.

Before Martin could think of how to inject some sanity, Isaac Ludlam raised a reasonable question. "Are ye certain the Midlands are ready for this, Oliver?"

Sidmouth's man looked at him, surprised and a perhaps a little annoyed. "O' course I am, Isaac. Half the country is organized, 'specially the manufacturing districts. I tell ye, the men are ready to rebel against the government. It is time for all good men to have a vote!"

"That may be, Oliver, but I still have a few concerns," said Isaac's friend William Turner. "People are unhappy, and some in dire straits to be sure, but not many would fight the government. 'Tis like fighting against the wind."

Oliver was undaunted. "Yer wrong, Will. It was only with a great deal of explaining that I was able to prevent some towns from taking up arms too soon."

"I grant ye there's been trouble," Turner continued, "but while many families have faced grave difficulty, Derbyshire seems set in the ways of the past."

Oliver looked around, and his eyes came to rest on Jeremiah Brandreth. "That will soon change. I would ask ye good men of Derbyshire to do something, even if 'tis only a token gesture. My London Committee will expect it. The main business will be done there, o' course, where seventy thousand armed men can be raised at an hour or two's notice."

Martin was appalled to see how far matters had gone and the direct way Oliver, fluent know-nothing that he was, actively encouraged impoverished and reticent men to revolt. He was calling for nothing short of a march on London, telling these poor country fools there were thousands of men willing to join them. Like lambs led to slaughter, they were unaware of the perfidy of the goat that was drawing them ever nearer to disaster.

He and John exchanged a look of concern, his young assistant appearing equally disgusted at the sheer folly of the course of action being advocated. Oliver wanted a demonstration of force that would satisfy his superiors in London, but Martin hoped to forestall such an event. A rebellion might never occur without such an *agent provocateur*. Perhaps Ormond would, in response to Martin's note, persuade the Prince Regent there was still time to stop what was developing in this peaceful Derbyshire. Martin prayed it was so.

A slightly crazed look about him, Jeremiah Brandreth suddenly exclaimed, "Well, I for one am ready to join those in London. I've had enough of the government's bare rations of liberty. Oliver's right. We must have change!"

That frenzied gleam in his eyes was worrisome. Of all the men Martin had met on this mission, the Nottingham Captain appeared the most dangerous. If Oliver was a schemer, Brandreth was a zealot. It was impossible to predict what he might do. Worst of all, he seemed able to stir the men of Derbyshire into an action they would not otherwise take. Active rebellion suddenly loomed large.

The man set eyes on his partner in lunacy. "Will you fix a date for the general rising, Oliver?"

"Aye, now that you have assured me the Nottingham folks are with us. We can talk of that when we meet again in a few days. And once the date for the uprising is set, I will be returning to London to make sure all is ready there."

Chapter 17

Entering the Dog Inn, Kit set her sketchbook aside and looked around its common room. A cheery place, several sets of windows bathed the space in warm sunlight. Only a few villagers were eating: it was too early for a crowd in the tavern.

An older woman with gray hair greeted her. "Good day ta ye. I am Martha Onion. You must be visiting Pentridge."

Kit said, "Yes, Mrs. Onion. I'm Mrs. Donet. Pleased to meet you."

"The wife of the gentleman at the meeting upstairs?"

"I'm sorry," said Kit, surprised. "The meeting upstairs?"

"Why, I do believe that a Mr. Donet, a Frenchman and his friend, were two of the ones who came to see Mr. Oliver today."

Kit was confused. What could he be doing here? She hadn't known Martin was meeting someone at the Dog Inn, and neither had she known he was posing as a Frenchman, even if it made sense considering the name he was using. But, then, he'd left the inn before she arose and was therefore given no time to inform her. Perhaps she should act like she was aware of his plans.

"Yes, my husband did mention a meeting," she allowed. "Upstairs, you say?"

"Aye, the lot of them. Drinking and planning for the uprising, you see. 'Twill be a grand affair when the new government is in place. My own husband John is there with them. He's hoping to gain a position 'longside Mr. Oliver and Capt'n Brandreth."

"Of course," Kit said. Then she smiled and asked for a table, deciding to have some luncheon while she pondered the woman's words.

A Frenchman! What could he be doing in Derbyshire posing as a Frenchman? Frustrated by being left out in the cold and wondering what her new husband was up to, she slammed her sketchbook down on the table. Then, after quickly eating a bowl of mutton stew and crusty bread, she tucked her sketchbook under her arm and quietly stole upstairs. If Martin wasn't going to tell her what was happening, she would find out for herself.

A door in the corridor was ajar. As she approached, the sounds of men's voices floated out to where she was standing. Through the slight opening Kit saw a handful of men, including Martin and John and George Weightman from the White Horse, sitting around a table. She listened attentively, hoping to catch a word but never expecting to hear what she did. There sat her handsome husband, John next to him, drinking with men who spoke about taking up arms against the British government. The face of the one called the Nottingham Captain was particularly arresting.

Aghast, Kit flattened herself against the wall, heart thumping. Had she heard right? A march on London! Was the man to whom she'd given her heart and body a traitor? Was he plotting revolution? No wonder they were here under an assumed name! Did Mary and her husband know of this? She was certain they did not, since Mary had been unable to give Kit any details of Martin's work or why they were even traveling to the Midlands.

Images of Martin darted through her mind. He had been in France, and his voice still carried traces of that time. Had he been working for England's enemy even then? But, Mary had told her he'd toiled with Ormond. Kit's thoughts were a jumble as she considered the possibilities. Perhaps he'd once worked for England but now sought revolution. After all, his grandfather was a French pirate.

The men continued to talk, their conversation focused on a meeting to set the date for an "uprising." *Oh my God.* How was she to live with a traitor? How could she be loyal to him and loyal to her country? And, if he did plot against the Crown, should she try and stop him?

The noise of chairs sliding back over the wooden floor announced the men were rising to leave. She couldn't be caught there. Not by revolutionaries. Turning, she fled down the stairs and out the door.

* * *

Riding along the dirt road to Pentridge, the Earl of Rutledge contemplated what manner of chap was Castlereagh's man in Derbyshire. Could this William Oliver actually rouse the north counties as Castlereagh hinted during their meeting in London? Rutledge hoped it was so, for if it was, and if he himself could manage things from this end, assuring there were enough men to put down the manufactured rebellion, assuring the rebels were captured, Castlereagh and Sidmouth would have all they needed to justify the additional measures the government intended to impose on the populace. Then he, the Earl of Rutledge, would finally have the reward he'd been seeking: a new position in Liverpool's government and the recognition he well deserved.

Along those lines, he also wondered if he could believe the words of the magistrate with whom he'd just spoken.

"My lord, all has been made ready, I assure you," Edward Mundy promised, albeit nervously. A man going to fat with bulging eyes, he didn't seem much the magistrate. Rutledge had expected a man with proper military demeanor and discipline. "I've been told by my men over a hundred of the seven hundred workers at the Butterley Ironworks just down the road from Pentridge have been sworn in as special constables, and we've twenty fully armed officers of the Fifteenth Light Dragoons on hold at Nottingham in anticipation of the uprising."

"And when might you be expecting that uprising?"

The magistrate squirmed under Rutledge's harsh glare. "Oliver says 'twill be the ninth of June, my lord."

Rutledge allowed his most imperious scowl to fix the fidgeting man. "See that a messenger is sent to Castlereagh on my behalf so advising him. And these special constables you speak of must be ready to move on the day set." He'd turned to leave then added, "They'd best be ready or there will be hell to pay."

Now entering Pentridge, he was still lost in the recollection, pondering whether or not the jittery magistrate could be counted upon, when a woman darted across the path of his horse. With a start, Rutledge reined in to avoid her. *Fool chit!*

Her auburn hair immediately drew his attention, and from the direction she was fleeing it seemed she'd just left his intended destination, the Dog Inn. Then he noticed the familiar profile as she paused before hurrying down the road.

My God. It's Katherine.

He would know that face, that hair anywhere. But what the devil was she doing in Pentridge? Had she flown so far to escape him? A smile slowly formed on the earl's face as he considered the possibility. By Jove, what a fortunate development. Small wonder his runners could not find her. Ah, but this was too sweet. The hare had come to the hound!

He veered from his course, slowly walking his horse a short distance behind her. Oblivious to his presence, Katherine ducked hurriedly into the White Horse Inn.

Rutledge pulled up before the stone lodging house, dismounted, and tied his horse to the post, carefully stepping inside. Katherine was nowhere in sight, but a young man with blond hair approached.

"Good day to ye, sir. My mother the proprietress is not in at the moment. Would ye be needing a room?"

"No, my good man. I require only information," Rutledge said. Then he allowed a brief inspection of his fine garments, knowing they would get him information that would not normally be shared.

"Of course, m'lord," the proprietress's son said. "What information would ye be wanting?"

"The young woman who just entered. The redhead. Is she a guest of the inn?"

"Why, yes, m'lord. Ye speak of Mrs. Donet."

"*Mrs.* Donet?" Rutledge repeated, dubious.

"She and her husband, a Frenchman, are guests of the inn. Did ye want me to tell her she has a caller?"

"No, I must have been mistaken. I only saw the woman from the back. Thank you."

Having what he needed, Rutledge left the establishment, fuming as he did. So, Katherine had rejected him, a peer of the realm, to marry a commoner? And a Frenchie no less! How dare she! Why, the wench had likely married the first man she encountered—if she was married at all, he decided. The little tramp might be only the man's mistress.

Rutledge calmed himself, finding comfort in his luck at stumbling across her. Soon enough he would reclaim what was his. Yes, even if it required the use of his sword, the Frenchman would not have her for long.

* * *

Married to a traitor!

Kit threw her sketchpad on the bed and dropped her cloak over the chair, all the while hearing the same voice in her head she had heard as she fled the Dog Inn. She stood in the middle of their bedchamber, mind awhirl, thinking of first one scene then another, but she had only an incomplete patchwork of knowledge about

Martin, the man she had wed, the man to whom she had given her body and her heart.

She reached for her sketchpad and flipped to the drawings of Martin she'd made during their trip to the Midlands. His handsome, intelligent face stared back at her from the page. Thick ebony hair with a lock fallen onto his forehead, raven-wing brows over eyes of darkest blue. Even though the drawing didn't show the color of his eyes, she'd captured the heat of his gaze. And his mouth…those sensual, curving lips had kissed her most intimately. A man of great yet tender passion. A man of mystery.

Mystery. Was this the face of a traitor as well? Is that the reason they were here under an assumed name? And, if it was, what was she to do? Could she betray the man she loved? Could she live with his treachery if she did not?

The door to their bedchamber suddenly opened, and Kit whipped around to see the man of her many questions. Martin.

"Ah, Kit, you're here." He closed the distance between them for a kiss, momentarily confusing her. "Did you have a pleasant morning in the village, *ma cherie*? I have missed you."

Kit was glad she had made some drawings of the church, though unfinished, and hastily turned to them. She had to keep a calm demeanor. He could not see the shock she carried within her at learning she was wed to a blackguard. "Y-yes…it was m-most interesting." She handed him the sketch of the old medieval structure she'd worked on before taking her luncheon. "I visited St. Matthew's."

The charcoal made the stone edifice seem even more a cold monument to the past. Her heart thundered in her chest as she waited for his assessment, hoping he didn't detect her rapid pulse. But his eyes were not on her, only the drawing.

"You're a wonder with those pencils, Kit. I think these splendid. Was the church as magnificent once you were inside?"

"I thought so." She reached for what she could say. "The colored-glass windows, the old tile-work and the carved wood of the nave are beautiful. The new curate paused in his work and gave me a tour."

"That was most thoughtful of him," Martin offered, setting down the sketchpad. "Did you have something to eat?"

"I did. A bowl of stew." She would not mention that she'd eaten that stew at the Dog Inn or that she had witnessed his meeting with the other conspirators. She could not.

"I had only ale and could use something more in my belly," he said, patting his stomach. "Oh, and I met the father of the child that John and I snared from the horns of that bull."

"Where?"

"At one of the inns. I spent most of the morning with him and some other villagers, paying a call on a man John and I had to see. You know how men blather on when they sit around drinking."

Kit knew exactly how *some* men spoke when they sat around drinking, having heard it for herself. The man, Edward Moore, the father of little Johnnie, must be one of the men Martin had been meeting with at the Dog Inn. She wondered if Moore's wife knew the treachery her husband was involved in. Kit recalled that Mrs. Weightman had encouraged her son to attend the meeting, and Mrs. Onion was enthusiastic about a new government as well. So, yes, Mrs. Moore likely knew of her husband's treasonous activities.

Another thought struck her. A fear, really. Was the whole village of Pentridge swept up in such madness?

* * *

She feigned illness that night, too upset to make love to the man she had married, the man who had lied to her or at least failed to tell her the full truth. He was kind, which only made her dilemma more difficult. She could not find the courage to address the situation and fell asleep with her emotions in turmoil.

The next morning she woke to a knock on the door to their rooms. Martin stirred beside her and she felt his weight lift from the bed. Opening her eyes, she could see faint light coming through the nearby window.

Her husband quickly donned his breeches and boots and strode into the sitting room. Through the open door Kit heard, "'Tis John, Martin. I have more on that matter we discussed last night. The news is urgent."

Martin opened the door to the corridor and John stepped inside. Before Martin spoke, he shut the door to the bedchamber, effectively closing Kit out. But she was curious to know what John considered urgent, so she lowered her feet to the floor and tiptoed to the door, listening intently to hear their exchange.

"I met a man at breakfast," John said, "a printer and bookseller from Dewsbury named Willan. We got to talking about conditions in the Midlands. As he rambled on, he told me William Oliver came to his shop and tried to convince him to attend a meeting of unhappy workers. Oliver pleaded, saying his London friends were almost heartbroken that the people in the country were so quiet on such a great matter. Willan, who seems a sensible sort, thought the whole thing strange and did not take up with the man. I knew ye'd want to be aware, sir. Oliver is recruiting more men."

"You did well, John. I think we'd best attend Oliver's gatherings as the time for his planned uprising grows close. Did you learn where the next meeting will be held?"

"In a barn on the far end of town on the road to Belper. Ye have some time. 'Twill not happen till noon."

"Very well. I will see to my lady and my breakfast and then join you."

Kit scurried back to bed as Martin returned.

"Anything wrong?" she asked, hoping he would share with her his knowledge of what this man Oliver was about. Would he tell her about the meeting to plan a revolt?

"No, nothing wrong, Kitten," Martin said as he leaned down to kiss her. "Just some business John and I must attend this afternoon." Sitting next to her he added, "Much as I'd prefer to spend the morning in bed with you, we'd best get dressed and have some breakfast."

He seemed distracted, and saddened by his vague answer Kit complied. But then, did she really expect him to confess his treachery?

As she dressed for the day, her thoughts scattered. Glancing at Martin as he pulled a shirt from his trunk, she watched his back muscles flex and remembered the feel of his skin, like satin over steel. How could he do this? And how could she not worry about the man she had married, the man she loved? He was an intelligent, resourceful man, not at all foolish. Why, his good friend was a marquess! Yet she could not dismiss how comfortable he was with weapons, how easily he had taken on the highwaymen and how blithely he had faced a maddened bull. Would he apply those same skills to treason? The whole situation seemed unbelievable and frightening.

Torn between love and what she had heard with her own ears, she wondered if she should tell someone. A magistrate, perhaps? But the idea of betraying her husband was a loathsome thought like a punch to her stomach. No, she could not do it. She could not reconcile the man she had known in London with the man he seemed here in the Midlands.

She tried to put the best light on the situation, tried to imagine a world where she could accept what he plotted. Perhaps by keeping her in the dark, Martin was trying to protect her from the consequences of his activities. But, she didn't want to be protected and lose him, not to any criminal activity let alone treason. It wouldn't just be prison. This would mean a traitor's death. His might be one of those new graves in St. Matthew's churchyard. The thought was terrifying.

Martin called her name, and setting aside her concerns Kit twisted her hair into a knot at her nape and rose to follow her husband to the inn's common room where other guests lingered over breakfast. There a smiling George Weightman served up steaming bowls of his mother's porridge with bits of dried fruit and nuts, accompanied by bread still warm from the oven.

Kit fought back a grimace as Martin exchanged a greeting with his co-conspirator. Then, as the handsome young lad hurried off to answer his mother's call, Martin leaned in to whisper, "That young man's quite enamored with you, Kitten. Whenever he looks at you, he reminds me of a lovesick swain. Should I be worried?" He raised a teasing black eyebrow, a devilish grin spreading across his face.

"Well, he does have the face of an angel," Kit said, hoping her husband did not hear the anxiety in her voice. "I've sketched him along with others in the village. And he was nice to me when I dined alone." Wondering if he'd admit their connection she asked, "Do you know him?"

"Only from some encounters with the men of the village. He is one of four brothers, but the others don't seem to work at the inn. At least, I've not seen them about."

He was too good at this! Encounters with men of the village, indeed. Of course Martin would never tell her he had discussed rebellion against the government with this same young man at the Dog Inn; he would never tell her anything. So, while they finished breakfast, Kit decided it was time to don the stable boy's clothes Mary had given her. With all the men congregating at the barn, surely no one would notice a single lad. Perhaps she could learn more of their plans if she observed this next meeting.

Martin set down the newspaper George Weightman brought him, one that was shared around the village. "What will you do today, Kitten?"

"I thought perhaps I'd draw some of the cottages—"

"Do not wander far," he interrupted. "I need to know you'll be safe and remain close."

"I cannot go far without a horse," she said with a smile. "Or did you forget you forbade me to ride without you or John?"

"Stay close is all I ask," he said with a voice of authority.

"I will."

She consoled herself that her words weren't a lie. She'd stay close to the village.

Chapter 18

Some hours later, Kit walked along the side of the road, her head down and her cap pulled so low she could barely see where to step. It had rained during the night, clearing the air, and though the path before her was quite muddy in places the entire village seemed cleaner. The scent of wet grass and soil, the smell of the country, was refreshing.

It was quiet. She saw no men in the fields. While the women might be working in their homes, were all the men at the meeting? A chicken followed by her chicks picked at the sparse grass next to a cottage Kit hurried by.

She had gone a good distance before she noticed several men entering a barn next to a large cottage at the end of the village, on the edge of a field where wooly ewes grazed with their lambs in the sun. As the men disappeared into the worn wooden building, Kit followed silently behind, staying in back, hidden from view by a large plow. A circle of nearly twenty men sat in the middle of the wide space, all in heated conversation. A few stood at the edges leaning against wooden posts, listening. Martin and John were not among them.

"I say we must join with Oliver and let the government know the people are tired of the laws the rich lords force upon us," said one man dressed in worn trousers and a woolen jacket. "We might send a petition to London."

"Aye, Isaac," said another. "We dinna have any say in them laws! 'Tis got to change, that."

"Dear members of the country delegation," said a man Kit recognized as Mr. Oliver. She vividly recalled his whiskered face and light red hair from the Dog Inn. "I represent the Radicals of London, as ye know. We argue for parliamentary reform that would change your circumstances for the better. But petitions will not bring the change you seek. There must be action! I have just come from Nottingham, from a meeting with our good Captain Brandreth and the others there who stand with us. They are prepared to fight. And my friend at the ironworks John Onion tells me there are many men at the factory who will join with us. The time is ripe to—"

A loud bang sounded as the door of the barn was thrown open, barely missing Kit where she lurked. She jerked away just as a portly man holding a pistol in his outstretched hand entered with two men behind him, one much taller and in the dark blue and white uniform of the King's Hussars. The man with the pistol said, "I am the Sheffield magistrate, and this gathering plotting action against the government is at an end. You're all under arrest!" The magistrate turned to the man in uniform. "General Byng, please place these men under arrest and transport them to Wakefield for questioning."

The would-be revolutionaries scattered, fleeing in all directions like rats before a fire. One escaped through a side door, followed by another. Then another. The general and the man at his side began grabbing whomever they could lay their hands on.

Kit waited, pressed against the barn wall until she saw a chance to escape. Dashing out the front door, she looked frantically around, wondering where to run. A fleeing revolutionary knocked her to the ground.

"Kit!"

She recognized Martin's voice, but before she could rise his strong arms lifted her from the ground. She twisted to stare into his anger-filled eyes, dark and menacing.

"Martin..."

"Come, I'll get you out of here," he growled. John ran up, and Martin said, "Hurry. Into that copse of trees," indicating a cluster of birches a short distance away. "We'll wait until they depart."

The confrontations inside the barn were loud in Kit's ears as Martin dragged her off. Just as he'd pushed her behind a large rock in the stand of birch trees, a pistol shot shattered the air. Kit's heart pounded in her chest, and she glanced at her husband. Anger was reflected in his tight jaw and furrowed brow, and he glared at her clothing.

John peered over the boulder and said, "They've rounded up some of the men."

Martin continued to study Kit, his blue eyes so dark they appeared nearly black. His voice was low and harsh. "What are you doing here, Kit? And why are you dressed like that?"

Still panting, she spouted her prepared alibi. "I only wanted to be less noticeable as I sketched. Then I was drawn to the barn and the conversations of the men." She glared back at him in defiance. "I was only observing."

"You cause me to wonder," he said with a frown. "Perhaps I should not have brought you here. You might have been arrested, or worse. For all that's holy, the magistrate might have killed you with that pistol he was waving about."

She tried to look contrite, but it clearly didn't work. He said, "Perhaps I should send you back to London."

London? Did she want to go back to London? Strangely, the thought did not appeal. She wanted to be with him, traitor though he was.

John, who'd been keeping watch as Martin scolded her, cast Kit a sympathetic glance. Peering once more over the rock he took that moment to announce, "They've gone, sir. I think we can leave."

* * *

"She could have been killed!"

Martin sat in a nearby tavern with John, each man holding a tankard of ale. Much as he disliked the taste, he was downing the liquid just to calm his nerves. The tavern keeper had just told them that ten men, including William Oliver, had been arrested and taken to Wakefield for questioning, but Oliver was seen walking free in town not a half hour later. The others had yet to be released.

An ache gripped his chest at the thought of losing Kit. He couldn't imagine being without her. His wife. His kitten. His life. The redheaded vixen had captured his heart, so now he must protect her—even from her own foolishness, it seemed. He'd left her in their room with instructions to stay there.

At the moment he was so angry he'd had to leave, unable to remain with her for fear he would shake her until her brain rattled. The memory of Kit on the ground had been all too familiar, a vivid reminder of Elise lying on that Paris street so long ago, of the nightmare he'd had in London. It had been the specter of harm to Kit that he had dreaded from the beginning. This was why he'd brought her with him, to protect her, though he was clearly failing. Again.

"Aye, 'tis possible," John said. "The magistrate seemed the excitable sort."

"It was reckless for her to be there. I wonder too what she heard of the men's conversations. I'd prefer she knew nothing of what may lie ahead."

"She did not tell ye?"

"No. She only spoke of men arguing as the magistrate and General Byng arrived. I do not think she was there long." He glanced up from his ale and added, "Oliver's quick freedom after the arrest confirms he is working with the magistrate. There is no other explanation for why he is loose and the others still held."

"'Tis not surprising," John said. "He had that letter from Sidmouth's brother introducing him to all the local magistrates. 'Twould seem he's made use of it."

"This part of England is a pot ready to boil," Martin said. "It won't be long before something happens."

"Aye," John agreed. "Brandreth will see to that."

"We must do something to prevent it. I have a few ideas—"

"Oh, ye remind me, sir. A message arrived from London," John said, reaching into his coat and pulling out a letter bearing the seal of the Marquess of Ormond.

Martin tore it open. "I hope this is the answer I've been looking for, the chance for us to intervene. If Brandreth and Oliver are working toward the date they've set for their march on London, I am hopeful we..." He read the message and his heart sank. Staring at his tankard of ale, he saw nothing and let out the breath he'd been holding.

"Not the news ye were looking for, sir?" John inquired.

"Damnation. No, it isn't. The Prince Regent does not want me to confront Oliver directly or make our identity known. We are just to observe, working only from behind the scenes if we wish to discourage the villagers from participating." He crumpled the letter and stuffed it into his pocket. "I suspect Prinny is curious to know how far this will go, content to watch, knowing he has the power to quash any rebellion."

"'Tis frustratin'," murmured John. "To be forced to watch while Oliver's wolf approaches the sheep."

"Yes, Brandreth is a wolf. While I find myself having some pity for him, pauper that he is, he is more worrisome even than his leader. Find out who manages the ironworks in Ripley, John. It's time we paid the man a visit."

* * *

Badly shaken by the debacle at the barn and the argument with Martin that followed, Kit tried to settle her mind by finishing her sketch of the man called the Nottingham Captain. She worked from memory, her pencil moving quickly over the paper as she focused on recreating his eyes. The intensity of that gaze had been unusual, striking. Perhaps even a little frightening. And as she captured his eyes in the sketch, her mind strayed to the last words she'd exchanged with Martin.

"You disobeyed me, Kit. It might have cost you your life. Can you not see it is dangerous for you to go about the village dressed as a lad and hiding out in barns where men are meeting? Are you perchance aping Lady Ormond? Did the idea for this masquerade come from her?"

Dismayed, she'd lowered her head. "No. It was my idea. Of course, you are right. I did not realize it would be dangerous."

That wasn't quite true. She did know if she were to enter a barn full of men plotting treason there was the possibility of danger, which was the reason she'd gone disguised. And because she would not have been admitted otherwise.

"That is why I confined you to the village and the inn, Kit. Much is going on in the Midlands just now. I am trying to keep you safe. You must trust me."

She'd seen his exasperation. And, she realized, anger. Perhaps like Ormond's for his wife, the emotion had an origin in a need to protect what was dear. Did he love her? She had given Martin her love. Could she give him her trust?

"I do *want* to trust you, Martin," she said. *But there is so much I do not understand.*

"I wonder if you do. Perhaps I should send you back to London," he repeated. "At least there Ormond has the resources to see to your safety."

He'd stormed out, leaving her shaking. Would he send her away? She couldn't imagine being sent from him, now that she realized she loved him, now that she wanted his love. No, she would not go. She would stay with him. Perhaps she could persuade him to leave off this treachery. Deep within her she believed he was a good man. But she had trusted her father to care for her and Anne, had trusted Baron Egerton to provide for her, had trusted Lord Rutledge to be honorable. She could not trust so easily now.

A gentle knock sounded at the door. Rising, she opened it to find a smiling George Weightman carrying a tray.

"Yer husband has sent ye tea, ma'am. And he's ordered a bath for ye, which the boys are bringing behind me."

"Thank you," she said, setting aside her sketch. "Tea and a bath would be lovely."

It was a marvel, really, Martin's kindness. He'd been so angry stomping out of their rooms. Or was this bath to prepare her to leave for London? Fear and anger warred within her. He'd confined her to their rooms and might be sending her back to London. Casting her away like an unruly child. Hadn't he been at the barn where the men were meeting? Likely it was only luck that he wasn't inside when the magistrate arrived. He, too, could have been arrested or shot. But, of course he'd refused to tell her why he was there when she'd asked, though he insisted on knowing all she had done that morning. She had not been candid in telling him how she'd discovered the meeting, but then what could she say—that she worried the man she loved was a traitor to the Crown?

An hour later, Kit had bathed and was dressed in a blue day gown. Her nerves much calmer, she had just set down her empty teacup when Nanny Weightman appeared at the door to tell her she had a visitor, a solicitor named John Highmore. Kit knew no man by that name, and she could not imagine what business a solicitor might have with her, but she thought it best to learn why he had come.

"Thank you, Mrs. Weightman. Could you send him up and arrange for more tea?"

The proprietress graciously agreed, and soon there was another knock at the door.

Kit welcomed the older gentleman into the sitting room as he handed her his card. Dressed like a country squire, in a soft brown wool jacket and tan trousers, the slight man with silver hair seemed frail. His face was kindly, however, and just now it bore a smile as if he were greatly pleased with himself.

She accepted his card and directed him to one of the large chairs in front of the fireplace. "Mr. Highmore, please be comfortable. I've ordered some tea. Have you come far?"

"Thank you, Lady Powell. It's been a long journey." Setting down the case he carried, he focused on her with a satisfied look. "It's taken me a long time and many inquiries to find you."

Kit was surprised. Everyone in Pentridge knew her as Mrs. Donet. "Sir, how do you know me?"

"Oh, I have known of you for years, my lady. You see, I represented your late husband, Lord Egerton."

"The baron?" No one had mentioned her first husband since she and Mary discussed him briefly in London.

The older man nodded and leaned down to open his case.

"How did you know to find me here?"

"Ah…that, too, is a Canterbury story," he said, his eyes twinkling. "After several inquiries that led nowhere, and remembering the baron once remarked you and your sister had a nanny named Abigail Darkin, I searched for her. That took some time. When I finally found her, she was quite guarded. When I managed to convince her I only meant you good, she sent me to Lady Ormond. Now, there's a smart one. Lady Ormond demanded to see all the records. Fearing I would not find you without her assistance but being assured of your friendship with the marchioness, I complied. She was the one who told me I could find the former Lady Egerton at the White Horse Inn under the name Katherine Donet. *Mrs.* Donet to be precise."

"And why would you be looking for me? The baron's estate was settled long ago. As you must know, I took very little from him, which soon dwindled to nothing at all."

"I represented Lord Egerton in matters of his *country* estates, my dear. He wished to keep them separate."

"You are not the London solicitor who spoke with me upon the baron's death." Kit spoke her recollection aloud. That man, dour-faced and unpleasant, who had told her in no uncertain terms she would be receiving only a pittance from the baron's holdings, did not have the kind demeanor of this one.

"No. That was by the baron's design. You see, my lady, the baron was quite fond of you, even before your marriage. He would have offered for you even if the circumstances—your father's death—had been different. He wanted to provide for you. Being aware of his advanced age and knowing of his sons'…proclivities, he thought it best his provision be accomplished outside the normal channels. Before you'd even married, he settled a fund upon you and asked me to handle it. His instructions were to see that you had the money upon his death. The sum has grown quite large, I am happy to say."

"But it has been so long since he died. How can this be?"

"Well, it took a while for me to become aware the baron died. My home is some counties away from London, and he and I were not always in regular contact. Then I had to deal with the business of tying up his affairs. By the time I traveled to London to find you, the trail was quite cold."

Kit was shocked. She'd had no idea the old baron, who in many ways was like a grandfather, had felt so strongly. But hadn't he always told her not to worry, that he would take care of her? He must have realized the perfidy of his sons and how ungenerous they would be. He had not violated her trust after all.

"How large is the fund, sir?"

"Twenty thousand pounds."

Kit's hand went to her throat and she took a deep breath. Tears welled in her eyes as she thought of the generosity of the man she first called husband. "Oh, my." She drew her lips together, fighting tears. If she had not been sitting down she might have fainted. "Twenty thousand? I had no idea."

"No, I was certain you did not. Before I spoke with Miss Darkin and found Lady Ormond, I tried to reach you at the home of your brother-in-law, Lord Rutledge."

Alarmed, Kit blurted out, "You didn't tell him I am here, did you?"

"Oh, no, my lady. I did not tell him the nature of my business at all. And he told me nothing either. It was Lady Ormond who kindly explained your new marriage and where I could find you."

Relieved, Kit listened as the man continued.

"The funds are on deposit in your name with the Bank of England on Threadneedle Street in London. Originally I placed it in the name of Katherine, Lady Egerton, but I have had that changed to Lady Katherine Powell in light of your subsequent marriage to Sir Martin."

"*Sir* Martin?"

"Why, yes," the older man said, looking puzzled. "Your husband."

"Of course." Kit feigned a calm exterior but her heart was jumping in her chest. The title for her husband shocked her. How did she not know he'd been knighted? This changed everything. A knight would not rise against the very crown that had bestowed such an honor upon him, would he?

Oh, Martin, have I misjudged you? Her eyes grew moist.

Mr. Highmore reached down to his case and pulled from it a folder containing a sheaf of papers that he handed to her. "These documents provide evidence of all I have told you, my lady: the instructions of the baron, the original sum, the accounting for its growth under my management and the new deposit with the bank in London. I trust all is to your satisfaction?"

Kit hurriedly skimmed the papers. "Yes, it's all here, just as you say. Oh, I cannot tell you how much this means to me! It gives me great joy to know that the baron did not forget me."

"I thought it might, my lady. Even though the money is now your husband's, from what I know of the Powell family Sir Martin needs no money from you. I would like to believe he will give it to you freely so that you may do as you please, which was what the baron intended. By the by, may I congratulate you upon your new marriage?"

"You may," Kit replied. The reality of the money and the baron's kindness had begun to sink in, and a broad smile spread across her face. She finally had the means to be independent. Just what she'd always wanted! But what should have been a moment of triumph was not. Did she truly want to be alone? Martin was now her husband in truth, and she didn't want to be free of him. The man she had chosen in a moment of weakness was a man she wanted in an hour of strength. She only wished the money had come sooner. Perhaps she could have given Anne a better life and taken her away from the cruel Rutledge.

"Mr. Highmore, thank you for traveling so far to give me this wonderful news."

"My pleasure, my lady. It is only what my friend the baron wanted for you." Eyeing her with benevolence he added,

"Sometimes when a man takes a wife late in life, especially one much younger than he, there is a special fondness for that woman, an appreciation for her character that would see beyond his age. Such was the love the baron had for you."

She'd never realized. Whisking away the few tears that had stolen down her cheeks, Kit smiled at the solicitor and grasped his hand. "Thank you, Mr. Highmore. Thank you."

The solicitor stayed for tea. He seemed pleased to be at journey's end and to have discharged his last obligation to the man he had served for so long. Kit shared with him the few stories she had to tell of the baron, all while wondering what this latest development would mean for her marriage.

Her marriage to a *knight*.

Chapter 19

"The baron left you what?" Martin exclaimed, eyeing his wife. He'd only been half listening, still angry at the events of the day, still trying to decide what to do with her.

"Twenty thousand pounds, Martin. It seems the baron did not forget me in his plans for what would happen at his death as I'd always assumed."

"Twenty thousand pounds is a lot of coin, Kit. You're a wealthy woman in your own right." A sudden fear reached deep in his mind. Would she ask for the funds and use them to leave him? They had argued and he'd been most cross—justifiably, he reminded himself. Letting his words reflect his thoughts he said, "You don't need my money now, do you, Kit?" He wondered if she needed *him* any longer. "Would you have married me if you had known about the money?"

Her pause told him the answer was not an easy one. "Does it matter now, Martin? We *are* married, and…I would not change that. You are my husband in truth and I am content for you to remain so. I want you, Martin, not for your money but for what you've come to mean to me. I meant it when I said I love you."

Martin felt the tension he'd been holding fall away like a castoff cloak. He had feared her answer would be far different than the one she'd uttered. "Good, for I would not change it either, Kit. That you have the means to be independent and still want to be my wife says much. You see," he added, turning to face her, "I do not desire to live without you, Kitten. I love you."

"You love me?"

She seemed so surprised, Martin almost laughed. Could his intelligent vixen really be so unobservant? "Silly goose. Have you not seen it when I look at you? Felt it when we make love? Why do you think I am so protective of you, so cross when you disobey me and wander into danger?" Pulling her into his arms he said, "You are my wife for always, Kitten. So please take more care with your person in future. I do not want you harmed. I live in fear that something might happen to you. That I might not be able to protect you."

While she considered his words, he leaned down and kissed her, enjoying once again the softness of her body as she melted into him. She could not know how real his fear was. Though his nightmares had not returned since their marriage, he still harbored a vague disquiet about the future. If Oliver or his cohorts ever discovered his game, they might take revenge on her as well as him. She could not know how badly he wanted to end their time in the Midlands.

* * *

Kit returned her husband's kiss, allowing the familiar feel to comfort her. He loved her! The death of her parents and that of her sister had shattered Kit's life. Only a man like Martin, whose life had once been torn apart, could understand, could help her heal. From that first night at Willow House he'd been helping her do just that, putting her life back together.

When he broke the kiss, she leaned back in his arms and looked into his face. Did his reminder to take care evidence his continuing anger at her sneaking into that barn? She supposed he had a right to be upset. But she had been angry as well. He'd never told her he was one of the Prince Regent's knights.

"Why did you never tell me you are *Sir* Martin?" she asked.

"Oh, that. It was Prinny's idea and I've never made overmuch of it. I am still the man I was before. I only become the baronet when I must. My plan, when this is over, is to return to my family's business where I am merely a merchant."

"Will you tell me for what great act of bravery you were knighted?"

"One day soon, but not now. Suffice it to say it was not for any act of valor in battle. There were many who deserved the honor and I do not count myself among them. The Prince Regent was being overgenerous."

Kit was frustrated that he would not tell her of the heroic task that led to his knighthood. Surely he must be proud of it...but she also believed he was a humble man.

"If you won't share that with me, can you at least tell me why we are here in Pentridge and living as Mr. and Mrs. Donet? We've nothing to hide, surely."

"There is nothing you need worry about, Kit. I've done nothing wrong," he assured her. "The name Donet is perfectly respectable. It is the family name of my French mother." Then he grinned and said rather sheepishly, "Though I told you my grandfather was a pirate, I'm given to understand he was an honorable sort. As for my purposes here in the Midlands, the name suits. You must continue to trust me a little while longer."

It was like pounding her head against a stone wall. For reasons only he knew, he would tell her nothing.

"I'm not happy with that, Martin. I don't like living as someone I'm not."

"Trust me, Kitten. All will come right in the end."

"So you say."

* * *

"Come in, gentlemen."

Martin and John stepped through the narrow door leading into the office of George Goodwin, manager of the Butterley Ironworks in Ripley, and the man wiped his hands on a cloth and offered them a welcoming shake. His office was in a small hexagonal brick building that also served as the gatehouse, nestled among the surrounding factory structures. In his fifties, Goodwin had face stubble the same gray color as the hair on his head, evidence he didn't always bother to shave.

As he entered the office, Martin focused his attention on the pictures of furnaces and some of the factory's recent products nailed to a board on one wall. One structure displayed was Vauxhall Bridge, parts of the iron edifice obviously made at Butterley drawn in detail. Other projects, graphically displayed on large sheets, were scattered about Goodwin's desk, some smudged with oil and iron dust.

The man gave Martin a skeptical look and his bushy gray brows drew together. "Why are you here, Mr. Donet?"

Martin and John took the chairs Goodwin offered on the other side of his desk, and Martin settled back knowing the next few minutes would tell him if he'd have an ally or an enemy. He had been told the man could be trusted, but he needed an assurance that would allow him to share things about himself he did not want generally known, at least not yet. "What I am about to tell you is confidential, Mr. Goodwin. Do I have your word it will remain so?"

The manager paused, doubt in his eyes, but then Goodwin seemed to make a decision and sat down behind his desk. "You have my word. Now, what is it that is so private and pressing?"

"I will be most direct, sir. There are some men in Derbyshire who are planning an uprising, a rebellion against the government."

Martin saw in Goodwin's eyes the recognition he expected. "I'm aware there are some who would like to see changes in the way the country is run, even some of my own workers. Are you referring to such?"

"Unfortunately it has gone beyond a mere desire for change. I have been sent here by the Crown to learn the true source of the planned rebellion."

The older man pursed his lips. "Assuming I can believe that, and I'm not certain I do, what interest has the Crown in the Midlands? Surely this is a local matter for our magistrates."

"Unfortunately, the Midlands has become involved in schemes that reach as far as London." Martin gave a slight nod to John in acknowledgment of what they both knew had to be revealed.

"London?" The manager looked at him askance. "What does London have to do with some unhappy men in Derbyshire? The magistrates have already been to see me and sworn in a hundred of my men to act as special constables should there be any trouble." He gazed out the window. "Even that seemed too much."

Martin and John exchanged glances. Though new information, it was not surprising. Martin expected both sides to recruit support from this large a pool of men. "I am hoping you are right. It is my desire to avoid violence if at all possible."

The manager's shoulders visibly relaxed. "That is my hope as well, Mr. Donet. My men have been through much in recent times."

"My real name is Sir Martin Powell, Mr. Goodwin. I come from London, sent by the Prince Regent himself. Our monarch is most anxious to know what is going on here. I bring you both a message and a request."

An expression of surprise flickered on George Goodwin's face. "*Sir* Martin?"

Martin nodded.

Goodwin's surprise faded, and he leaned across his desk. "What message?"

"I believe the good men of Derbyshire, for the most part, do not seek active rebellion, but their unhappy condition of late has rendered them vulnerable to a man who would, for his own purposes, urge them to violence. The *agent provocateur* is one William Oliver, who works for men in Sidmouth's government seeking to incite the very rebellion the magistrates have asked you to help quash."

Goodwin stared down at his desk, his hand nervously fumbling with a paper. "I have heard of this man Oliver. He's a bad one, I think. But why would men in the government want to incite a rebellion? That makes no sense."

"To justify repressive measures and, once they see the rebellion put down, send a message to all of England that there will be no revolution here as there was in France."

Raising his head Goodwin said, "I begin to see. And do the magistrates know of this?"

"They know Oliver was sent by some in the government because they were asked to cooperate with him. So, yes, I believe they know. Undoubtedly, the request for your special constables is the direct result of their complicity."

"Where is all this leading, then?" asked Goodwin.

"It is possible," Martin said, "even likely, that you or your men will be approached by the leaders of a group of rebels seeking weapons, or the makings of such, as well as men to join their cause. If you can convince them to turn from their path and go home, to avoid an altercation with the authorities, it would be a gift to the people of Derbyshire."

"It pleases me to hear you say so, Sir Martin. I worried when the local magistrate asked me for the special deputies. To me it only spelled violence."

"You may be the key to keeping the countryside calm, perhaps even a voice of reason in the midst of a growing insanity, Mr. Goodwin."

The older man squared his shoulders as if accepting the responsibility Martin offered. "When do you expect this to happen?"

"Soon. Though I cannot give you a date with any confidence, I have heard Oliver mention the ninth of June. I will get word to you through John, my assistant here, should we catch wind of a more specific time."

Goodwin gave John a measured look as John nodded and said, "Aye, ye'll be seeing me afore long, I expect."

"I will gladly do as you ask," said Goodwin. "I have no wish to see the men of Derbyshire involved in any uprising. 'Tis only foolishness. No good can come of it."

Martin and John rose from their chairs, and as they did Mr. Goodwin stood to shake their hands. "Thank you for coming, Sir Martin."

"Mr. Donet, please."

The older man nodded, and Martin was assured his message had been well received and his confidence kept. Now, if they could only assure no lives were lost.

* * *

Kit had come to enjoy the peace of the village, notwithstanding her displeasure at her husband's continued reticence to tell her how he was involved in the plans for an uprising in Pentridge. She took long walks and, during the days following the skirmish at the barn, sometimes rode with John or Martin to the neighboring towns of Belper, Ripley or South Wingfield. It was the end of the first week in June and the days were long. Though sometimes they were favored with sunshine, more often a cold rain fell upon the village. Today, observing the chill in the air and dark clouds on the horizon, she determined to take her sketchbook outside to draw while she could.

From her seat on the wooden bench in front of the inn, she could see lambs grazing in the far distance on the green hillsides and thought perhaps it was a sign that times would be better for the people of the Midlands. She hoped so. Watching the endless circle of life in the farm animals was peaceful and reassuring. Pentridge had brought a quiet to Kit's life so different from the frantic pace in London and the tragic events of her past.

She'd become a familiar sight as she sat on a stone wall or bench drawing the faces of the villagers going about their day, working in the fields, tending their sheep or feeding their chickens. There were always children running with dogs, too. Many waved or bid her good day as they passed. Not a few times George Weightman, sometimes accompanied by one of his brothers, stopped to chat. On this particular morning he was alone when he paused to speak to her, just on his way out of the White Horse.

"Have ye finished my picture, Mrs. Donet?" he asked, flashing his blue eyes at her.

"I have. Would you like to see?" She flipped through her sketchbook until she came to one of the earliest sketches she'd completed since coming to Pentridge and showed him.

He studied it for a moment then said, "'Tis a nice picture. Better than my true face, I think."

"Not to me," she replied. "I've made one for your mother, too. You're a handsome fellow, George. Have you never noticed the attention village girls pay you, or does it take a woman to see that?"

A red blush crept up his face, and he dropped his gaze to his shoes. Well...I suppose I have noticed a few."

Kit pondered the man before her. He still seemed more like a younger brother to her, even though his ruddy complexion and wavy blond hair would never have been seen in her family. Perhaps his youthful demeanor came from living in the country where life was simpler. His eyes did not speak of experience. In London, she had seen so much at such an early age she felt a decade older.

"There, you see? Even you have observed the girls of Pentridge watching you from beneath their lashes. When it comes to choosing a wife, you will have your pick."

"Do you think so, ma'am?" he asked.

"I do." And when she smiled up at him, he returned the expression and sauntered off with a lighter step, leaving Kit pleased she could bring him some joy. It saddened her to think that the fair-haired young man was involved with the men planning an uprising, even at his mother's insistence, and she worried for him.

A moment later two little girls rushed by at play, teasing each other. Kit hurriedly flipped her sketchbook to a new page to capture them. One had blonde curls and the other a more common brown. Though very different in appearance, they reminded her of two other girls the same age a long time before. Kit remembered again the day that she had rescued Anne's doll from the bullies; they had played together just like these two. Pausing in her drawing, she realized not for the first time that she would never again hear Anne's sweet voice, never again have the chance to comfort her. Kit had said a brief good-bye, and that was the last memory she would have of the sister she loved who called herself the brown mouse.

* * *

That evening, after dinner, Kit and Martin wished John a good night and entered their rooms. Martin settled into a chair in the sitting room, while Kit went to the bedchamber.

"What's this sketch?" Martin called.

Kit glanced over her shoulder to see her husband studying her sketchbook and remembered the drawing she'd left open when she'd returned that afternoon. "Two village girls I was watching play near the inn." She put on her blue wrapper, tying it in front of her waist and went to retrieve the book, worried he'd see more.

"There is something about this drawing," Martin continued. "So much emotion between the two girls."

"Perhaps it's because they reminded me of my sister and me," Kit said, taking it from his hand.

He must have heard the quaver in her voice, for he rose and followed her into their bedchamber where she took a seat and began brushing her hair. Leaning down, he wrapped his arms around her. "What's wrong, Kitten?"

"There are times, like today," she explained, setting the brush down, "when the loss of Anne overwhelms me. I'm reminded..." She turned to the side as her voice caught and took a deep breath before continuing. "I will see something, like a pale pink ribbon she would have loved, and I want to buy it for her. But then I remember she is gone and I'll never again share such a gift with her." She turned to find his indigo eyes filled with sympathy. "I'll never see her again, Martin. Not in this life."

"I know, Kitten," he said, pulling her up from the bench and drawing her against him. "I know."

He reached his hand to her face and wiped away the tears she could feel spilling down her cheek. She supposed he did know, for he too was living with the loss of someone he loved.

"Come," he said. "Let me help you forget the sadness."

Willingly she let him undress her and, having doffed his clothes, he gently pulled her to the bed. He kissed away her tears and loved her with his gentle hands just as he had that first night they came together. The scent of him and the heat of his body surrounded her, and she pulled him closer. He kissed her deeply as she delighted in the rough hair on his chest teasing her breasts.

When his lips trailed kisses down her throat to her breasts, she responded. His warm flesh pressed against her caused the tension to quickly build, and her woman's center grew wet and eager for him. His erection pressed into her mound; then his body slid down hers as he kissed her stomach, her belly, and finally the sensitive flesh of that responsive bud where he lingered.

"Oh, Martin," she sighed as she pulled him back up to her.

He was so perfectly formed; she slid her hands over his back and rubbed her face against the rippling muscles of his chest. "You smell good, Martin. An unusual spicy scent, all earthy man."

He chuckled. "Enough of that. I want you."

She reveled in his weight upon her and opened to him. With one thrust, he was lodged deep within her. She raised her hips and moved with him, the friction of his slow slide in and out of her sheath bringing her quickly to the fever pitch of their lovemaking. And when release came for both of them, the echoes of her spasms held him deep within her.

She clung to him, cradled in his arms, and Kit let out a sigh of contentment. Her husband stroked her arm, tender in his touch, and she was reminded that she had made a wise decision in marrying him. No matter the questions that still remained, she would trust him.

"I love you, Martin," she said.

"Ah, Kitten, you've made me a happy man. I'll never grow tired of hearing those words. I love you, too."

"I wanted to tell you for a long time, but I was afraid. I didn't know if I could trust you," she whispered in a revelation.

"And you do now?" Martin whispered back, softly kissing her temple.

"Yes," she admitted, shivering.

"You and I are very much alike, you know."

"How is that?" she asked, nestling deeper against his body.

"We both want to control our lives. It's why you wouldn't have married me when I asked, not if you'd had the baron's money then…and it is why I gave up the sea and left my father's ships. You're brave, independent and curious, and you care for others, like your sister Anne and even the people of this village. You make me care, too, Kit. It's because of you I have more sympathy for the plight of these people of Pentridge."

She kissed him then, a soft thank-you for who he was: her knight. There had never been anyone like him in her life. Not her father, who loved her but failed to understand his younger daughter, nor Anne, who admired her strength but did not share it. Martin understood her and loved who she was. He encouraged her drawing and gave her time many husbands would have denied. He'd met her need for small comforts on their trip north. He sent her a bath and tea even when he was angry. And, too, there was that first night at Willow House. In some mysterious way she could not explain he'd understood what she'd needed.

She wanted to be the wife who met *his* needs. "I don't care about having control anymore, Martin. I care about sharing a life with you. Please don't do anything that would jeopardize that life."

Chapter 20

Kit stretched and yawned, the soreness in her body reminding her of the previous night. She had known Martin was a wonderful lover, known he could be tender and gentle, but this time he had been so much more. He'd been voracious, murmuring French words of love as he took her again during the night, like a man long without food finding himself at a banquet. She had never felt more desirable.

As she lay next to him, she thought about how intimately they shared their bodies and how eloquently he spoke of his love while sharing nothing of his work. Perhaps that would soon change.

"Martin, how much longer will we be here?"

"Ah, Kitten." He gave her a squeeze. "I see you grow tired of this village life. I do not blame you. So do I. It won't be much longer that you'll have to endure this slow pace."

"It is not the pace I mind. I rather enjoy the calm of village life. But it's not *our* life, is it? I trust we have a future that is not here in the Midlands."

"We certainly do. And I am anxious for it to begin, to sweep you away on a wedding trip we've yet to take. Trust me, it won't be long now. But stay close to the inn and the village."

Always there was that caution. He worried about something that was coming, a dark cloud on the horizon. The uprising, she supposed. Again, for the hundredth time, she wondered how involved he was, and whether the disgruntled workers would truly march on London. At times it all seemed like a dream. The Midlands were so beautiful, and the idea of any kind of revolution in England seemed impossible.

On the eighth of June they went to church at the ancient St. Matthew's. In a bizarre turn of the weather it had snowed the day before, and, though much had melted, white patches remained in shadows under the trees. Stepping out of the church at the end of the service with Martin at her side, Kit gathered her cloak more tightly around her, and stopped to talk to Lydia Moore, the cobbler's wife, wondering aloud how the weather would affect the local wheat crop. Only yesterday the tender green stalks had been blowing in the breeze.

Martin excused himself, saying he and John needed to speak to the curate. Kit half listened to Mrs. Moore speak of how well her young son Johnnie was doing, half watched Martin and John walk to where Mr. Wolstenholme stood bidding his parishioners good-day. The three men stepped aside and huddled together to talk. Kit wondered if the curate was involved in the planned insurrection. His views seemed more those of a revolutionary than a man of the cloth, but if he was involved it was surely because he cared about the people and wanted justice for them. What a strange place Pentridge was.

Later that day, after they'd shared a meal, Martin excused himself again to leave her alone in their rooms. Kit could sense something was afoot and was curious to know what it was.She allowed some time to pass then started downstairs. Nanny Weightman was welcoming a score of men through the front door, urging them quickly into the back room. A few allowed their gazes to drift to where Kit stood on the stairs, but none paused as they strode to their destination. From the looks of them, they were from the ironworks, large muscular laborers with rugged features dressed simply in brown woolens as she'd observed the day she and Martin rode to the factory.

As Kit descended to the base of the stairs, the one they called the Nottingham Captain walked through the door. Her drawing of him was nearly done, and she could see it was a good likeness. It depicted the man's thin face, thick curly hair and intense dark eyes, the scraggly dark beard and mustache that cried for a trim. His shoulders were slight but he stood erect.

Only when he joined the others assembling in the back room did Kit approach the proprietress. "Mrs. Weightman, may I ask, do you know that man who just passed by?"

"Why, yes, that'd be Mr. Brandreth, m'dear. He once destroyed those infernal textile machines, but he's taken on a greater role now for the good of the cause. He's arrived in Pentridge for some final planning with the men of the village, including me own sons. Did ye know me boys are to have positions in the new provisionary government? And me brother Thomas has been participating in the meetings in Nottingham. He believes, as I do, 'tis time the workers have their say."

Kit could hardly believe the pride shining in the woman's eyes as she spoke of her sons and family rebelling against the Crown. "I see," she said, still shocked by the possibility the townsfolk could endorse the man known as the Nottingham Captain and think a revolution likely to succeed, even encouraging their sons to join up. Kit would have considered persuading her to see reason, but the conviction in Mrs. Weightman's voice did not invite debate.

"Why, yer own husband Mr. Donet be with them!"

"Yes…yes, of course." Kit shouldn't have been surprised to hear that, but she was. She decided to pretend Martin participated with her knowledge, certain it was the only reason the woman was sharing information so freely.

Nanny Weightman turned to greet more men entering the inn, and Kit wandered toward the back listening for voices. She paused near the doorway, hearing the large room crowded with men, and slipped along the back wall to sit on a keg behind a stack of crates.

Through an opening she saw Jeremiah Brandreth at the front of the crowd.

Gesturing to the man on his right Brandreth announced, "The rising is nearly here. Meet my good friend from South Wingfield, Isaac Ludlam. He lost his farm to bad times and has been using his stonecutting skills to develop weapons. Thanks be to God he escaped the scrape with General Byng!"

Ludlam rose from his chair. Tall and powerfully built, the man had hair the same tan color of the stones of the Pentridge inns. "I've some pikes stored at my quarry on the way to South Wingfield not two miles away. They'll arm some of us at least. My friend William Turner here"—he gestured to a man next to him— "has more."

The thin and wiry Turner joined his friend at the front of the crowd. "I can get us weapons, but they be of little use if'n we don't first get rid of the magistrate, Colonel Hatton. He's the one who had those boys arrested that even now rot in gaol, waiting to be hung for the hayfield burning. I've a plan to lure Hatton out of his house by setting fire to some straw on his doorstep, and then we can shoot him as he comes to investigate. 'Twill be easy."

The men seemed to consider Turner's idea, some shaking their heads, some nodding. Kit was horrified. The man openly urged murder! She remembered what the curate had told her of the four young men whose bodies he expected would soon be buried in the church graveyard, and she regretted that their lives might be forfeit, but revenge such as this was appalling. She was relieved when, after some discussion, most of the men dismissed the idea of killing the magistrate.

"I be John Onion"—a man rose from the barrel upon which he rested—"and I speak fer the Butterley Ironworkers here. Six of our men were just sacked because they are members of the Hampden Club led by our friend Thomas. They argued for reform of

Parliament and the vote for all men, but the factory manager claimed they were rebels and troublemakers and threw them out. I say they are men we should follow!"

Listening, Kit wondered if that was the reason Martin had taken her riding near the ironworks. Somehow she felt certain their ride and the involvement of the men from the factory were two threads in the same twist. Why else would Martin want to see the ironworks? Did he plan to return with these men?

"Aye, you're right, John," called Brandreth. "You mention my friend Thomas Bacon. I met with him in Nottingham just a day ago. He thinks Pentridge should be our base of operation for the rising. I agree. Great events will shortly come to pass, and the countryside is only waiting for the men of Pentridge to join."

"We're with ye!" a man shouted from the back of the room. Raised voices began a chorus of agreement.

Brandreth calmed the men with raised arms. "It makes sense to me we begin here. Pentridge is near the ironworks, where John Onion has assured me hundreds will rise with us."

"Aye, Capt'n," said Onion. "Some I know were none too happy about the sacking. Those were men with families to feed. 'Tis only right that the iron bars lying about the factory should be given to us as weapons when we come a-calling." The big man gave Brandreth a knowing smile, as if they shared some secret. Kit decided the ironworks must be the key to their success.

The Nottingham Captain drew a large map from the floor behind him and set it on a crate in the middle of the room, and the crowd drew close, straining to see. It looked to Kit like there were more than thirty of them gathered around.

"Oliver tells me the whole country is ready to rise. This is the route we'll take to join the others in Nottingham. We'll travel the few miles south from Pentridge to Ripley and then east the fourteen miles to Nottingham. And from there to London! Along the way we shall gather more men and weapons." Brandreth picked up a stack of circulars and began to pass them around. "I've written some verses to inspire ye," he said, then he began to recite:

Every man his skill must try,
He must turn out and not deny;
No bloody soldier must he dread,
He must turn out and fight for bread.
The time is come, you plainly see,
The government opposed must be!

The room was quiet for a few seconds and then erupted with shouts of, "The time has come! The time has come!"

Kit watched in horror. Could they not see what idiocy this was? Soldiers could kill them all! She wanted to cry out their folly but knew they'd never listen to a woman, and certainly not a Frenchman's wife.

Brandreth raised his hand to silence the men and began once more to speak. "Tomorrow night we'll gather at Hunt's barn. From there we'll march together to Nottingham, where my own men await. Clouds of men from the north will come alongside, and we'll sweep all before us!"

"What will happen at Nottingham, Captain?" shouted a man from the back of the room, not far from where Kit was hidden.

"There'll be ale and beef for every man, and a hundred guineas apiece. Over sixteen thousand men will rise there to march with us," Brandreth promised with obvious confidence. "Oliver has assured me that, by the time we reach Nottingham, London will have fallen into the hands of the new government he is organizing. I'm dispatching young George Weightman here," he added, gazing at the young man of whom Kit had become so fond, "to check on the men at Nottingham and return with a report for us tomorrow."

Kit struggled to absorb the gravity of what she heard even as the men shouted, "Hear, hear!" No longer could she deny the purpose the men were pursuing, or their determination, even if it be madness. Though the stuff of dreams, she knew the promise of a hundred guineas would lure many of the villagers to join the insanity. It was an outrageous sum that none would ever see.

She raised her head to peer over a crate, watching as the men gathered around George Weightman, wishing him well on his journey to Nottingham, some even handing him coin for his travel. And that was when Kit saw him. *Martin.* Sitting on a barrel in a corner of the room, still as a stone, his blue eyes full of fury he stared straight at her.

Without hesitation, heart racing, Kit slid out of her hiding place, ducked out of the room, and ran for the stairs.

She slammed the door to their rooms, pressed back against it. Her heart pounded in her chest. What could she tell him? But before she could gather her thoughts, the door struck her back as it was forced open. She turned and stepped farther into the room.

A furious Martin stalked toward her. She gasped and ran into the bedchamber. The sound of his booted footsteps followed.

"Just what did you think you were doing, Kit?" His expression thunderous, he stood legs spread and hands fisted on hips. Never had she seen him so angry. Backing up, she watched him while desperately trying to think of an explanation he might accept.

Her retreat was stopped by the bed. "I...I just went downstairs when I saw the men pouring into the inn and I was curious to know what they were doing here." Reminded that her husband had been one of the men, she found herself asking, "And why would *you* be calmly listening as men urged murder?"

He glanced down for a moment as if reluctant to answer then returned his gaze to her. The fire in those dark blue eyes was only just banked as he repeated, "You must trust me, Kit. I know what I'm about."

"Why can't you tell me what's going on?" she almost shrieked. His continued refusals drove her mad. She knew of his involvement, of his assumed name, but had no reason for it or what he'd dragged them into. Would he follow that madman Brandreth? She could not believe it of him, not unless there was some other part of him she truly did not know.

"I do not want you involved, Kitten," he said in a softer tone. "I brought you here for your safety, not to involve you in this mess in the Midlands. The less you know the better. You must promise me to stay in the inn and our rooms for the next few days. Please, promise me."

"Why do you try and restrict me so? Can you not trust my judgment?"

She saw pain in his eyes as the anger faded. "Recall, Kit, that I was married before."

"I never knew how your wife died..."

"I lost my first wife in France, years ago on a night when I failed to protect her. I have even wondered many times if she was killed in place of me. I have never forgiven myself, and I don't want to repeat that mistake." He closed the distance between them, taking her into his arms. "You are so precious to me."

"Do you still miss her?" *Love* her?

"I can't say I don't think of her. I do. That I was the cause of her death haunts me—but it is only you I am concerned about now. Only you I love, Kit." Stepping back and raking a hand through his dark hair, one hand on his hip, he added, "Only you *I must protect*."

His words caused her anger to fade. She was precious to him. He was worried about her. He'd said it again: he loved her. How could she not love such a man in return?

He drew her to him, and his lips captured hers in a gentle kiss. But when he raised his head, she came back to a nagging question that still plagued her. She had to know. "Martin, those men are planning a rebellion. Are you a part of it?"

Still holding her he said, "I have a role to play in this, Kit, but it is not what you may suspect. Soon I will explain, but there is no time now. I must return to see what John has learned. Tonight will be critical."

"I don't want to stay here alone, Martin."

"You must," he replied. "I need you to be strong now, and I need to be sure you are safe while I deal with what is about to happen. Trust me for a little while longer."

He left without saying more. Kit was torn, thinking of how much she loved him but also tired of being told what to do and offered no information. Did he truly feel justified in leaving her to wonder about his part in this fomented rebellion? Did she truly think that she would not worry about him as he worried about her? No, she would not sit and wait as he urged. If he did not tell her the truth tonight, if he gave her some excuse or forgot to bring it up, she would plan to be at Hunt's barn in South Wingfield where the men were to meet. If he was there, perhaps she could talk him out of madness.

* * *

Rutledge stood in front of the White Horse Inn, content with the way his plans were coming together. The house he had leased from the Duke of Devonshire's agent lay in a dell, hidden and isolated, most suitable for his purposes, and he'd been having Katherine watched. All was ready.

Though his finding Katherine had come at an inopportune time, it could not have been helped. He was delighted to have found her at all. And then, perhaps the business that brought him to

Derbyshire might take care of his other problem. Yes, the timing was perhaps perfect after all. Wasn't the Frenchman Katherine married one of the insurrectionists plotting that doomed rebellion? The hussars might take care of him. In that case, he would not have to kill the man himself to render Katherine a widow, soiling his hands where it wasn't truly necessary. He might have a word with the hussar captain, though, to assure they did not miss that particular traitor. Yes, that could be easily arranged.

He had brought an unmarked carriage to the inn, equipped with curtains covering the windows. Taking one of his guards with him and leaving the other with the carriage, he ordered the coachman to wait and entered the inn to find the proprietress just inside the door. He knew of Nanny Weightman from Oliver, for she was active in the workers' cause, even urging her own sons to become involved in the planned insurrection. The woman was a fool but she might be helpful.

"Good day ta ye, sir. May I be of service?"

"Why, yes." He forced a smile. "I'm here to escort Mrs. Donet to her husband, who, I understand, is attending a meeting. I believe you are aware of the…meeting at Hunt's barn?"

"I am, good sir. 'Tis an important day here in Pentridge. Did ye want me to tell Mrs. Donet she has a caller?"

"No. Mrs. Donet and I are previously acquainted. I am expected."

"Well, then, ye'll find her upstairs. First door on yer left."

"Thank you." Rutledge tipped his head to the innkeeper then signaled his guard with a raised brow to keep the woman occupied.

As he ascended the steps, Rutledge once again gave thanks for the fortuitousness of these events. As it was June ninth, Nanny Weightman's sons and most of the men of Pentridge were already at Hunt's barn. There would be few, if any, to see him leave.

Chapter 21

Kit paced before the fireplace in the sitting room. The crackling fire wasn't soothing her as it often did. Martin had been gone all afternoon, and though she did not expect him to return until late that evening she was worried. He had not discussed with her further the events of yesterday, but she was nonetheless having second thoughts about attending the rally at Hunt's barn. If Martin was there and caught her, she wasn't certain how he'd react to a third flaunting of his request. Then, too, she'd have to walk to the town of South Wingfield.

He had asked her to trust him. Could you love someone you didn't trust? *Yes.* But she not only loved him, she also had faith in his goodness. He was a man to be trusted, no matter that she did not understand all he was about. He was one of the Crown's own knights. Perhaps he was even now working for the Crown. She had watched John speak with Martin, following him around like an eager puppy. That young man, ever her husband's eager pupil, had nothing save respect for him. So how could she, Martin's wife, doubt him?

No, she decided, the answer was clear. She would not doubt him. She would trust him and stay as he'd asked. She would not go to Hunt's barn.

A knock sounded at the door. *Martin?* No, he would not knock. Likely it was Mrs. Weightman.

As she opened the door, her blood ran cold. Rutledge stood before her, a sardonic smile on his face.

"Ah, Katherine, do not look so shocked. Did you think I would not pursue you?"

Fear coursed through her, setting her every nerve on end as she realized he blocked the doorway. She was trapped. Just like the first time.

Backing away, she reached for the right words to hold him off. "I…I am married now." Surely he would honor her vows and cry off. He had refrained from assaulting her while married to her sister.

"Ah, yes, the Frenchman," he said with a smirk, looking down at the simple gold ring on her hand. "So I've been told. Not to worry, m'dear. Soon he will be a matter of the past. I told you once that you have always belonged to me. And, so it is. You will be my wife."

"You are mad!" Kit stared at him in stark terror, and more frightening than his statement of possession was his calm, snide smile. She had to get away and warn Martin. She didn't know what Rutledge planned, but it could not be good.

Before she could move, the earl reached out and grabbed her arm. She struggled to pull free, but he held her firm. She twisted desperately in his grip, all to no avail.

"Let me go!"

Without warning, he backhanded her, hard. Kit felt a jarring wrench in her neck, and her body slumped to the ground. The room faded into blackness.

* * *

Rutledge considered the woman lying on the floor at his feet. He regretted having to temporarily damage her face. After all, he took care of his property. But, even with threats, she would not have come willingly. This way was better.

Once he had her in his bed she would change her mind, of course. Or he would hide her away in one of his country estates until he got her with child. Though a marriage to his sister-in-law could be voided if someone were to object, he doubted anyone would dare challenge the union. And once Katherine delivered his child, she would do nothing to jeopardize the legitimacy of her babe. She might be willing to live with her own shame, but he knew her well enough to know the daughter of an earl would never bring shame on a child.

Lifting her into his arms, he carried her out the door and to the top of the stairs. Looking into the entry below, he waited for his guard to wave him down before descending. Once outside, he laid Katherine on the seat of the waiting carriage, climbed in beside her and shut the door. The trap was sprung.

* * *

Kit slowly opened her eyes to find herself lying atop a strange bed in a darkened room. Casting a quick glance around, she recognized nothing. It was not her room at the inn, of that she was certain, for she could see opulent furnishings far exceeding the simple accommodations of the White Horse.

Where am I?

A violent pounding in her temple reminded her she'd been struck. Gently touching the lump on the side of her head, she winced at the pain. Rising up on one elbow, she felt the room shift and her stomach lurch. She froze. Gradually the room righted, and the memory of her altercation with Rutledge flashed in her mind. She could still see his sickening smirk as he informed her she belonged to him. Truly, the man was unhinged. What made him believe he could take whatever he wanted? That he could take her?

You have always belonged to me.

All this time, had he never cared for her sister? She could well believe it.

Another thought came to her. Had Rutledge something to do with the baron's death? She considered it might be true. Baron

Egerton was older, yes, but he had not been unhealthy until the day of his death. The Earl of Rutledge, she now believed, was not above murder.

Sitting up, Kit slid her legs over the side of the bed and was relieved to find herself still dressed in the blue muslin gown she'd been wearing when Rutledge abducted her. With trepidation she stood, careful, but even keeping her movements small she found the room swam before her and a nauseated feeling crept into her stomach. Reaching for the bedpost, she hung on until the room stopped moving and her unsteady stomach calmed.

At the door, she tried the handle and was unsurprised to find it locked. Crossing the room to the window, she opened the shutters and peered out. The room where she was confined was on the second story. Green lawn stretched away from the house. The clouds lying low and heavy in the sky rendered the ambient light a dim gray, and she could not be certain but thought it might be early evening. The branches of the ash trees just outside swayed in the rising wind. A storm was on the way.

Dropping her eyes, she noticed the nails pounded into the window frame on the outside, and her heart sank. She was well and truly trapped. Did Martin even know she'd been taken? Where was her fierce protector? He would be mad with worry when he discovered her missing. Was she even still in Pentridge? She had no idea how far Rutledge had traveled to bring her to this lavish prison. On this side of the house she could see no stable, horses or men, but she was certain such a fine house would have a stable of some sort. And she was certain Rutledge would have posted a guard.

The door behind her suddenly opened. Kit started and stepped back, pressing her body into the wall next to the window. Rutledge stepped inside, shutting the door behind him as a loathsome grin spread across his harsh face.

"M'dear, how nice to see you are awake. I trust you are no worse for my having to…ah, render you more amenable to transport."

A deep anger rose within her. She stiffened her back and raised her head in defiance. "Where am I? Where have you brought me?"

"You are still in the Midlands if that is what concerns you. I have a bit of business tonight that requires my presence, but you can be sure I will return so we can become…better acquainted." His eyes raked her body, came to rest on her full breasts.

He walked slowly toward her as if approaching a wild animal. She felt like a caged one. Reaching out his hand, he ran the backs of his knuckles over her temple. She jerked her head away, repulsed by his touch, and he withdrew his hand.

"The bruise is unfortunate. I would not have marred you, but it seemed required at the time. It will, of course, heal. But then the mark you left me was much more…evident," he added coldly, touching briefly the scar on the left side of his face. "Perhaps we are even now."

He stepped closer and took a strand of her hair in his hands. "Your hair has always fascinated me. Most unusual."

"Don't touch me!" Kit stepped to her right, pressing her back to the shutters. He stared at her as if perusing a piece of porcelain for his collection.

"Oh, I intend to touch you, Katherine. I most definitely intend to touch you."

He reached toward her again. Kit recoiled, drawing as far away as she could. His hand stilled in midair and dropped to his side. "But unfortunately having my pleasure of you will have to await my return. I am needed elsewhere this evening."

Relief washed over Kit like a wave, but her heart still pounded out a fast rhythm. She knew it was only a brief reprieve. She had to escape before he returned. Could Martin find her here?

"You cannot keep me imprisoned in this room," she announced.

"Why, yes, m'dear, I can. Do not think to escape. There are guards. Of course you will be fed. I would not want you hungry for ought but me."

"That will never happen!"

"I assure you, it will."

"Why me? I belong to another," she tried again.

"I do not recognize the Frenchman's claim," Rutledge said, waving his hand dismissively. "As I have mentioned, you have *always* belonged to me. It was not your sister I asked for. It was you."

Kit stared, stung. *Me?*

Rutledge's eyes narrowed, and his face froze in a scowl. "That bumbling guardian made a grave error when he drew up the papers to give you to the baron. You were intended for me, but they were signed before I discovered his mistake."

Kit wondered if the baron hadn't tried to save her from this man. Perhaps, if he had been fond of her, as the solicitor said, it might have been so. She owed him so much more than she'd realized.

A smug smile spread across Rutledge's face. "You need not look so surprised. Why do you think I invited you into my home when the baron so conveniently died soon after you were wed? For charity's sake? Hardly."

"My sister suffered so—"

"Needlessly. Ah, but at least she had the good grace to die along with the baron."

"You are insufferable and cruel. I only came to your house to help my sister—"

"Perhaps you did, no matter your motive. I intended you come to me and you did. I am not a patient man, Katherine. I have waited long to have what is mine. You *shall* be my wife."

Then he turned, dismissing her, and as he closed the door behind him Kit heard a key turn in the lock.

Crushed by despair, she sank onto the edge of the bed. As much as she hated her brother-in-law, she would have become his wife if that had been the only way to spare her sister a horrible marriage. Anne was not as strong as she was. Perhaps that is why Anne grew ill, even content to die like their father. Kit would have survived.

Her mind raced for ideas to escape before he returned. Surely it could not end like this! And what of her husband? The words Rutledge had spoken earlier came back to her. *Soon he will be a matter of the past.* He planned to kill Martin! No! She must find a way to get to him, to warn him. He had been terrified for her, but he was the one truly in danger. She could not lose him, not now.

Chapter 22

It was the ninth of June, Martin noted as he and John sat waiting at Hunt's barn that slowly filled with men from the towns of Belper, Ripley and South Wingfield, a day that he hoped would not go down as a blot on England's history. He observed with irony the good humor the men demonstrated as they filed into the building, laughing and telling jokes among themselves. Almost the atmosphere resembled a country fair, so confident were many of the success of their venture. Fools every one. But there was little he could do. The Prince Regent had tied his hands.

By nine o'clock at least forty were assembled, and the speeches, which he'd heard so often he could now recite them himself, were beginning in earnest as the ringleaders shared their thoughts, hoping to stir the minds of any still reluctant to join the march. All he could think of was the way he'd left things with Kit yesterday, her face full of doubt and despair at wondering what his part was in all this, just like she'd wondered the night before after the meeting in Pentridge. He had chosen not to bring it up again, too afraid she would involve herself. He wouldn't be surprised if she returned to London on her own. She had money now and could go wherever she wanted.

He thought again. No, Kit would not leave him. They had grown close these past few weeks. Their nights had been nothing short of wonderful, and they had confessed their love. She would trust him. And when it was over and he was certain she was safe he would tell her all there was to know of his work for the Crown and Prinny's last assignment.

He glanced around the room, which was overflowing with men. He counted three pistols and some eight-foot pikes that were little more than sticks with a piece of iron attached. From their faces it seemed to Martin that only Brandreth was truly serious about violence. Many of the rest played at revolution. Oliver was notably but unsurprisingly absent. The deceitful fox had likely already dispatched a message to Sidmouth and was now on his way back to his London den.

Undertaking a march to Nottingham, some fourteen miles to the east, on a night when the sky threatened rain, was to Martin's thinking nothing short of harebrained. But none of the men present seemed to recognize that small bit of good sense. He knew Brandreth's plans were to first march to the ironworks where he intended to gather men and weapons, so Martin had taken all the measures he could, John having warned Goodwin to be ready for the unruly band should they get that far tonight. Personally he hoped the expected rain and eventual weariness of the men would quickly send them home.

He had learned Oliver's agreement with the magistrates included soldiers at the ready who would engage with force should the Midlands men persist in this cause Oliver had urged upon them. Martin prayed it didn't come to that. The last thing he wanted was anyone harmed. He had come to like the villagers. They were good men, if simple in their understanding and sadly misled. Plots such as Sidmouth's and Oliver's would never occur to them. Thankfully, the private urgings he and John had made to leave off had been successful in at least some cases. Judging by the men pouring into the barn, however, many others had been unconvinced by their words. Some might just be spectators, attending to watch what happened, to share in the fellowship of other men, but Martin couldn't be certain of that.

When the last speech ended, Brandreth walked to the center of the room. Standing on the hard-packed dirt floor, he surveyed his audience and gestured to a man leaning against the side of the barn to come join him. The man, whom Martin had met first at the Dog Inn, was a stonemason.

Draping his arm around the man's shoulders Brandreth said, "I've appointed William Turner here to be my lieutenant, if there be no objection."

Murmurs of agreement rose from the crowd.

Brandreth clapped Turner on the back. "Then I say 'tis time we begin our march!"Several ayes were heard and Brandreth continued. "For those who don't know, we'll first travel the few miles to the ironworks in Ripley, and on our way we'll stop at farms to gather weapons, provisions and men. There will be none gainsaying us this eve!"

The men filed out of the barn and into the night. Martin gave John a nod, and they followed. It was now ten o'clock, according to the wedding gift Kit had given him, his treasured pocket watch. Martin was hungry and suspected the other men were as well, for none had left to eat. He didn't see any leaving now, though.

Marching briskly down the road at their leaders' direction, the men headed south to Ripley, where they were joined by a group from the nearby town of Swanwick bringing the number of men to near seventy. Acting as if he were still in the militia, Brandreth formed them into columns. Martin and John hung to the rear. Martin saw few real weapons, though the Swanwick men were armed with hayforks and freshly peeled tree poles studded with nails.

It was late when the downpour that threatened all afternoon finally arrived, and though it came in fierce sheets of cold, biting rain, to Martin's dismay it did not slow the march. A crowd of men stirred by flowery speeches decrying the treatment of the government and the poor condition of their lives was not easily turned, though they might regret their discomfort.

"'Tis a bad night for our march," muttered one of the men walking near Martin and John, lifting their spirits. But when John nodded in agreement, the man said, "But that might discourage any who might oppose us."

"I only wish I'd brought me winter coat," said another.

"And me boots," said a young man who pulled his foot out of a hole filled with mud.

Knowing the night was only beginning, Martin and John exchanged a weary look and drew their coats tighter about them.

Along the way Brandreth, now armed with a shotgun as well as the pistol he'd displayed earlier, went from house to house, hammering on doors and forcing men and boys at gunpoint to join him. "A gun and a man" were demanded at each stop. Though some of the men came unwillingly, all the same they came, so the crowd progressing toward Ripley grew with each mile, one hundred in number as best as Martin could count in the drenching rain.

As the mob—for it was now a mob—approached a farmhouse, Brandreth yelled to the closed front door that they needed provisions. Martin feared he would have to intervene if violence erupted. As it turned out, Brandreth did not have to press his demand. The farmer—one Samuel Hunt, who insisted all know his name—welcomed them onto his land. He must have emptied his stores, for he freely dispensed bread, cheese and beer to the crowd pressing close to his house. After they'd finished, Hunt wished them well in their venture and waved them good eve. Martin wondered what price the farmer would pay for that generosity.

When they got to the home of Colonel Wingfield Hatton, John Onion again threatened the violence he had urged in the prior meeting. However, his diatribe fell on a servant's deaf ears. Much to Martin's relief, Squire Hatton was not at home.

Martin was thankful that thus far he'd not had to intervene, though he suspected it might eventually be required of him. The Prince Regent asked only that he learn the truth of what transpired in the Midlands, and the role of Sidmouth's spies, but neither he nor John could refrain from wanting to turn the tide of men bent on their own destruction. So he stayed, hoping to make a difference. His only warm thought was that this night his kitten was safely ensconced at the inn. While his instincts told him her appearances at the meetings in the barn and at the White Horse Inn were not coincidental as she suggested, he believed that this time she would listen. He did not fault her curiosity. He had told her little and supposed it was her nature to get involved. That was why he had tried to keep her away from all that was happening. Now he was glad she was safe. It wouldn't be long before they could leave the Midlands and begin the rest of their life together. A life he very much wanted.

With difficulty, he turned his thoughts back to what lay ahead and followed the marching men.

Soon after they left Colonel Hatton's home, Brandreth halted the march and divided the column of men into two groups, one on his right, the other on his left. The rain came down in a steady downpour.

"I will lead the first group with my lieutenant William Turner and my friend Isaac Ludlam," Brandreth shouted, pointing to the men on his right. "The second group," he called, gesturing to the men on the left, "will follow George Weightman and Edward Turner, William's brother."

George Weightman had returned earlier from Nottingham with good reports that all there was ready; throngs of men waited to attack Nottingham Castle before they moved on London. Watching

Weightman receive the thanks of Brandreth for this news, Martin thought the young man lied to please his captain. It was obvious George considered this the most important thing he had ever done, and likely he was amplifying the good news to the men above him far above the real truth. Martin wanted to believe so.

His coat soaked from the constant rain, Martin drew John aside as the men finished dividing into two groups. Speaking softly so only his young assistant could hear, he said, "Go with Weightman's group and, if you can, try to urge men to leave off this insanity. Unless the rain turns them back, I expect this will become ugly at some point, so take care."

"Aye, sir," John agreed. "'Tis not hard to see where this is leading. I'll keep me eyes open."

"Meet me back at the White Horse when this is over."

"Aye, sir. Or, if they make it as far as Nottingham, I expect I'll see ye when the two groups come together."

Martin nodded and watched John's head of dripping curls as he stalked off to join the column forming behind George Weightman. Soon that group slogged away over the muddy ground.

At eleven o'clock, the Brandreth-led group reached another farmhouse. Martin knew from his earlier research on Pentridge that the Widow Hepworth lived there with her servants and two sons.

"Mary Hepworth!" Brandreth shouted over the noise of the incessant rain as he pounded on the door. "We would have yer pistols and any other weapons stored on yer farm."

The widow, who was not about to be cowed, shouted back through a window, "Ye'll not be having anything of mine! So ye best turn yer horde around and leave. What you're doing is all wrong, and I'll not be a part of it."

Martin was pleased to see that the Widow Hepworth was a tough old bird. He had heard she was a most independent woman.

After what happened at the first farm, he'd been worried all the surrounding farmers would only encourage Brandreth with food and provisions and was gratified to see this woman take a stand against the Nottingham Captain.

Notwithstanding Mrs. Hepworth's discouraging words, the mob of men searched for a way into the farmhouse. Martin was preparing to argue against a forced entry when he heard the sound of glass breaking at the back of the house. Brandreth strode to investigate, and Martin followed, close on his heels. As they neared the broken window, the Nottingham Captain raised his pistol and pointed it into the jagged opening. Realizing what he was about to do, Martin lunged—but not soon enough.

Brandreth fired, and a moan sounded from inside the house followed by a woman's scream. Martin peered over Brandreth's shoulder to see a man slumped onto the floor of what appeared to be the kitchen, and a woman, presumably Mrs. Hepworth, bending over him. She turned, staring over her shoulder at the men on the other side of the window and shouted, "Ye've shot my servant!"

"You idiot!" Martin shouted at Brandreth. "You've shot an innocent man! This has gone too far. Enough!"

Brandreth rounded on him. "It was my duty," he said coldly, glaring back. "And if you say anything more I'll blow yer brains out, Frenchman."

He'd stowed his pistol but waved his shotgun menacingly at Martin, who pulled a pistol of his own from the back of his breeches, and with fierce disdain for the crazed convert Martin growled, "You can try, *Captain*." He slurred the title in mockery.

Brandreth must have seen the ice in Martin's eyes in the light shining from the farmhouse window, or perhaps he didn't want the men to see one of their own cut down, for at Martin's words the Nottingham Captain turned away and ordered his followers to

"March!" For one brief moment Martin regretted the lost opportunity to end everything there.

At this point, some of the men who'd been pressed into joining the march ran away under cover of darkness. Martin speculated, not unreasonably, they agreed with him that the attack on Mrs. Hepworth's servant had indeed been "enough," and now that they'd seen their captain was not above murder likely feared for their own lives. Martin was encouraged to see the men dropping out and prayed there would be more deserters when they reached the ironworks. His last hope to end the madness rested on George Goodwin.

By the time they'd traveled the few miles to the Butterley Ironworks, notwithstanding those who'd deserted the march at the Widow Hepworth's house, Martin was dismayed to see the number of men in Brandreth's group bulging with new recruits that had joined on the way so that they again numbered nearly one hundred. Brandreth had explained earlier that his plan was to kill the three senior managers at the ironworks and ransack the factory for weapons, but he was in for a surprise as he beat on the gates with the butt of his pistol. Thanks to Martin's earlier meeting with George Goodwin, and the message John had carried to the man earlier that day, Goodwin was prepared.

In a moment the ironworks manager crossed the short distance from his office to the gates to meet them, a score of tall, powerfully built men at his back. Martin recalled the special constables Goodwin had been forced to provide, and he assumed the men were a part of that group.

"You'll give us men!" Brandreth demanded of Goodwin. Isaac Ludlam, with a spear, and William Turner, brandishing a pistol, flanked him. "We're marching to London to stand up a new government for all of us."

Goodwin surveyed the waiting mob and, with only his eyes, acknowledged Martin's presence. "You shall not have a one. You are too many already, and your purpose is not a good one. Disperse!"

While only twenty men stood behind Goodwin, it was a formidable rearguard, armed and by the looks in their eyes ready to wound or kill if necessary. Brandreth's men fell back. If Brandreth and Oliver had had any supporters inside the ironworks, they were not present.

"We've no intention of doing that," said Brandreth with firm conviction.

Goodwin was not to be daunted, either. "The laws are too strong for you. You are going with halters about your necks."

Martin was pleased Goodwin had raised the specter of hanging, which caused many in the crowd to murmur. More men slipped away while Brandreth and Turner were too occupied to notice.

In an apparent attempt to reason with Brandreth, Goodwin invited four men into his office to talk: Brandreth, Turner, Ludlam, and with a scowl from Brandreth Martin. The hexagonal brick office was just as Martin remembered, but the desk had been cleared as if the manager were expecting company.

Martin was happy to be out of the driving rain. The group sat in rough wooden chairs as their host offered the four men hot coffee. One of Goodwin's guards stood at the door. Martin gratefully accepted the mug warming his cold wet hands before taking a large swallow of the hot brew. He waited expectantly, hoping Goodwin would be able to pull the men back from the brink of disaster.

"You must leave off this foolish venture," urged the ironworks manager. Looking at Isaac Ludlam, whom he apparently knew,

Goodwin counseled, "Isaac, you must convince these men not to go on. This is beyond folly."

Ludlam shook his head, eyes downcast. "No, George. I cannot go back. I'm in too deep."

Martin joined the plea for reason. "Perhaps Mr. Goodwin has the right of it. It is a bad night for revolution. The men are wet and tired and have had no sleep and little to eat. Surely this is not well thought out." He looked into the hostile, angry eyes of Brandreth and sadly realized the man was beyond hearing logic.

Goodwin seemed pleased by Martin's words and nodded, but Brandreth rose scowling. "We'll have done with this! If ye'll not give us men or weapons, we'll continue with the hundreds we have. Thousands more wait at Nottingham." He turned and stalked out of the office.

Turner and Ludlam followed, but Martin remained behind to shake Goodwin's hand. "Thank you for trying to end this."

"Are you staying out there with those men tonight, Mr. Donet?"

"I must see this folly, as you well named it, to its conclusion, doing what little I can to deter the good men among them from continuing. That madman Brandreth has already engaged in one shooting, and I am worried there will be more. Not all the men marching with him came willingly, as you might imagine." Martin then thanked Goodwin for having prevented the factory from contributing men and weapons to the uprising, and reluctantly trudged back out into the rain.

The remaining mob was a dreary band: wet, tired, worn. Some of the reluctant marchers seized the opportunity and stepped forward to take sides with Goodwin, who had followed Martin out and now stood as sentinel watching at the open gates. Goodwin ordered the mob to leave the factory land, which they did, and at

Brandreth's command to "March!" those who remained determined resumed the long grind southeast toward Nottingham.

* * *

Following Brandreth and his rain-sodden troops, Martin grew weary. Like the others, he was cold, wet and tired. The rain had tapered off as the dawn neared and they reached the town of Codnor and the Glass House Inn, another brown stone public house. Brandreth must have recognized his rebels would never make it to Nottingham without sustenance, because he waved them to the side of the road.

"We'll stop here for ale and food."

Shouts of acclamation went up as the men stumbled into the tavern, wet, muddy and bedraggled, grumbling about the weather and the long night. The inn filled with murmuring as the men greedily reached for the ale and bread brought by serving wenches obviously roused early from their beds. With little in their stomachs, the men were soon slurring words as they complained about the hard times in the Midlands.

Though Martin would not have favored ale for breakfast, he was glad for the drink handed him. His body clamored for food and rest. His feet were tired and his boots muddy. But there was another reason he was grateful for the pause. It was an opportunity to send men home.

He grabbed a piece of bread and washed it down with a gulp of ale. Around him sat half a dozen men wearing discouraged and exhausted looks. With the remaining time being short in which to end the uprising, he reminded those sitting closest to him that they might have already witnessed a man's death, not to mention the treason to come. The men stared down into their tankards, shamed by what had taken place.

"There's still time to leave," Martin prodded. "You know this will not end well."

"Ye might be right, but we've come this far," said one.

"London is farther still," Martin reminded him. Several others nodded their agreement and cast furtive glances toward the door as they downed the rest of their ale.

A half hour later, when Brandreth ordered the march resumed, the men, many of whom were swaying with drink, stumbled out of the inn. Martin heard Brandreth promise the innkeeper he would be paid for the ale and bread when the revolution saw its rightful end. Martin doubted the man would see a farthing, so he left several coins on the bar as he departed.

The smell of wet earth rose to Martin's nostrils as he stepped outside. Shivering in the cold morning air, he drew his damp coat tightly around him. The rain had diminished to a mist. Still, a number of the men he'd been speaking with were so soaked, dispirited and disturbed by talk of hanging they apparently took his advice and decided to retreat to their homes and their work. Martin was heartened to see them go. Perhaps the budding revolution would die here and they could all go home.

Thoughts of Kit made Martin restless and increasingly anxious to leave. She would be worried by now. Long past worried. He was warmed again by the knowledge she was safe in Pentridge, perhaps still tucked up in their bed. She had often reminded him of a red tabby cat when she curled up to sleep, and it was that image that heartened him now. He wanted to share with her all he'd withheld and join her in that bed. The very thought that his new wife loved him lifted his spirits more than anything. He couldn't wait to sweep her away on the wedding trip he'd been planning in his mind as he'd slogged through the night. But first he must see an end to this Midlands madness.

At Langley, not halfway to Nottingham, Brandreth's men fell in with George Weightman's group. Together, notwithstanding the desertions, Martin could see in the clear light of the new day the two groups numbered more than two hundred men. He wondered how many were still committed to the venture and how many remained from fear of Brandreth's wrath should they try to leave. Some, he knew, were still there because they'd been pressed into joining. Day was dawning, and it was now more difficult for any to sneak away.

Brandreth paused in his march to question Weightman on what he had learned. The young man answered his comrade's inquires with what Martin was certain to be an improbable lie.

"All is right, lads," George declared. "You have nothing to do but march on. At two o'clock this morning, Nottingham was given up to us."

John found Martin and gave his own report. "Weightman's become as unhinged as his captain, sir. He only wants to look good in Brandreth's eyes. Ye'd not believe the wild actions I've witnessed. 'Twas just an excuse for mayhem."

"I'd believe most anything," said Martin. "My own eyes have witnessed what may have been murder." With a sigh he added, "One way or the other, it will soon end. With the dawn, let us hope the men who remain will see reason and take their leave even if they must face Brandreth's wrath to do so. Did you have any luck turning some back?"

"Aye, I did, but not all as ye can see." John gestured to the throng of men, discouraged.

"If only they carried no weapons," Martin said aloud, "they might be seen as the Blanketeers, but even that did not end well. I would send them all back now if I could."

"'Tis sure some are leaving. See there," said John, gesturing to a group of men scrambling over a small hill in the direction of

Pentridge. "Those are Ripley men who were with us all night. I guess they disbelieved Weightman's words."

Martin watched the men, mud-splattered and rain-drenched, struggle up the slippery incline to depart as fast as their tired legs would take them. "We can only hope there will be more."

Once more, with Weightman's encouragement and Brandreth's order, the men who remained plodded on through the cold.

"I can scarcely believe so many are still about this fool's errand," Martin muttered to John a short time later. "Even with the desertions, there must be over a hundred men still blindly following...though half appear foxed."

"The mud would have discouraged me long afore this," said John, raising his boot. The mud sucked at his sole and made a popping sound. "Were I my own man."

Martin chuckled. "Ah, but you weren't raised in country mud, John. They were. Up to their knees and still marching forward."

"'Tis enough for me," an older man suddenly growled in front of them and peeled off.

"I've still me west field to tend today," said another, departing with him.

The desertions became more frequent, and Martin's hopes rose for a fully peaceful end to the cold, gruesome night. But it was not to be. Two miles further on, a report was shouted back that a group of Derbyshire Yeomanry, voluntary cavalry, were headed their way, and with the threat of real opposition Brandreth's mob panicked. The lines broke apart and the tired farmers and laborers scattered like flies, running as fast as the mud allowed, dropping weapons as they did. It was then that more than a dozen hussars of the Fifteenth Regiment came into sight over a ridge, their flashy uniforms of dark blue splashed with silver braid and white breeches ending in black Hessian boots an impressive symbol of the Crown's authority.

"Bloody hell!" said John in a hoarse gasp.

"Precisely," echoed Martin. "The cavalry has arrived. It was only a matter of time."

Martin had no intention of fleeing but pulled John from where he stood transfixed to the side of the road and into the trees, out of the line of fire. They watched as Brandreth's remaining men faced the dragoons' sabers with only a few pistols, spears and pikes. Shouts filled the air, and Martin saw Brandreth running away as the mounted soldiers plunged into the disbanding rebels. All was chaos as the last of the men soon fled from the charging horses.

Martin lingered only long enough for the seized men of Derbyshire to be rounded up before he and John approached the hussar captain who was taking charge of the captured rebels. As the orders were given concerning the prisoners, Martin stepped up to where the dragoon officer sat his horse. In his most proper British accent, Martin identified himself.

"Captain, I am Sir Martin Powell, on assignment for the Crown." Pointing to John, he added, "This is my assistant, John Spencer."

The uniformed man eyed them critically, taking in their simple clothing. Martin observed the doubt written in the lines of his face, and seeing no alternative he pulled from his jacket the oilskin pouch that protected the letter Ormond had given him on their last day in London. He had hoped he wouldn't need to use the communication from the Prince Regent, but it now appeared he must. "I believe this will clarify my purpose in being here."

The captain leaned down from his horse, took the proffered letter and read it, then leaned down to hand it back, offering his hand to Martin. "Captain Philips at your service, Sir Martin. It's not often the monarch sends his own man to the Midlands. Were you with this rabble all night?"

"We were, sir. Trying to send as many home as we could and attempting to prevent violence. Not that many were truly committed to the uprising. Some only joined after they were threatened with force. I had hoped more men would leave off this folly." Suddenly reminded of the crime he'd witnessed during the night he inquired, "Have you been to the Widow Hepworth's farm?"

"I dispatched one of my men there earlier. The news is not good. The servant who was shot succumbed to his wound. Did you happen to see who fired the shot? Mrs. Hepworth did not know the brigand."

"Yes, I did. It was Jeremiah Brandreth, the one they call the Nottingham Captain."

"I know of him. The reports have identified him as the instigator." The hussar captain turned back, gesturing to the group of rebels his men had confined. "Is he among these?"

Martin and John surveyed the group of more than forty captured. In the morning sun they appeared bedraggled, muddy and dazed. "No, not one of them," he said. "He must have gotten away."

"No matter. We will find him. With a fifty pound reward on his head, I suspect he will soon be produced."

Chapter 23

Martin and John's trip back to Pentridge took less time than expected, owing to the horse the good captain loaned them. Martin sent John to tend the animal and arrange for its return, and to get some breakfast. His only thought was only to find Kit.

Knocking the dried mud from his boots on a stone outside, he hurried into the White Horse Inn and up the stairs to their rooms, anxious to finally share with her all that had happened. He had told her he would be late but had not expected to be gone all night. By now she'd be worried.

She was not in their rooms. All his instincts were on alert as he gazed around the sitting room and saw no signs of his wife's having been there that morning, no breakfast tray, newspaper, or teacup where she often left them. Striding to the bedchamber, he saw the bed still turned down for the night, not mussed from sleep as he would have expected. Dread crept up his spine like icy fingers. Something was terribly wrong.

Could she have left him? She'd been angry with him for refusing to tell her why they were here or what he'd been doing at the rebels' meetings. It was for her own protection he hadn't told her. If she knew he was working for the Crown, Kit would have been in the middle of it, maybe even would have tried to help. He wasn't taking that chance with his kitten. She had finally given herself to him and told him she loved him.

For that reason, despite the state of the room, he knew she would not leave. Certainly not without talking to him or leaving a note. Not without taking her clothes.

There was no note, so he made a quick search of the bedchamber's armoire and her trunk. His fear grew, a brooding omnipresence, as he realized not a thing was missing. Not her reticule, not even her brush and comb. Then he saw the sketchbook.

He picked it up and flipped to the last page she had drawn upon. It was his face as seen through the eyes of love, different from the first one of him she had drawn. No, she would not leave him, he felt certain. This image was proof. But had she followed him to Hunt's barn? He had not seen her there.

He set the sketchbook down. She had been gone since at least last night and had not left on her own, of that he was now quite certain. Hastily descending the stairs, he spotted Nanny Weightman staring out the front window of the inn. Glancing through the glass, he saw nothing of note that she could be watching.

At the sound of his boots on the floor, the older woman turned to face him with an anxious look. "Oh, Mr. Donet. It is terrible, terrible! My sons have been arrested. Have ye heard? Were ye there? Did ye see what happened?"

He joined her in the entry. "I am afraid the rebellion was doomed from the start, Mrs. Weightman. The hussars have arrested many of the men and are searching for the others."

She sank into a chair. "It was to have been so grand, a new government where the common people had something to say…."

Her words trailed off and she stared into space, and Martin was tempted to express his opinion about a mother who would push her sons into joining an uprising against the Crown, but he could see she was hurting so he refrained. Likely her sons would go to prison, or worse. Based on what he knew of Sidmouth's plans for quashing the stirrings of rebellion, he held little hope they would remain free.

"I am truly sorry your sons and you were involved," he said. It was the only comfort he could give the woman. The weight of Kit's disappearance was heavy on his heart as he asked, "Have you seen my wife, Mrs. Weightman? She is not in our rooms, and it does not appear she slept there last night."

"What?" Nanny Weightman stared at him then shook her head as if coming out of a dream. "Oh. A gentleman called on her yesterday. He told me he was to bring her to ye." She eyed Martin, a puzzled expression on her face.

"What gentleman, Mrs. Weightman? What was his name?"

"Didn't give a name. But I could see he was a gentleman by his clothes. There was a man with him, a hired man I'm thinking, and they had a carriage. At least I saw a carriage waiting. I returned to the kitchen before they left."

Speaking slowly, as if to a child, Martin commanded, "Describe the man for me. The gentleman."

"He was tall, though not as tall as ye. He had dark brown hair and eyes, and he was well groomed and clean-shaven. His face was most stern, now that I recall, even when he smiled."

That described half of London. "Was the man from these parts?"

"No, I don't think so. I've never seen him afore. His speech was very proper. Such men as that are rare in this part of Derbyshire."

"Think carefully, Mrs. Weightman. Was there anything unusual about him, a mark of any kind?"

"Why, yes. There was a scar on his left temple."

A stern-faced gentleman with a scar on his left temple? Suddenly Martin knew who it was. But how could that be? How could Rutledge have found Kit this far from London? There were only two explanations that made any sense. Either he'd followed them, which Martin doubted; he felt that his instincts would have told him if that had been the case. Or, more likely, Rutledge was somehow involved in Sidmouth's plot in the Midlands. Either he or Castlereagh might have asked Rutledge to do the dirty work of assuring there would be armed men to shatter the rebellion urged on by Oliver. Martin had always believed someone else in the peerage was involved.

Rutledge has Kit. Tightness seized his chest as he considered the possibility of what the evil earl might already have done to his beautiful bride.

John was just sitting down to breakfast when Martin found him. "John, Kit is missing and I believe her brother-in-law Rutledge has taken her."

John dropped his bread and nearly choked on his egg. "The same Rutledge yer lady was running from in London?"

"Yes. The same. While you saddle the horses, I'll check the other inns in Pentridge. Perhaps I'll get lucky and he'll have been staying in one of them. Otherwise, we'll have to go to South Wingfield. The magistrates there will know if a peer has been involved in this business."

It didn't take Martin long to end up at the Dog Inn. As he entered, he recognized the obviously distraught woman who approached. He'd seen her before. He was loath to press her for information, but there was no choice. "Madam—?"

"Mrs. Onion, sir," she said anxiously.

No wonder she was upset. If she was married to John Onion, her husband might not have come home. "Mrs. Onion, I am looking for a man. Lord Rutledge. Might he have been a recent guest of the inn?"

"Aye," she said. "We don't get many gentlemen like that. I'd not be forgettin' him. His lordship stayed with us several weeks, though he was gone much of the time. He left a few days ago."

"This is very important, Mrs. Onion. Do you know where he went when he left?"

"I did ask him," she admitted, crossing her arms over her chest and drawing her brows together as if pondering. "I recall only that he said he'd taken a house nearby."

"He didn't say where?"

"Nay. At least, I cannot recall if he did."

Martin started to thank her for her time, but another thought occurred. "Would you by chance know from whom he rented the house?"

"Why, there be only one man ye can rent from in these parts, sir. That would be His Grace, the Duke of Devonshire hisself. He's landlord to us all."

Of course! Hadn't Ormond said the duke owned the lands of Pentridge?

He returned to the White Horse, and there Martin hastily explained what he'd learned to John and sent him to South Wingfield to get a report from the magistrates. He himself hurriedly changed from his muddy clothes, donning those more appropriate for the road north to Chatsworth and an urgent call on Ormond's friend.

* * *

After twelve miles of hard riding, Martin was relieved to finally cross the stone bridge spanning the Derwent River to Chatsworth House. His raw anxiety for the terror Kit might be experiencing was the only thing keeping him in the saddle. His fear was a stark contrast to the calm picture of sheep grazing on the grass-covered grounds in front of the majestic stone estate the young Duke of Devonshire called home.

He could feel some of the tension ease from his body when the duke's butler told him His Grace was in residence and could be found in one of the gardens undergoing expansion. Martin was not surprised, as Ormond had told him the duke had a reputation as an accomplished horticulturist.

Martin wasted no time in bringing his desperate errand to the fore when he found the duke. "Your Grace, I am Sir Martin Powell, a friend of the Marquess of Ormond. I believe he sent word I might call without notice."

The duke held out his hand to shake Martin's. "Ah, yes. I recall the mysterious message. I must get to London soon to visit him and his lady. In the meantime, would you like to see the latest additions to the gardens and then stay for luncheon? We can dine on the terrace."

"On another day I would gladly accept your invitation, Your Grace, but I've come on a desperate errand and must return immediately if I am to prevent disaster. A man to whom your agent leased one of your houses in Derbyshire has abducted my wife, and I believe he is keeping her there to evil purpose. I do not know which house, and that is why I've sought you out. When it comes to my lady, the man is obsessed and has previously threatened her with violence."

The duke's face twisted in puzzlement. "Obsessed? I daresay. Who is this man?"

"The Earl of Rutledge."

"Rutledge…?" The duke drew his brows together as he considered the name. "I cannot recall the man's face. But I do know the name. Seems I recall he has a bad reputation." He looked up, and as if catching the energy rolling off of Martin gave him a quick glance and began to stride back toward the estate indicating Martin should follow.

"Let us return to my study where I keep the estate books. My agent can tell us what property he rented to the earl and when."

* * *

The duke spoke briefly with his agent, who handed him a ledger. He turned to Martin and said, "The house Rutledge leased is one of several I reserve for visiting members of the nobility and gentry." He pulled a map from a file and spread it on his desk. "It's near the village of Cromford, south of Chatsworth and about eight miles north of Pentridge. It was vacant only a short time before Rutledge arranged with my agent to take it."

"I thank you, Your Grace. I must leave immediately."

"Seeing how the man may have sequestered your wife in one of my properties, it seems only fitting I should accompany you, Sir Martin." The duke looked again at the map. "I know the house well, and since Prinny is a good friend and you're on his business, it is the least I can do."

"Are you certain, Your Grace? The task will be dangerous. He has stooped to violence more than once." In fact, he had already attempted rape, but Martin wouldn't mention that. Kit would be thought less of in the eyes of some if others knew she'd been subject to Rutledge's barbarity. It was one reason he'd been glad she didn't have to face a trial for the man's death. Today he would risk that the duke could be trusted.

"I'll not let you go alone. Oh, and do call me Hart. I prefer it. Ormond knows the name well and uses it most freely." The duke was already striding out the door and toward the stables when he shouted over his shoulder, "We can take one of my footmen with us. I've had the usual training with pistols myself, of course."

Martin caught up and, on the way to the stables, explained the uprising that had delayed his learning of his wife's abduction, so he was half-expecting the duke's next statement.

"The people of Pentridge are my responsibility, and if there have been crimes against the Crown I must know which of my tenants has been involved. These are difficult times for the people of the Midlands, but I cannot tolerate those who would rise in revolution."

"I doubt if they would have without prodding," Martin said as they reached their goal. "They were urged on by Sidmouth's spy, and his protégé Brandreth."

The two men mounted horses made ready for them. A footman joined them, and as the duke settled himself in his saddle he asked, "Sidmouth's spy?"

"With your permission, Your—Hart, I'll explain as we ride." Martin wanted to tarry not a moment longer.

"You will need to speak up, then, as I'm not likely to hear all you say with the pounding of the horses' hooves. My hearing sometimes fails me!"

The travel south was fast and hard. Martin and the duke rode abreast, followed by the duke's footman, a burly servant who carried himself like a former soldier. The duke had graciously granted Martin a fresh mount, one of his own grand Thoroughbreds. By now, only his fear for Kit kept Martin awake, as every muscle in his exhausted body protested the grueling pace.

He had a foreboding that he might be too late, and that dread of it drove him onward. Pictures of his smiling auburn-haired kitten flashed into his mind. When had she become all to him? His chest ached with the thought that he could lose her. He knew well that in one tragic moment she could be gone. If Rutledge had been involved in Sidmouth's business in Derbyshire, by now he might be leaving and taking Kit with him, what with the rebellion quashed. She would fight as she had once before. What would that fight lead to this time? The thought tore at Martin. Losing her would destroy his world. He desperately wanted that world.

As they covered the miles, Martin had to shout at times for the duke to hear him over the pounding of the horses' hooves, just as the man warned. He responded to questions pertaining to all that had happened. The duke grew angry when Martin told him of Oliver the spy, retained by the government to stir unrest in the duke's own lands.

"It is not just the harsh winters, crop loss and machines that have replaced workers," Martin explained, "they are unhappy at having no direct say in government." Having listened to all the speeches and complaints, he had a good feeling for what had led the people to join the ill-conceived rebellion.

"I myself favor the vote for the populace," the duke offered, his voice rising to be heard over the galloping horses, "but it cannot come about this way."

"They are poor and ill educated. When the spy Oliver told them all of England was ready to rise and demand change, they believed him."

The duke seemed to consider this as he shouted back, "Perhaps if the people had been better educated they might have known a ridiculous claim when it was presented. They might have come to me. I shall look into it."

Martin vaguely nodded in agreement, his thoughts having long ago left the matter of interest to the duke. His only energy was focused on reclaiming the object of his heart's desire. He must reach her before Rutledge could harm her.

* * *

"But there must be a Frenchman among the rebels arrested!" Rutledge demanded of the cowering magistrate behind the desk. He had to shout to be heard over the din of the waiting room behind him where prisoners were being questioned.

The rotund magistrate peered up at him, speech faltering. "But m-m'lord—"

"Look again, you idiot! You must have missed a name. He's one of them!"

The room behind them suddenly stilled. Feeling eyes boring into his back, Rutledge grew impatient. He was weary of the ineptitude of the local populace.

The magistrate returned his attention to the paper he held in trembling hands, but Rutledge cared not a whit if he disturbed this incompetent man's day; these country bumpkins were getting on his nerves. He pounded his fist on the desk to warn the magistrate he was serious. "Look again!"

"I'm s-sorry m'lord," the man stammered, "but the list the hussar captain gave me of the men he arrested this morning contains no Donet, nor any French name at all."

"I waited all night and all morning for this paltry result? Surely your men can do better."

"There are still dragoons in the field rounding up rebels, m'lord. I think they may find him today," the magistrate offered, sounding hopeful.

Rutledge doubted the man thought of anything save his next meal. Grabbing the list, he studied the column of names. "'Brassington, Hill, Hunt, Ludlam, Moore, Onion, Swaine, Turner, Weightman,'" he recited under his breath as he ran his finger down the list. Raising his head from the paper to peer down at the magistrate he repeated, "No Donet?"

"No, m'lord."

The noise of the waiting room behind him resumed its former hum as the soldiers went about the business of dealing with the aftermath of the rebellion that had ended only a few hours before. Rutledge glanced again at the list he held. A name at the bottom of the page, set apart from the others, drew his interest:

Sir Martin Powell, Crown's Agent.

"Who is this?" he asked, wrinkling his brow in consternation and shoving the paper in front of the magistrate's nose, finger pointing to the name. "I am not aware of any representative of the Prince's government here save me."

"Apparently he was dispatched by the Prince Regent himself, m'lord. Captain Philips assured me he is a most agreeable fellow. Stayed with the rebels all night trying to talk the local men out of following that rascal Brandreth. It seems he turned many back."

"Odd that Castlereagh never mentioned him," Rutledge murmured to himself. "Ahem…*well,*" he spoke up, returning to his original subject that was of more interest. "Please inform me should the Frenchman Donet be apprehended. You can reach me through my man who will check with you daily while I am in Derbyshire."

"The prisoners will be taken to the Derby gaol once we're through with them," the magistrate called to his departing back.

Still fuming as his boot heels hit the steps leading down from the office, Rutledge pondered his next move. Katherine was now his. He could take his time marrying the girl, but he first wanted the Frenchman arrested. No, he wanted him dead. A hanging would take too long.

Ah, yes. Much too long.

Katherine. Pleased he had her hidden away good and proper, he decided the Frenchman could wait. Katherine, however, could not.

Chapter 24

Kit woke from a restless, uncomfortable slumber as a shaft of light shot through the shuttered window and fell upon her face. She had slumped against the wall and fallen asleep, curled into a ball, tears streaking down her cheeks. She'd never considered sleeping in the bed on the chance Rutledge might return during the night and incorrectly assume she'd accepted her fate. She was thankful he had not.

She wondered if Martin was searching for her. Surely he had returned to their rooms last night and found her missing. What would he think? Might he consider she'd run away? No, he would know she had not. He might have been angry with her but surely he would not believe she would leave him. But when he found her gone, he would not know that Rutledge had taken her. He didn't even know Rutledge was in Pentridge! How would Martin ever find her?

Perhaps he would not.

The thought of never being in his arms again, of never being able to share with him all that was in her heart, caused Kit to despair. Eventually Rutledge would have to return to London, and she might escape him there, as she had done once before, but what if he left her imprisoned her in the Midlands? That thought sent cold chills through her body. Somehow, she had to escape. She had to get back to Martin.

It scared her to think that somewhere in all that had happened she had come to love Martin with the passionate love her father had for her mother, an irresistible, unstoppable love. Perhaps, in the end, one really had no choice but to accept the love the heart gave in full measure, and all the risks than went with it. Even if the loss of it could break one's heart.

Her feelings softened toward her father as she remembered the kisses he'd bestowed on her mother, the way he used to wrap his arms around her in delight. He had been smitten, just like Kit was now smitten with Martin. In the end, the loss of that love had robbed her father of his will to live, and that was the part she thought wrong. But it was possible to love like this and still live to celebrate that love if it were ever taken from her. She prayed she would not lose Martin.

Kit had searched the room in which she was imprisoned and knew it to be devoid of weapons. With the window nailed shut, the small panes of glass would render escape through that exit impossible. A sharp piece of glass could be a weapon, but could she break a pane without making a noise that would immediately draw the guard's attention? She thought not. And she might as easily cut herself as anyone else while trying to use such a crude blade. In her desperation she had even considered the chimney, but the passage was too narrow for her body to fit. No, she would have to go out through the door.

When that same door was opened last evening by the guard to permit a serving woman to carry in a tray of food, Kit had scanned the tray for weapons, disappointed to find only a spoon. She'd tried to catch the serving woman's eye, hoping for sympathy or possibly an indication of a willingness to help, but the older woman kept her head down, likely thinking the lord from London kept an unruly mistress who needed taming. But Kit's spirits rose when, as she sat staring at the pot of tea on the tray, she had an idea. If this morning's breakfast tray brought another pot of the nearly boiling liquid, she would use it to escape. It was her only chance, and though it was a slim one, she would take it.

Rising from the floor, she stretched out the kinks in her back and braced herself for what lay ahead, her mind racing with all she had to do. She didn't have long to wait. The door slowly opened, just as it had the night before. The guard allowed the older serving woman to carry in the tray then stepped into the doorway to watch. As the tray was placed on a small table, Kit took a deep breath and moved quickly to the teapot.

"Thank you," she said to the woman. Picking up the pot of tea, she removed the lid. Her hands were trembling as she took the few steps to where the guard stood, but his manner was unwary. Perhaps he thought she'd come to offer him a cup. She mustered her strength and hurled the scalding liquid into his face.

The old woman shrieked. The guard bellowed in rage and covered his scalded face with both hands. Using all her strength, Kit shoved him aside and hit him over the head with the teapot, shattering the pottery. Then she flew down the stairs and out the front door.

She'd covered only a short distance when she heard heavy footfalls behind her. Suddenly grabbed from behind, she tripped. A man's body slammed into hers, and they both hit the ground. Air was forced from her lungs and for a moment Kit just lay there panting, bruised and defeated.

"Not so fast, missy," the guard said, rising from the ground. "Ye'll not be leaving until his lordship says so." He pulled her up, and she saw that this burly guard was not the same one she'd assaulted with the tea. She recalled Rutledge had said there were *guards*.

She tried to shake off his grip. "Let me go! I'm being held against my will! My husband will have his vengeance on all of you."

"His lordship said to expect ye'd give such an excuse. Yer his to deal with, not mine." Then, thrusting her roughly before him, the guard ordered her back inside.

* * *

Rutledge reined in his horse and handed the reins to the guard he'd ordered remain in front of the house he'd leased so conveniently from the Duke of Devonshire. Just as the housekeeper opened the front door, however, the guard said, "Yer lady tried to escape this morning, yer lordship, but she's in her room now."

Rutledge paused to consider this new bit of information, then shrugged and entered the house. He was not surprised Katherine had attempted to flee. Hadn't she done the same in London? But soon, very soon, he would make the girl his own. In time she would come to accept her future with him. After all, he was not a bad lover, and though well-born she had few options. No woman could prefer a common Frenchman—a criminal, no less—to an earl. Then, too, he was certainly higher in rank than her first husband, the old baron. Yes, she should be content as an earl's wife.

And if she was not? Well, then, he would follow his plan to get her with child. She would not flee after that.

* * *

Kit had been dreading what she knew would surely be a fight she must wage even if she lost and was bloodied in the process. Unsurprised when the door suddenly opened, she braced herself against the wall.

"There you are, m'dear," Rutledge said, eyeing her like a hunter sighting his prey. "Did you have an active morning?" he asked, raising an eyebrow. When she said nothing, just stared, he went on. "Any attempt to flee will not go well for you…and, as you've seen, will be unsuccessful."

His dark hair was mussed and his elegant clothes wrinkled as if he'd slept in them. Never had she seen him so disheveled. Usually every hair was in place and he was flawlessly attired. Always he'd been particular in his ways, fastidious to a fault. Where had he been all night?

She watched as he slowly began to unbutton his waistcoat. Though she thought she knew quite well his intention, she couldn't help asking, "What are you doing?"

"Why, undressing, of course, m'dear. Did you think I would have you fully dressed?"

His demeanor was cold, his tone detached and passionless, his only hint of emotion the lust in his eyes. Fear crawled through her veins like cold sap. He was evil.

"You cannot do this!" she yelled. "I am married!"

"Ah, yes. If that bothers you, it will soon be remedied. Even now they are rounding up the rebels who last night marched, weapons in hand, determined to reach London. Your husband the Frenchman—Donet, isn't it?—was among them. He, too, will soon be arrested and, I daresay, await the hangman's noose."

"My husband with the rebels?" Kit was horrified. Could it be? She had convinced herself Martin was no party to the insurrection planned by the men of Pentridge and their Nottingham Captain. No, Martin was a knight awarded the honor by Prince George. Her husband had asked for her trust, and she had given it as well as her heart. She would no longer believe he had anything to do with treason, no matter his reasons for associating with the treasonous.

"I have it direct from the magistrate that they are even now rounding up more traitors. The hussars dealt with many this morning. Soon they will have your Frenchman."

It was then Kit realized Martin might not even know she was gone from their rooms, not if he'd never returned. Hopelessness swirled around her like a black cloud. Where was he? Surely he would come for her if he knew where she was. He loved her. She believed that.

Down to his shirt and breeches, Rutledge approached. "Come, m'dear. I had a long night and I am tired, so this first time will be rather quick. But there will be many more…opportunities for us to take our pleasure."

He reached for her hand and she pulled away. "No!"

"Oh, yes, m'dear," he said, grinning, and Kit wondered not for the first time if he was out of his mind.

"You're mad!" She shouted the words as if throwing them at him might hold back his lechery.

"Consumed with the thought of finally having what is mine? Yes, I freely admit it. But mad? Certainly not."

He cornered her and this time successfully gripped her wrist to swing her up and onto the bed where she landed with a thump. Determined to escape, Kit quickly sat up on her knees and backed to the far side of the bed, all the while watching him to anticipate his next move.

He was fast, and he leapt upon her. After a brief struggle he pinned her, but writhing under him she fought with all her strength, grabbing fistfuls of his shirt and trying to force him back. When his mouth slammed down on hers, she bit his lip. He reared back, glaring at her, and then he grabbed her hands, holding them away from her body.

"It will do you no good to fight me, Katherine." Shifting his body over hers, his heavy weight stopped her futile struggling. "It seems we were here once before," he reminded her, huffing with exertion. His face was only inches from hers, and she felt his arousal press hard against her.

He tried to kiss her again, but she jerked her head to one side, avoiding what would have been a punishing kiss. "No! Let me go!"

"Take your hands off my wife!" Martin bellowed from the doorway, and he stomped into the room.

"Martin!" Relief flooded Kit at seeing her husband stride toward the bed like some fierce dark angel of wrath. He had come for her!

Rutledge let go of her hands and started to move, but Martin's eyes were frozen blue flames and his intent more terrifying. Grabbing Rutledge by his shirt, he dragged the earl from the bed and in one lightning strike slammed his fist into the earl's face.

Kit scurried from the bed and watched as the two men grappled. She'd never seen Martin use fisticuffs, but given all she knew she was unsurprised that he had the speed of a wildcat and the force of a lion. Yet the earl fought back, determined and mean.

Breaking free of Martin's blows, Rutledge staggered backward, hand to his jaw. Blood trickled from his mouth. "*Your* wife? And just who are you?"

Ignoring his question, Martin drew his pistol from his coat and trained it on the earl.

Kit rushed to her husband's side and welcomed his arm around her shoulder as he drew her close. His eyes still on Rutledge, his voice full of concern, he said, "Did he harm you, my love?"

Her heart still pounding in her chest, she said, "No, but thank God you appeared when you did. I was so afraid you didn't know where I was. How did you find me?"

"It will soon be apparent. Now I must remove this vile creature."

Rutledge scowled, wiping the blood from his face, and arrogantly said, "You have not answered my question. Just who in the hell are you?"

"Your hell, perhaps. I am Sir Martin Powell. And the woman you have twice tried to violate is my wife. Now, down the stairs with you!" He gestured to the open door with his firearm. "Your landlord, the duke, would have a word."

Rutledge seemed to accept defeat and proceeded haltingly through the doorway. As he stepped into the corridor, over his shoulder he said, "Powell? The Crown's agent? I understood she was married to a Frenchman named Donet, one of the revolutionaries."

"It is not important what you know," Martin sneered. "Twice you have tried to force yourself upon my lady. If you want to remain among the living, you will never come near her again."

Martin prodded Rutledge with his pistol, forcing the earl into the corridor and down the stairs. Kit followed. From the top of the steps, she glanced down to see a tall man with chestnut-colored hair standing in the entry next to a footman in livery bearing a pistol. Kit realized the elegantly dressed man must be the Duke of Devonshire, Ormond's friend. She'd not met him before and was surprised at his youth, for he was barely older than she.

The two guards who worked for Rutledge were tied up on the floor. Standing nearby, the old housekeeper wrung her hands and trembled in obvious fright.

With Martin's continued prodding, Rutledge arrived at the base of the stairs, still wiping blood from his face.

"Wasn't my doing, Yer Grace," the old housekeeper assured the duke, her gaze darting between all the men in the room.

Devonshire nodded his acceptance and then said to Martin, "All in hand, I see. Well done!" To Rutledge: "You have much to account for, sir."

Martin shoved his pistol into the earl's back, and the duke stepped aside to allow them to pass through the entry hall. Kit felt the tension in Martin's body as he reached out with his free arm to pull her to him.

As he passed the footman, Rutledge grabbed the pistol from the servant's hand. The footman reached to retrieve it but was too late. Kit gasped. Rutledge backed out of the house, pointing his weapon at Martin. Slowly, Martin retreated with Kit back toward the stairs.

It all happened at once. Kit heard Rutledge cock the weapon, the sound echoing off the walls. Martin thrust his body in front of hers, shouting, "Get down!" Then, before she could move, two gunshots sounded.

Martin's body slumped, his weight driving her to the floor. She looked out the door and saw Rutledge lying on the ground in front of the house. The entry was full of the familiar bitter smell of gunpowder. The duke held a smoking pistol.

Kit struggled to move from under Martin, gently laid him on the floor and saw the blood oozing from his jacket. "He's been shot!"

The patch of blood on his jacket was growing larger, and Martin's unfired pistol dropped from his hand to the ground. The duke set aside his weapon and knelt next to them. Martin, still conscious, looked up and said, "It seems I was a bit slow."

"Not slow," replied the duke gravely, "just protecting your lady. And had you not made that sudden move to put yourself before her, I suspect the ball would have struck your heart."

Kit lifted Martin's head onto her lap just as he closed his eyes. "Martin," she whispered.

He must have heard the fear in her voice as it faltered. Opening his eyes slightly he said, "Not...fatal, I think." Then he closed his eyes, and his head rolled to the side.

Feeling the warm blood soaking through her husband's shirt, waistcoat and coat, Kit reached down and tore a strip from her petticoat to staunch the bleeding. Shouting to the housekeeper she demanded, "I need clean cloths and hot water."

The old woman, eyes dazed and mouth agape, came out of her stupor to respond.

The duke reached inside his coat and took out a cloth. "Here," he said, "this should help until she brings more." He faced his footman. "Get a physician, and on your way check on the earl."

"Yes, Yer Grace." The footman hurried to where the earl lay on the ground in front of the house. Shortly, he returned. "I'm leaving now, Yer Grace, to fetch the doctor."

The duke eyed the door where the footman stood. "Rutledge?"

"Alive, though he needs a healer if he's to stay that way. He's bleeding like a stuck pig."

"We'll do our best for him while you summon the physician. Be quick."

Kit heard a horse's hooves hitting the ground as the footman galloped away, and she pressed her cloth to Martin's wound, now a pool of red on his chest. The blood quickly soaked through the duke's handkerchief, a warm wet heat under her palm. She stared down at the man she loved and knew fear.

The housekeeper returned, stepping around the two guards lying tied up on the floor, handed Kit several linen cloths and set a bowl of steaming water on the floor. Ripping open Martin's shirt, Kit pressed linen to the wound, tossing aside the blood-soaked handkerchief and strips from her petticoat.

The duke, watching, said, "I am hopeful, Lady Powell, that Sir Martin has the right of it. The wound does not appear fatal. The physician is not far, just in Codner. He'll be with us soon."

"I do hope you're right," Kit said, still staring at her unconscious husband.

The duke spoke to the waiting housekeeper. "More cloths, good woman. Bring them to me outside where the earl lies. We must see what we can do."

The old woman nodded. Hastening to another room, she soon returned with more cloths and another bowl of water and followed the duke through the open door. A moment later, the duke returned.

"Is he still alive?" Kit asked.

"For now, yes. I hated to shoot a peer, even this one," the duke said, wrinkling his brow, "but I had to stop the man before he killed your husband. It seems I was not entirely successful."

Kit wasn't at all sure she cared for Rutledge to survive. He had tried to kill Martin and violently attacked her. She gazed down at her husband, pale and still, though she was glad to see him breathing steadily. With her free hand, she brushed the lock of ebony hair from his forehead and stroked his cheek.

"You have my gratitude, Your Grace," she said to the duke. "You saved his life."

"It was an honor to help Prinny's man, Lady Powell. I wasn't aware until your husband paid me a visit that Rutledge had even rented this house."

She gazed up at him. "Thank you for aiding in my rescue. I will be forever in your debt."

"My pleasure. How is he?"

"The bleeding has slowed, I think, but I will be more at ease when the physician is here. The ball needs to come out of his shoulder."

It wasn't long before the physician arrived. He first assessed the earl and, with the footman's help, both Rutledge and Martin were moved to beds. Shortly thereafter, the duke informed her that Rutledge was not likely to survive, a major vessel having been severed.

"Yet another pistol wound," the physician said to Kit as he dropped his bag and leaned over the bed Martin lay upon.

"I think the bleeding is stopped," she told him. "I've not disturbed the wound."

"You did fine."

Kit forced herself to watch, and she assisted as she could while the doctor cleaned the wound. She was glad Martin was unconscious when the physician removed the shot from his shoulder and stitched up the flesh; it appeared a painful and bloody process. And she was worried. While she was relieved to learn the shot embedded in his shoulder had severed no major blood vessel, she knew men could die of such wounds, especially with fever.

"Will he recover?" she asked anxiously.

"If a fever does not claim him, he should recover with rest. See that the bandage is changed once a day."

The duke stepped into the room as the physician completed his work. "I insist you and Sir Martin return with me to Chatsworth, Lady Powell," he said. "He'll be well cared for, and you can rest. My carriage should be here soon."

Kit was only too happy to agree to the duke's kind invitation, though she had no intention of leaving Martin's care to others.

Soon the footman returned with the duke's carriage. Another footman was dispatched to take a message to John. Arrangements were made for the care of Rutledge and for the two bound guards to be taken to the nearest magistrate.

Martin, still unconscious, was carefully lifted into the carriage and settled onto the seat. Climbing in with the duke's assistance, Kit lifted her husband's head onto her lap. The duke followed, sitting across from them, and as the carriage departed he said, "I had intended to offer you and Sir Martin some time at Chatsworth as my guests, a beginning of your delayed wedding trip. It seems you will be my guests after all, but under slightly different circumstances."

"Your Grace," she responded with a grateful heart, "we cannot thank you enough for all you have done." She could not imagine taking Martin back to Pentridge in his condition.

"When Sir Martin is better," the duke said reassuringly, "and he *will* be better, Lady Powell, then we will see about tidying up this business he was handling."

"He has told me little of his affairs in Pentridge, Your Grace," Kit admitted. "Perhaps as we travel to Chatsworth you might illuminate me?"

"I can at least share what I know," the duke offered. "And you may call me Hart. All my friends do."

Chapter 25

Fever could kill!

The words were a shout in Kit's mind, reminding her what a thin thread held Martin to this earth. She'd refused to leave his bedside when, shortly after they arrived at Chatsworth House, his temperature began to rise.

Martin's face was flushed with the fever that consumed him. He faded in and out of consciousness, restless in the huge and elaborate bed he'd been given. Bathing his sweating body with cool wet cloths and changing his bandage, Kit cared for him the best she knew. She had taken care of her sister and her mother in their last months of life, and the foreboding she experienced tending her husband was a familiar constant worry she wore like a cloak.

She kept watch by his bed should he wake and need her. When her fatigue proved too great, she sat on a chair and leaned onto the edge of the bed, resting her head on her folded arms. Occasionally he woke and looked at her as if through a haze, only to fall back into a restless sleep. In his dreams, he murmured of France and relived the night his wife Elise was killed. It pained Kit to hear him cry out for the young woman, but it told her what a horror that night had been and why he felt so responsible, why he had been so concerned for Kit's own safety.

Tonight he rambled about the man named Oliver. "Sidmouth's spy" he called him, and the man Brandreth, the one she knew as the Nottingham Captain. The duke had told her much of what happened and she could still scarcely believe it. All those Derbyshire men led astray by a treacherous viper.

"Must get a message to Prinny. Must do something," he mumbled over and over.

From what she had learned, all along he had wanted to prevent the rebellion that was eventually stopped by the King's Dragoons. She watched as he became more agitated, tossing and turning on the bed. Fearful lest his bandage come off, she drew close to soothe him, but his head rose off the pillow and his glazed eyes stared straight ahead, not seeing her.

"Kitten!"

Wiping the moisture from his fevered brow, she gently lowered his head to the pillow and took his over-warm hand between hers. "I am here, darling. I won't leave you. I love you."

At some level he must have heard her, because he calmed and succumbed to a deeper sleep.

If it were possible to fall more deeply in love with him, she did. It didn't matter he was unkempt, sweat-soaked and smelled as if he long needed a bath. He was hers, and as his fever raged, the thought she could lose him caused tears to flow unimpeded. The duke's servants were ever gracious, looking in on her and Martin several times a day, bringing food and asking if they could help.

"Why don't you get some sleep, child? There's a bedchamber just next door you can use," said an elderly servant one night, stopping to inquire of her needs and frowning at her disheveled condition.

"I will when his fever breaks," she promised the gray-haired woman. "I don't want to leave him until then. He is often delirious, and bathing him with the cool water you bring seems to help."

"I am only too pleased to help the duke's friends. There's more water on the side table when you have need of it."

"Thank you," Kit said, but she kept her eyes on her husband.

Making ready to leave the woman said, "The lad John Spencer has arrived, my lady. He brought your trunks. If you will allow it, I will bring you a change of gowns."

"Certainly," Kit said, grateful to be free of such duties.

"There's a tray of food on the table should you be hungry, and some broth for Sir Martin if you can get him to take any. You must keep up your strength, child. His Grace has been most insistent that we see to your health as well as your husband's."

John stopped by shortly after she changed gowns, concerned about Martin and also agape at the grandeur of Chatsworth. "'Tis a palace, my lady. Have ye seen it all?"

"No." She smiled. "But I can imagine the rest from the halls and rooms I saw when I first arrived."

"Should you wish to take a walk, I will stay with Sir Martin," the young man promised. "'Tis my duty, and he is my friend. I'll never be far."

"There is little to do, John, save watch him, feed him broth when he'll take it and bathe him. I will let you know should I need your assistance."

Too tired to keep up the conversation, after hearing of the meals John was sharing with the duke and the luxurious bedchamber he'd been assigned, she sent him away. She knew from the servants that, as he said, he never went far.

She refused to allow the physician to bleed Martin, telling the affronted man, one Dr. Wendell, that her husband had lost enough blood already. The next night, however, when she removed the bandage, what at first appeared to be a normal wound—though awful as one could imagine sewn-up flesh to be—had become a red swollen mass seeping pus-like liquid with a foul smell. Feeling the rising heat of Martin's body, Kit's concern rapidly turned into alarm.

He could die!

Panicked, she wondered if the doctor had closed the wound too soon; she recalled her father telling her of men who died of battle wounds when the surgeon in his hasty attempt to deal with too many wounded men at one time failed to properly drain an injury before stitching it up. She was no doctor, though she had cared for her sister until the end. But her efforts to save Anne had ended in her sister's death. Would she be equally unsuccessful in trying to save Martin?

Calling for a servant, she asked for a clean sharp knife and someone knowledgeable in herbs. She would do all she could. He had to live.

A woman she'd not seen before appeared a few minutes later with John Spencer behind her.

"What has happened my lady?" John asked.

"The wound is festering and I must cut it open to drain the purulent liquid."

John and the woman came closer to examine the wound. "Aye, 'tis bad," John acknowledged. "Tell me how I can help."

"You can summon the physician and let the duke know."

John left immediately, and Kit turned to the female servant. "Did you bring the knife?"

"Yes, my lady." The woman handed it over. "'Tis new and sharp. I've also brought supplies for wound-stitching as well as the ingredients for poultices to reduce the redness and swelling."

While not trained in the healing arts, Kit knew enough to know the wound had to be cleaned and drained. She poured a small amount of brandy onto the cut then carefully sliced through the stitches. Making a small cut, she pressed gently on the sides of the reddened area, draining the wretched fluid. She grimaced at the foul odor and forced herself to go on. This could save his life.

She didn't re-stitch the wound but drew the sides together, cleaned the area and applied the poultice the woman gave her.

Then Kit bound the wound tightly with a clean bandage. She feared it was not enough.

"We must get his fever down or he will die," she exclaimed. They could immerse him in cold water, she knew, but he was too weak to take to the river. And then she remembered that Chatsworth was a grand estate. Grand estates, Kit recalled from her visit as a young girl to Petworth House, had ice houses.

"Chatsworth has an ice house, does it not?"

"Yeah, we have one," said the woman helping her. "For many years, since the time of my grandmother. 'Tis just south of the canal pond. In the winter the men carve ice from the canal to store there."

"We must have enough ice to surround his body."

The woman hurried off. Not long after, the duke entered, followed again by the female servant. "John tells me Sir Martin has taken a turn for the worse, and Alice here says you need ice. What has happened, Lady Powell?"

"Martin's wound turned angry and his fever soared. I have drained the wound and applied a poultice Alice gave me, but I need your help to deal with his fever. If he is to live, we must cool his body. Can we get some ice from your ice house to surround his body?"

"Of course. My footmen will go at once."

The duke disappeared and a short while later returned with two footmen unloading blocks of ice from a cart and several servants anxious to help. The men carefully lifted Martin's body from the sheet to lay an oilcloth underneath him, then placed thick cloths next to his sides and set the ice they had broken into smaller chunks around him, packing it close to his body. Kit placed small pieces of ice in cloths and set them on his forehead and chest, careful not to wet the bandage. It was all she knew to do. Then, holding the bagged ice to his forehead, she prayed.

"Oh, Lord, please do not take him."

Perhaps in comfort, the duke said, "John and one of my footmen have ridden for the physician. If he can be found, he'll be here soon."

Kit prayed he would.

The physician didn't arrive until early the next morning, the same Dr. Wendell she had encountered before. John told her the man was delayed by complications with a birth. Immediately upon entering the bedchamber, he checked Martin's wound. He peeled back the bandage, and Kit was relieved to see the swelling reduced, though her husband was still warm to the touch.

"You have done well, my lady," said the physician. "Continue to keep him cool. If the fever persists, perhaps he might be immersed in a tub of chilled water. Then all we can do is watch and wait—and pray."

Kit kept vigil over her husband for another night. She told herself he could not die, not now. She wouldn't say any more goodbyes. To him she would not, could not, say those words. He must live.

He awoke on and off, and when he was awake she got him to take a few sips of broth or a mixture of brandy and water. And she scolded him. "You must not leave me. It would be most inconvenient. I…I could not bear it. You shall get well."

Two days after they first applied the ice, his fever dropped enough that they removed it. They changed the bed linens, too, carefully lifting him. It took several footmen and John working with Kit to accomplish that, while thankfully Martin was unaware. Kit breathed a sigh of relief. Her prayers had been answered.

On the following morning, a sudden movement woke Kit from where she slept exhausted on the edge of Martin's bed. She looked up to see his head lifted off the pillow.

"Hello, Kitten," he said weakly, smiling.

"Martin!" she said, excitement rising in her chest. "You're awake."

His eyes were clear as they had not been before. She touched his forehead. Cool. Studying his face for a clue to his health, she noted his color was better. She leaned in to kiss him gently and sat back.

"Yes, it would appear I am," he said. His voice was a bit weak, but his customary grin was back in place as he reached for her hand. Warmth infused her from the joy of knowing he was out of danger.

"I've been so worried about you. I nearly lost you. How do you feel?"

"Sore." He reached for his bandaged shoulder. "And a bit bedraggled. Thirsty. Some water?" he croaked.

"Yes, of course." She hurried to pour him a glass from the pitcher on the dresser. Setting the glass aside, she propped up his pillows. "When your fever lessened, I tried to get as much broth down your throat as you would allow, but I was not always successful. It might take a while for you to come fully right. But the wound is healing well now," she added, handing him the glass. "I just checked it some hours ago."

"How long have I been out?"

She sat on the edge of the bed. "Most of this last week."

"And you've been my nurse?" He had the audacity to wink.

"Who else? I would not leave your care to others."

He squeezed her hand. "Rutledge?"

"It seems the duke's pistol dispatched him to the next world. He's dead, Martin." Her voice sounded cold even to herself, but she couldn't deny she was glad the man was gone.

"Saved me the trouble."

"The duke insisted on bringing you to Chatsworth," she said, looking around the overlarge room. "If you're wondering about this grand bedchamber."

The corners of his mouth hitched up in a grin. "Yes, that occurred to me. Nowhere else in the Midlands looks like this."

She glanced toward the fireplace, following his gaze. "It seems the duke favors marble...and books. I've seen a lot of both everywhere, and John tells me he has seen even more."

"John is here?'

"The duke insisted, and it seemed a good thing to me. I thought you might need him."

"Yes, that was wise."

"Hart put you on the first floor so that his servants could better see to our needs. He's been very kind, Martin, even sending a message to Ormond to let him know you were injured."

"Hart, is it? Well, I suppose that is to be expected. Seems to be the name he prefers."

He pulled her onto the bed and winced, and observing his expression Kit said, "Do you think we should be doing this? You're not well."

"It's part of my recovery having you next to me, Kitten."

She smiled in agreement, turned in to his side and nuzzled the base of his neck, reveling in the now cooler touch of his skin.

"I seem to recall in my foggy dreams a woman's voice telling me she loved me. Your voice, Kitten."

"Yes," Kit admitted. "I was reminding you that you were not free to leave this world."

"I have no desire to leave it," he announced, leaning down to kiss her. "And it sounds like I owe my recovery to Hart as well as you."

"The duke doesn't think you owe him anything, Martin. He's been telling everyone you're the Prince Regent's man and a hero.

But I agree with you: We do owe him. If we hadn't been here, if we hadn't had the ice he provided and the care..."

Her words trailed off as Martin drew her tighter into the curve of his body. She kissed the skin just below his ear and said softly, "The duke thought to offer us a wedding gift with some time at Chatsworth, but you getting shot changed that a bit."

"I'm certain we can make up for it," he said, teasing her lips with a gentle kiss.

Seeing Martin brought back from death's door had drained all the prior anger she'd experienced at his having failed to tell her what he was doing in Pentridge. Those nights of sitting with him while he was lost in fever had bonded her to him in a new way. But she hadn't forgotten. As she leaned into his side and returned his kiss she whispered, "You might have told me you were working for the Crown and not against it."

"Did you truly worry I was a traitor, Kit? You were supposed to be trusting me, remember?"

"I did trust you—and I did worry. Recall we did not know each other very well."

"Ah, my kitten, you keep saying that. But, as I keep telling you, we did know each other *very* well."

The look on his face was most definitely a satisfied grin, and she would have slapped him except for the huge bandage wrapped around half his chest and injured shoulder. Instead, she cast him a sardonic smile. "Ah. So you will continue to act the spy for the Prince Regent."

* * *

Her statement surprised him, but more unsettling was Kit's clear concern. Martin watched her brows beetle with fresh worry, and he knew he could never put her through this again. "No, Kit.

This was my last assignment. Our future together will be very different, I assure you."

"That sounds good, husband."

"I hadn't planned on being wounded. I was just exhausted and so angry at Rutledge's perfidy and worried about his shooting you I was slow to act." The fear Martin had felt when Rutledge snatched the footman's pistol was still so real he shuddered at the memory.

"Not so slow to act, husband. You threw yourself in front of me. Remember? The duke said that move saved you from a mortal wound, and I am glad. It would break my heart if I were to lose you. I love you so." She did not need the dark of night to whisper the words any longer. After all they had been through, she would shout them from the rooftops.

"I love you, too, Kitten, most fervently. But it seems I cannot always protect those I love." He cast a side glance at his bandaged shoulder. "I cannot even protect myself. Life is a risk-laden business, Kit. At times it has left me with a deep ache for how precious it is—and how fragile."

"We both know how fragile life is." She let her gaze fall to the side as she said, "We've both lost people we love." Then, facing him, she added, "I was not going to lose you."

Martin knew well he could not love without accepting the risk of losing that love. Try as he might, he could not protect Kit from all danger. Whatever time life would give them, he would embrace it fully. But he would not be careless, either. Never again.

"And I do not intend to lose you," he said. "That is why I will always hold you close, Kitten." He pulled her atop him. "Come here. I'm tired of sleeping alone."

"You're not fully recovered!"

"I may be weak, but I'm not dead. And there are ways."

"But—"

He showed her the ways.

* * *

"You'll be pleased to know," the duke said, "my agent is conducting an inquiry into the tenancies of those involved in the insurrection."

Martin looked at Kit, sitting across the dining table in what the duke called his "small" dining room. The scale was more conducive to conversation than his grander rooms that would seat scores. Though not surprised by the duke's stated intention, Martin thought he saw a glimmer of concern on his wife's face. She cared for the families in the village.

"Will they lose their homes?" she asked.

"Possibly," replied the duke.

A footman served the next course: a pheasant displayed on the silver platter with its head attached and its feathers fanned out. Martin watched as Kit accepted a slice of the meat on her plate while trying not to look into the bird's eyes, and gazing at his beautiful wife brought a smile to his face, particularly when he considered their last two nights together. His lovely vixen was all he could hope for in a lover. And she'd been creative as to positions, accommodating his wounded shoulder.

Struggling to bring his mind back to the topic of conversation, he asked the duke, "Are they still rounding up rebels? John tells me the price on some heads is now up to the enormous sum of one hundred guineas."

John, sitting next to him, nodded. "'Tis what I've heard."

"It may be weeks before all are captured," the duke said, "but with that kind of coin as bait, they will soon all be reeled in." I intend to take away the property of any involved in this uprising and give it to tenants who refused to join the rebels' cause. I have already assured myself that woman, Ann Weightman, who forced her four sons to participate under diverse threats, will no longer be innkeeper on my lands. She has been arrested for permitting a seditious meeting in the White Horse."

"I feel sorry for the villagers," said Kit, vocalizing the concern he'd seen in her eyes. "I don't think they realized what they were doing. Not really. I became acquainted with Mrs. Weightman's son George while we were in Pentridge. He was a kind young man whom I believe only became part of the rebellion at his mother's insistence."

The duke wore a troubled expression. "Then you will not like my news, my lady. The magistrate Edmund Mundy has just sent word that George Weightman is one of those apprehended. I expect he will be tried for treason along with the others. The government is being quite serious about this incident and will, I expect, hang some as examples."

"They ought to be trying Sidmouth's spy Oliver," said John.

"'Ought' is the key word, John," said Martin. "The government will never call him at trial, because spies do not help the prosecution. Juries do not like the sneak, which he certainly was. Worse, he was working for the very government now crying treason, encouraging the villagers to rise against the Crown."

"There's to be a grand jury convened in Derby," the duke informed them. "My uncle George Cavendish has been asked to be foreman. Young Weightman may well hang for his role. As I recall, Martin, you told me he actually led a group of the men through the night."

"Oh, no," Kit said, looking anxiously at Martin. "We must do something to help him. Surely he does not deserve to die."

Martin felt an ache in his chest at the despair reflected on his wife's face and the sympathetic look John cast her way. Perhaps when they returned to London he would ask Prinny to commute the sentence should young Weightman be convicted, as he undoubtedly would.

The duke's brows rose in question at Kit's statement, so Martin offered, "My wife grew attached to some of the villagers, remember, young Weightman included. She made sketches of many of them."

"You draw, Lady Powell?"

"Yes, I do…a bit."

"More than a bit," Martin said proudly. "My lady is quite the artist."

"May I see? the duke asked.

"Why, yes," she said.

John was sent to find the sketchbook he'd retrieved from the inn with Kit's other things. He returned, and with Kit's nod he handed her drawings to the duke. The duke took some time to peruse them as his guests continued to eat.

The duke looked up, obviously impressed. "They are quite good. Martin has not exaggerated. Would you be willing to share these drawings with a friend of mine, Lady Powell?"

"Why, yes, if you desire it, Your Grace. Well, at least some of them," she added. Martin could only guess at the ones she would withhold.

"Hart," the duke reminded her. "You may call me Hart. The person with whom I'd want to share them is my friend Edward Baines, the editor of the *Leeds Mercury*. He is quite the thinker. We share many views on education. Knowing of my overseer role, he has sent me a message inquiring about my response to the uprising in Pentridge." Giving Martin a knowing look he added, "It seems he is pursuing a story of the rebellion."

Kit raised her eyebrow, eyeing him. "Martin?"

"I suppose it can be done, though he must not know of my position or my work for the Crown. And, he must not mention you, Kit—or me—in his article."

"If he were to use your drawings, my lady," the duke said to Kit, "I am quite certain I could persuade him to say nothing of you. Your name will not be mentioned."

The topic was dropped for a time, but on the way back to their room that night Martin took Kit through the long gallery the duke had converted to a grand library. He brought her hand to his lips and pressed a kiss to her knuckles. "You don't have to share your drawings if you'd rather not, Kit."

She looked up at the wall of books on both sides of the gallery as if pondering his statement and sighed. "No, I want to, but I will carefully select what he may use."

Chapter 26

Kit's meeting with Edward Baines was soon arranged to take place in the sitting room the duke called "the schoolroom." It was a small room with a white and gold mantelpiece over which hung a picture of a boy with a magnificent dog, though Kit did not know the breed. Kit had been a bit reluctant to meet with the editor alone and so asked Martin to join her, which as it turns out he had planned to do.

Upon greeting him, Kit thought Edward Baines had an interesting face, with a tall forehead, long nose and sparkling hazel eyes, framed by brown hair falling nearly to his shoulders. His friendly sincere smile instantly put her at ease.

"I am looking into some claims only recently brought to my attention about a man named William Oliver, Lady Powell. The duke tells me you may have a drawing of him."

Kit exchanged a glance with her husband sitting next to her.

"I see the name is known to you both," Baines said.

"Why, yes," Martin offered. "From time to time he was in Pentridge, the town where we stayed. The village is not large."

Kit handed him the drawings she'd brought. "There is one of him among those, I believe," she said, directing him to one particular sketch and then another. "This one." She pointed to the picture of the men sitting around a table drinking at the Dog Inn, and to another of Oliver's face alone.

When the editor turned to the drawing she'd made of the men meeting in the upper room, Kit saw a faint glimmer of surprise on Martin's face. She had purposely drawn different faces on Martin and John so as not to include their identities among those plotting treason. At the time she did it, she didn't know why, but now she did. In her heart, she had never counted them among the rebels. Never allowed herself to believe her husband was a traitor. Martin reached for her hand and squeezed it, giving her a grateful smile as he did.

"How did you manage to see this meeting, Lady Powell?" Baines inquired.

Thinking fast she said, "Oh, I was merely passing an open door and found the men's faces intriguing. I particularly like to draw faces, you see, but I have also made drawings of St. Matthew's and the cottages in the village. They are among the ones in the stack I've given you."

He seemed to accept her explanation. Then, focusing on the sketch of Oliver he added, "It's an interesting face, this one. From what I've learned, the man is a kind of Lucifer whose distinguishing characteristic is first to tempt and then to destroy."

Kit couldn't agree more. She'd heard the man encouraging the villagers to rise against the government.

"That would match all we have heard," announced Martin. "He led good villagers astray, and created a zealot in his protégé Jeremiah Brandreth."

"Ah…the Nottingham Captain," said Baines, setting down the sketch of Oliver. "It's certain that one will hang. Do you have any drawings of him, my lady?"

Kit had not brought all her work to show the editor, but she had the one of Brandreth's face that reflected his zeal for the rebel cause and offered it to Baines. He studied it for a long moment before saying, "The eyes…you've captured something there, I think. Perhaps a bit of fanaticism, no?"

"I could not say, sir," Kit admitted. "But I did see something unusual—a passion perhaps—and tried to draw it as well as I could."

Baines handed back the sketches. "My evidence suggests that the government was deeply involved in this uprising, perhaps even to the point of encouraging it. There have been allegations by several of my sources that Oliver, who came up from London, was a government man inciting others to illegal acts!"

"Would that be the focus of your article, Mr. Baines?" Martin asked.

"I intend to follow the thread and unravel this ball of twine. Should the allegation of Oliver being a government spy prove to be true, I will bring it to light." He focused his next statement on Kit. "Your sketches, my lady, will be a welcome accompaniment to my piece if you will allow me to use them."

"Our understanding from His Grace," said Martin, "is that you will not disclose the source of the drawings should you use any. And for my wife's safety, I'd ask you not to use any that would put her in the scene, such as the meeting she happened to observe. Just the ones of the faces you need."

"I can do that, certainly. I've no desire to render your lady the focus of public attention. No, I will be quite careful. I've many a source to protect with this story. Not all want to be revealed. She will not be the only one."

They agreed upon the few sketches the editor could take with him, and he left a pleased man. Once he was gone, Kit turned and said, "I'm curious, Martin. Why did you agree to our meeting with him?"

"Well, it seemed only right we should help the duke's friend after Hart's hospitality, but I was also interested to learn if Baines had uncovered Sidmouth's scheme. Seems he has. I believe in accountability, Kit. Sidmouth and Castlereagh should not be free from scrutiny, nor their spy Oliver."

"You said nothing of your own role, my love," she reminded him.

"No, I'll be saying nothing of my role. That is the Crown's secret."

* * *

The next day, Kit, Martin and John bade the duke goodbye and returned to London. The trip home was uneventful and the weather remained fair for the most part. After the quiet of the country, Town was a jarring assault on Kit's senses. The noise, the smells and the huge buildings were a decided change from the small white cottages of Pentridge. Even the majesty of Chatsworth had been softened by green slopes dotted with wooly sheep, chirping birds and sweet-smelling country air.

She stepped out of a shop with Mary at her side and let out a sigh as they walked toward the waiting carriage.

"What's wrong, Kit?"

"Oh, nothing really. It's just that I did not miss the noise of London and its many foul smells. Derbyshire was so quiet. Even in the midst of a plot to overthrow the government, it was peaceful."

"I daresay it will take you a while to become accustomed to Town once again," her companion offered.

"It would be pleasant to have some time with Martin before he is swept into matters of business," Kit said wistfully.

"Knowing what I do of your husband, Kit, and how very much in love with you he is, I expect you will see much of him despite the Powell family's tug upon his time."

"I do hope you are right," Kit said. "We've grown so close."

* * *

Ormond handed a glass of brandy to Martin and John as they sat conversing in the marquess's London study. "Mary and I are eager to have you and your bride stay with us for a while, Martin. Can you not spare a week or two?"

Seeing the hope of a positive response on his friend's face, Martin was reluctant to decline the invitation. "We'll not be here that long, Ormond. I've planned a wedding trip that I'm anxious to begin." Truth be told, though they had returned only a day ago he was anxious to leave immediately. He wanted his kitten all to himself.

"I do suppose that should come first," Ormond replied grudgingly. "At least your business for Prinny is done. By the by, how did your meeting with him go today?"

"My wife will be pleased," said Martin. "The Prince Regent agreed to commute Weightman's sentence to transportation if he's convicted, as he is sure to be after it is known he led the rebels halfway to Nottingham."

"I expect the trial in Derby will be nothing more than the government's scripted play," Ormond said from where he perched on the edge of his desk.

"Some of the Derbyshire men will certainly hang, Brandreth foremost among them," Martin acknowledged with a frown. "Particularly after his slaying of the Widow Hepworth's servant. The government is intent on assuring there will be no more revolutions in England."

"A sorry way they went about it," Ormond muttered.

Martin nodded and took another sip of his brandy, happy to have left the alehouses of Derbyshire behind him. "A sad chapter in our history, indeed."

"By the by," said Ormond, "Hart sends his regards and says he is planning a trip to London. Are you certain I cannot persuade you and Lady Powell to linger for his visit?"

"No, though perhaps when we return—"

"My wife will be most anxious to know just where it is you are sweeping her friend. I trust you will disclose that bit of information, won't you?"

"No, I don't think I shall," Martin said with a smile. "Only that it involves a ship."

"A ship?" said John, face agleam.

"Neither of you are to say one word to my wife until I've told her of my plans."

The two others nodded.

"So, John, you are interested in going to sea?" asked Martin.

"Aye. I am, sir."

"Well, then. I believe I can arrange for you to crew on one of the Powell ships—say, mine perhaps?"

"'Tis certain I would like that, sir."

"Oh, I almost forgot," Ormond interjected with a sigh. "Hart said in his letter he's seen the *Leeds Mercury* article on the Pentridge affair. Apparently it's a rather scathing indictment of Oliver, whom he asserts plainly was a government spy. He cites a printer named Willan as saying Oliver tried to recruit him to the cause. Now that I think of it, with that article published, perhaps it would be best after all if you were not in London. Questions might arise as to the Frenchman Donet."

Martin perked up. "Save that article for our return, if you will. I am certain Kit and I will want to read it. Some of her drawings may even be featured, though Baines assured me there would be no attribution."

A knock sounded on the door, followed by Lady Ormond poking in her head. "If you gentlemen can be pried from your brandy, dinner is about to be served and Kit and I are starving!"

"The mother of my child calls," said Ormond, setting down his glass and walking toward his wife. "We were just about to join you, sweetheart."

Over dinner, Lady Ormond excitedly told them of her day shopping with Kit. Martin was pleased his wife could spend time with her friend before they left London, and he was delighted to see her again wearing gowns that befitted her station after the simpler clothing she'd worn in the Midlands. The emerald silk she wore tonight with the amber and pearl necklace he'd given her made her auburn hair sparkle in the candlelight.

"Kit has told me all that happened in the Midlands, Martin," said Lady Ormond. "Well, most of it. I was not surprised to hear you'd kept your work for the Crown to yourself. You spies are all alike," she said, giving her husband a side glance. "And that highway attack...it must have been frightening!"

"Actually," Martin said, smiling at Kit who, he was pleased to see, had the cabochon ruby ring back on her finger, "my wife was very calm through that episode. Told me I was amazing, as I recall." He grinned mischievously at Kit across the table. Inwardly he'd been proud of her in return. Most females would have whimpered and swooned at the pistol-fire and blood.

"It's clear to me, husband, that you love the adventure of this business you're about," Kit said. Then her gaze settled on Ormond and John sitting next to him and she added, "All of you, I expect. Scoundrels every one."

"Hear, hear," said Ormond. At that moment he looked at his wife and said, "But a love of adventure is not limited to us men. As I recall, my own dear wife makes a rather convincing spy."

"Hmm," murmured the blonde beauty.

"Our time in the Midlands was an adventure to be sure," offered John, "though marching all night through the mud with a madman is not something I would soon repeat."

"I feel sorry for all the families of the men involved," said Kit. "Some will be hard-pressed to eat if their men are taken from them in punishment."

"Hart will do what he can to help the people of Pentridge," said Ormond, now serious, "but there is no doubt the men most involved will face hanging or transportation—or perhaps a further stay in prison. Of course, it is possible at trial they could somehow be found innocent…though that seems unlikely."

"I would do something for their families," said Kit, darting a glance at Martin. He could see she was worried and thought she might be considering using the funds that had recently come to her.

"We can work with the curate in Pentridge to assist those families in need, Kit, if it would make you happy."

Her brilliant smile was aimed at him. "Oh, yes!"

He loved pleasing her, and seeing those blue eyes sparkle at the chance to show kindness warmed his heart. How fortunate he was to have her as his wife.

When the evening was at an end, they bid their friends goodnight and Martin took his wife's hand and led her to their chamber, the same room in which they'd spent their chaste wedding night. "I'm of a mind to rectify that first night of our marriage, my love, when we shared this same bed but with little…activity."

Kit began to take the pins from her hair, letting her long auburn tresses cascade down her back. "Whatever do you mean?"

Shedding his coat and waistcoat, he wondered if the vixen knew how alluring she was. In the few months he'd known her he had come to love the way she could toss her beautiful mane of auburn hair and look up at him so innocently as she was doing now. From that first night at Willow House, he'd been enthralled, captivated. Tonight was no different.

"You know well my purpose here, Kitten. I intend to give you a new memory of our time in this room."

Then he took her into his arms and kissed her soundly, slipping her gown from her shoulders. With knowing fingers, he turned her and unlaced her corset. Once divested of that garment, she turned and ran her hands over his shirt, sending ripples of desire through him. Between playful kisses, they removed the remainder of their garments. Naked and laughing, they raced together for the bed.

* * *

The next morning was a sunny one. Kit had been told nothing of their errand. Martin was being quite mysterious. After a brief ride to the waterfront, the carriage stopped, and through the window Kit watched as the footman hurried to open the door. Martin stepped down then assisted her, asking the coachman to wait.

Kit took his hand, held her skirt with the other hand, and looked up to see a long line of ships lying at anchor in the river.

"Oh, no, *ma chère,* not yet," said Martin with a chuckle. "I must cover your eyes until I am ready for you to see my surprise." And with that he drew a black scarf from his coat pocket and loosely tied it around her eyes. "Ormond lent me his scarf."

She felt him wrap his arm around her waist, and then he led her along beside him. She was anxious to see the surprise. Martin had rarely shown this much excitement for anything save the night they consummated their marriage…well, and last night. The thought warmed her.

So, this must be something special. Slowly he guided her along the quay. Gulls shrieked in the background.

Soon he stopped, turned her toward the water and removed the scarf. "All right, Kitten. Open your eyes."

Kit slowly opened her eyes and blinked. In front of her was a beautiful sleek schooner, its sails furled. The hull was dark blue and, from what she could see, the wood of the two masts was polished and new. Martin stood behind her, wrapped his arms about her waist and drew her in to his chest. Her gaze drifted over the ship.

She could feel the tension in his body and wondered what she was supposed to see. Was his surprise a ship? And then she saw. The name on the bow.

The Sea Kitten.

It must have been the stillness of her stance that made him ask, "Do you like it?"

His voice was eager yet unsure, and Kit smiled to herself, emotion welling up in her throat. She was more like her mother than she realized. When she'd had the power to choose that day Martin asked her to marry him, without knowing it she had chosen love, and she had chosen a man more like her father than she'd have guessed. Both this man and her father would risk all to have the woman they loved by their side. But, unlike Kit's father, Martin understood her. His love for her was perfect and accepting.

Yes, she was pleased. Very pleased. And at that moment she sensed Anne would be happy for her. Kit would live the dream they both wanted, a man to love them and bring them children. If they had a daughter, she would name the child after Anne.

Turning in his arms, she stared into her husband's indigo eyes. "Yes, I do. I like it very much. When...when did you do this?"

"Ah. That morning after we were married, recall I disappeared for a while? Just long enough to make certain my schooner under construction was...modified. The captain's cabin now has a larger shelf bed. And the name, of course. Did you see the figurehead?"

Kit gazed again at the ship and saw the carved wooden figure of a woman's head. It was not an exact picture of her; still, the auburn hair that flared out behind the carved figure in wild abandon and the blue eyes were hers. Yet the body—the body was that of a red tabby.

She turned back to Martin. "The cat?"

He chuckled. "Why do you think I call you Kitten?"

She laughed. "I see."

"I only wanted to hint at your beauty, Kit, and capture your fire. I think the tribute is fitting. The ship is for you. For us."

"Oh, Martin," she said with a sigh, turning back to view the schooner and leaning against his chest. "She's beautiful. I think I have even grown fond of that name you call me."

He drew her against him and wrapped his arms around her. "Ah, *mon chaton*," he whispered into her ear, "come away with me, my love." He nuzzled her neck, sending shivers down her spine. "I will show you white sand beaches and blue lagoons. We'll make love in the warm tropical waters of another land."

She glanced again at the ship and then turned away from the gift and back to the giver. Martin's handsome face now wore his usual grin. Raising her gaze to his eyes, she wanted him to see all the love she had in her heart. Reaching up, she brushed aside the stray lock that had blown across his forehead and said, "I want those days with you, my love, my knight—all of them."

His grin became a tender smile. "Then you shall have them, Kitten." And he kissed her for all the world to see.

AUTHOR'S NOTE

After the war with France ended in 1814, England suffered from great social, economic and political problems. Many of the major issues were a direct result of the war, but others were the necessary product of changes occurring throughout society, some of which had begun earlier. The discontent that this change brought, and the distress in the lives of the working people, culminated in the series of events that occurred during 1811-1819, including the attack on the Prince Regent's carriage, the March of the Blanketeers and the Pentrich Rebellion in 1817. (Pentridge is the old name for Pentrich.) Dubbed "The Last Revolution in England," the Pentrich Rebellion was just what the leaders of the British government needed to justify sending a strong signal to the masses that no uprising would be tolerated in England such as occurred in France.

Lord Sidmouth, the Home Secretary, did send spies throughout England, including the Midlands. Among them was William Richards, better known as William Oliver or Oliver the spy, who became an *agent provocateur* inciting open rebellion where there might have been only discontent. Thus the men who rose that day in June 1817 did indeed fight against the wind—the power of the Crown. They stood not a chance. But for Oliver's lies, they might have realized that truth.

Years after the events, in a letter written in 1831, Lord Melbourne, a former Home Secretary, recalled that there was "much reason to suspect that the rising in Derbyshire…was stimulated, if not produced, by the artifices of Oliver, a spy employed by the Government of that day."

Notwithstanding the circumstances of the uprising and the involvement of the British government, the powers in London decided to make an example of the rebels. Forty-five men were tried for high treason by Special Commission. Three were hanged, including Jeremiah Brandreth, Isaac Ludlam and William Turner, all characters in my story. Fourteen were sentenced to transportation to Australia, including George Weightman, who lived to the ripe old age of 73. Several others were imprisoned.

In examining the causes for the uprising in the Midlands, one cannot discount that the people had been through much hardship and by 1817 were hungry and tired of laws and taxes imposed by a nobility that had little understanding of their needs. We who enjoy democracy might say their desire to rise against such hardship was not unreasonable. The motive of the government, of course, was to crush the yearnings for democracy and the vote so strong at that point among the common people, and to prevent a revolution like that which had occurred in France. The rebellion and other successive events were used to justify the Six Acts, adopted in 1819, summarized by the Whig leader in the House of Commons as taking away the right of meeting, and invading the broad liberty of the press.

As with all my stories, some characters are real—those involved in the Rebellion, and Lords Sidmouth, Castlereagh, and Eldon, and the 6th Duke of Devonshire—while many are fictional, including Martin, Kit, John, Rutledge, Miss Abby, the de Courtenay family and those characters from my first book, RACING WITH THE WIND. I have made some changes in the real characters as my story dictated and other minor changes in the locations of events. For example, the real George Weightman was a sawyer and married, but for my story it was best for the angel-faced man of 26 to be single and smitten with Kit. That first meeting of the rebels in Derbyshire that Kit witnessed actually took place at the Three Salmon Inn not the Dog Inn. William Cavendish, the 6th Duke of Devonshire, known to his friends as "Hart," did not shoot the fictional Earl of Rutledge, of course, but he was an acclaimed horticulturist and loved marble and books, and these are reflected in his changes to Chatsworth House, pictured on the cover of this novel. Although the duke was on the Continent when these events took place in 1817, he did take action by depriving the rebels involved of their tenancies and establishing a school for village children.

The inns mentioned were all in existence at the time. The Guardsman public house in the mews where Wellington's barracks once were located didn't open until 1818, however. After the rebellion, the White Horse Inn was torn down and Nanny Weightman, for her part in the rebellion, lost her license and thus her livelihood.

I hope you enjoyed this foray into a little-known and sad chapter in England's history, and I trust you enjoyed the romance between Martin and Kit that began so strangely. The third in the trilogy, WIND RAVEN, the story of Martin's sea captain brother Jean Nicholas Powell, whom you met in AGAINST THE WIND, will take you onboard a schooner and into the Caribbean where pirates lurked even in 1817. And you'll get to see Martin and Kit again!

Oh, and if you want the recipe for Nanny Weightman's famous porridge Kit ate at the White Horse Inn, you can find it on my website here: http://www.reganwalkerauthor.com/nanny-weightmans-famous-porridge.html.

Enjoy!

ABOUT THE AUTHOR

As a child Regan Walker loved to write stories, particularly about adventure-loving girls, but by the time she got to college more serious pursuits took priority. One of her professors thought her suited to the profession of law, and Regan realized it would be better to be a hammer than a nail. Years of serving clients in private practice and several stints in high levels of government gave her a love of international travel and a feel for the demands of the "Crown" on its subjects. Hence her romance novels often involve a demanding Prince Regent who thinks of his subjects as his private talent pool.

Regan lives in San Diego with her golden retriever, Link, whom she says inspires her every day to relax and smell the roses.

AGAINST THE WIND

A night in London's most exclusive bordello. Agent of the Crown Sir Martin Powell would not normally indulge, but the end of his time spying against Napoleon deserves a victory celebration. Yet, such pleasure will not come cheap. The auburn-haired courtesan he calls "Kitten" is in truth Katherine, Lady Egerton, a dowager baroness and the daughter of an earl as elusive as she is alluring. She flees a fate worse than death. But Martin has known darkness, too, and he alone can touch her heart—as she has touched his. To the English Midlands they will steal, into the rising winds of revolution.

Boroughs
Publishing Group

Did you enjoy this book? Drop us a line and say so! We love to hear from readers, and so do our authors. To connect, visit www.boroughspublishinggroup.com online, send comments directly to info@boroughspublishinggroup.com, or friend us on Facebook and Twitter. And be sure to check back regularly for contests and new releases in your favorite subgenres of romance!

Are you an aspiring writer? Check out www.boroughspublishinggroup.com/submit and see if we can help you make your dreams come true.

14642318R00175

Printed in Poland
by Amazon Fulfillment
Poland Sp. z o.o., Wrocław